Jewish Spirituality

Jewish Spirituality

Revitalizing Judaism for the Twenty-First Century

LEWIS D. SOLOMON

JASON ARONSON INC.
Northvale, New Jersey
Jerusalem

This book was set in 10 pt. Esprit Book by Pageworks of Old Saybrook, CT and printed and bound by Book-mart Press, Inc. of North Bergen, NJ.

Library of Congress Cataloging-in-Publication Data

Solomon, Lewis D.
    Jewish spirituality / by Lewis D. Solomon
        p.   cm.
    Includes index.
    ISBN 0-7657-6116-5
    1. Spiritual life—Judaism. 2. Jewish way of life. 3. God.
(Judaism). 4. Ethics, Jewish. 5. Judaism—20th century. I. Title.
BM723.S63 2000
296.7—dc21   99-37994
                                                      CIP

Printed in the United States of America on acid-free paper. For information and catalog write to Jason Aronson Inc., 230 Livingston Street, Northvale, NJ 07647-1726, or visit our website: www.aronson.com

In memory
of
my parents

Contents

CHAPTER SIX
Forgiveness: A Key to Loving Others and
Enhancing Inner Peace of Mind   **79**

CHAPTER SEVEN
Truthfulness: Another Key to Our Dealings with Others   **93**

PART FOUR
PERSONAL VIRTUES: BRINGING PEACE
AND HARMONY TO OUR INNER LIVES   101

CHAPTER 8
Striking the Balance between Humility and Positive Self-
Esteem   **105**

PART FIVE
DEALING WITH PAIN,
SUFFERING, AND TRAGEDY   191

CHAPTER ELEVEN
Facing Serious Illness, Curing Symptoms,
and Promoting Healing   **193**

Foreword

It pleases me greatly to introduce this important work by a scholar I have known and admired, whose ideas of Jewish Spirituality I share, and which I have put into practice as a rabbi for more than sixty-five years. My own philosophy expresses my approach to Jewish traditions and practices very simply: "Never instead of, always in addition." The ideas Professor Solomon presents here amplify and illuminate the ways in which Jewish Spirituality can continue to be real and relevant and valid in our new age.

Let me share with you a story. In the early 1940s, brand new to the United States, I was asked to perform a wedding in Staten Island. I did not know where Staten Island was, only that it was a part of New York City. The wedding was at six o'clock; I gave myself an hour to get there. What with the subway, the ferry, taxis, and so forth, I ended up arriving an hour late. The bride and groom, their parents, everyone was terribly angry with me.

During the reception afterward, I explained what had happened and I told them of a tradition that says when the rabbi is late for a wedding, it is a good omen for the marriage. It means their marriage will last.

One of the uncles present, a learned man, said to me that he had never heard of this tradition before. I said to him, "Of course not. We're just starting it! How else does a tradition start?"

So this is what came to me more than fifty years ago: Our function is, in addition to doing what our forefathers did, to add new traditions because we live in a new age. Our spiritual natures are timeless; to express that nature in the world today, it must take forms that are relevant in the world today.

Later on I went back to my roots as a Jew and looked at the traditions I had followed since childhood with my own eyes. I examined—and continue to do so even now—every tradition with this question in mind: "If I do this, will it make me a better person, a better husband, a better neighbor, a better rabbi, a better Jew?"

If the answer is yes, I do it, and it does not matter what kind of tradition it is. It could be mystical, kabbalistic, hasidic, Conservative, Reform, or even something I made up. If the answer to the above question is yes, I do it!

If the answer is no, I still do not throw it out. I simply put it aside. Perhaps tomorrow it will inspire me. That which inspires me I do, that which does not inspire me I put aside. All of it has value, but I choose the traditions and practices that inspire me to be more of a child of God.

So if you were to come to the services at The New Synagogue in New York City, you will notice that many parts of the service are mystical, many are hasidic, many are Reform, many are New Age, and many are altogether brand new ways to express ourselves as Jews. We are not against tradition; personally, I live very much in the traditions in which I was raised. Yet, Judaism for me is not a rote practice of forms and rituals that continue unexamined and without meaning in today's world. It is the living embodiment of all that has come before, shaping all that is to come in the future.

In this examination of Jewish Spirituality, Professor Solomon looks at the traditions we have lived with as Jews with new eyes. He looks at the historical authenticity of practices that we take for granted, at the fallacies that have been handed down to us as unbreakable tradition. With great integrity and courage, he excavates the foundations of the mountains of Jewish lore upon which modern Judaism stands, and sifts through the past to find the value there for the present.

What remains for him, as for me, is the core of Judaism, the great truth of our God-given spirituality, "God is One."

More than fifty years ago, the words came to me in an insight: "Never instead of, always in addition to." Don't throw it away, add to it. Take what is of value to you, and leave the rest. We do not have to divest ourselves of the old or deny it, as so many people are doing today who renounce the faith of their fathers. I strongly believe there is a reason one is born into a Jewish family, or a Christian one, or a

Hindu one. You cannot change that, just as there is a reason one is born a man or a woman.

To be a Jew is not so much a head thing as it is a heart thing. Can you feel the joys and sorrows of your fellow human beings? Can you feel your connection to God, your part in the great universe around us? If so, then join with Professor Solomon in examining the real meaning of Jewish Spirituality. It is a journey we each must make, with each other's help.

Shalom.

Rabbi Joseph H. Gelberman, Ph.D.
New York City

Acknowledgments

I owe two enormous debts of gratitude, first to Rabbi Dr. Joseph H. Gelberman, who ordained me, and, second to the late Rabbi Morris Lichtenstein, the founder of the Society of Jewish Science. Rabbi Gelberman introduced me to a spiritually-directed Judaism grounded in kabbalistic wisdom and healing. Rabbi Lichtenstein's voice reverberates throughout this book, illuminating Jewish Spirituality, an ethical, virtue-oriented monotheism.

This work had its genesis in the Pauline and Sidney Feiler Memorial Lecture, "What Happened at Mt. Sinai?," I delivered at the Arlington-Fairfax Jewish Congregation in Arlington, Virginia, on Shavuot, 7 Sivan 5757. Several sermons given in the Fall of 1997 while I was serving as guest rabbi at Beth Chaverim Reform Congregation in Ashburn, Virginia, form the basis for Chapters 10 and 11 of this book. I also want to thank the students in my Basic Judaism course at the Jewish Study Center in Washington, D.C., from whom I learned so much.

John Miller, Reference Librarian at the Jacob Burns Law Library of The George Washington University Law School, unfailingly helped in locating hard-to-find materials. Peg Northen-Cole, who also provided helpful editorial comments, and Dale T. Wise, Jr., diligently typed the manuscript.

PART ONE

INTRODUCTION

CHAPTER ONE

Rethinking the Jewish Tradition

Why be Jewish in the twenty-first century?

For many American Jews at the beginning of the twenty-first century, Judaism has lost its vital content and its enchantment. American Jews are threatened with communal extinction through assimilation and intermarriage.

We see a rising tide of assimilation marked by the merging of many Jews into the general secular community. These Jews have exchanged their religious souls for the right to thrive as individuals in an open society.

Runaway intermarriage rates also threaten Judaism in the United States. More than 50 percent of Jews intermarry and only a small fraction of the non-Jewish spouses, perhaps as low as one out of twenty, converts to Judaism. Only slightly more than one-quarter of the children of these intermarriage unions are raised as Jews and far fewer marry Jews.[1] Thus intermarriage reflects, consciously or unconsciously, a way of opting out of Judaism.

Yet in the midst of interfaith marriages, our children's questions about God, our stressful, two-career lives, our friends' cancers, the terrors of aging, and eventually our own mortality, many Jews sense a spiritual disconnectedness, an emptiness, a void. Something is stirring people's souls. They are searching for a deeper connection and yearning for a more profound meaning in lives all too shallow and rootless, in a world racked by alienation, loneliness, and family dissolution. In hungering for a meaningful existence, they are searching for a transcendent reality and spiritual fulfillment that will enrich their lives in the midst of our modern, materialistic, consumer-oriented culture.

Those who have achieved everything they once thought would make them happy (and even those who have not yet attained their earthly goals), experiencing their finiteness, declare at the end of their quest: "There must be more to it than this!" They see that the search for a materially good life does not bring happiness. Striving to be rooted in a spiritual tradition, they want to feel part of something greater than themselves.

In the midst of this malaise, the mainstream of American Judaism has become ossified. Increasingly, Judaism places an ever greater emphasis on tradition and ritual.

We are like Tevye in the 1960s musical play *Fiddler on the Roof*, which was set in a *shtetl*, a Jewish village, in czarist Russia in 1905. The musical recounts the struggles of Tevye, a milkman, to survive and keep his family together in the face of governmental repression and the forces of change that threaten longstanding Jewish observances. Tevye looks to "tradition."

Like Tevye, American Jews now look to tradition for comfort and sustenance. We look back fondly to idealized memories of the "old country," of our grandparents, of particular kinds of foods. We rely on nostalgia, a sentimental kind of Judaism. As an escape from the complexities and stresses of contemporary society, some of us say, "What was good enough for my grandparents is good enough for me."

We are witnessing a resurgence of traditional Judaism, marked by an emphasis on strict ritualism, the preservation of the ceremonial aspects of Judaism, a rigid body of observances and prohibitions, and the minutiae of Jewish law. For many, rituals, ceremonial practices, and Jewish law, which enabled Jews to survive in a hostile world for two thousand years, connotes Judaism.

This traditional approach to Judaism and, more generally, to living provides a lifestyle characterized by regimentation and apparent certainty. When so much of life seems confusing, the search for security and stability in "tradition" and an escape to the past serves as a survival mechanism for the modern, remaining Jewish remnant, meeting needs for those who feel inadequate or threatened, or who find it difficult to exist in an increasingly chaotic and ambiguous world. It is a throwback to our ancestors' centuries of separatism in the former ghettos of Eastern Europe.

THE NEED FOR A NEW APPROACH FOR THE TWENTY-FIRST CENTURY

When we think about Judaism, we usually focus on mechanical repetition and cookbook-like observances and rules. We think that Judaism is synonymous with an almost mindless performance of ceremonies and rituals, particularly with respect to observing the Sabbath and the dietary laws. The rituals have taken on a life of their own. Yet the ceremonies, rituals, and all the accompanying rules and regulations (Jewish religious law, or Halakah) are the byways of Judaism, not its highways or its essence.

For many, the ceremonies and rituals, although designed to open and touch the spiritual dimension of existence, often block their spiritual life and vitality. They find little value in observances and rules for their own sake. These rigid, ancient rites and indecipherable liturgies are often spiritually choking. Judaism has thus come to consist of an empty shell.

If not by rules and rituals, how then can we sustain, promote, and enhance Judaism? How can we formulate a core of Jewish belief and identity? How can we keep Jews as Jews and even attract non-Jews?

Today, just as in the first century of the Common Era, doubts exist that a new Judaism can be created. Yet rabbinic Judaism arose, vastly different from its biblical predecessor. It was and is a Judaism that did not need a Temple in Jerusalem or animal sacrifices. It continues to be a Judaism, focused on the local synagogue and rabbi, that could be transported around the world. However, there were and continue to be many forms of Judaism, a religion that has constantly changed and evolved over the ages to meet changing needs and conditions.

As discussed in chapter 2, "The Crumbling Foundations of Judaism," in the twenty-first century Judaism must offer some positive, affirmative identification beyond the Torah as a Divinely revealed document; victimhood, particularly remembrance of anti-Semitism and the Holocaust, as well as the perpetuation of a survivalist mentality; and a secular, political approach, namely, unqualified support for the State of Israel. Judaism must also stand for something beyond non-

Christianity, beyond rejecting Jesus as the Messiah and the path to heavenly salvation.

At the start of the twenty-first century, we live in an era of general change in religions and religious institutions. Old forms have lost considerable vitality. A revitalized Judaism must, therefore, offer a vibrant force, a life philosophy, a set of beliefs, and a method of living for people's entire lives. It must have a sacred core and vital content beyond its outward forms: rituals, ceremonies, and a code of rules. Providing meaning and a sense of purpose, it must affirm both a love of God and a love of life.

THE SPIRITUAL ESSENCE OF JUDAISM

To fill the need for a positive Judaism for the twenty-first century beyond rituals, victimhood, or Israel, I offer Jewish Spirituality, an ethical, virtue-oriented, monotheistic system, transcending the minutiae of the traditional legalistic rules and rituals designed to govern everyday living.

Filling our spiritual hunger, offering meaning to our existence, and providing a connection with the transcendent, Jewish Spirituality represents a nondogmatic, nonlegalistic path. It is a way of thought, feeling, and belief, not centered on rules or rote rituals and prayers, about God and the spiritual depths of our being. It welcomes all people who seek to attune to the Divine Presence in their lives. It offers the vision of a personal, intimate experience of a living God as the source of health, joy, love, abundance, and wholeness. It is designed to help us meet and surmount our daily problems as well as the crises we all face in living and, ultimately, in dying. True to its practical orientation, Jewish Spirituality focuses on an approach to living that is liberating, that promotes and unfolds our inner human possibilities, and that helps each of us realize his or her highest self and that of others around us.

Spiritually oriented Judaism strives to answer two fundamental questions: How can I personally access, experience, and relate to God? How can I daily enhance the quality of my life and those around me through ethical conduct and the practice of certain virtues? Thus, Jewish Spirituality informs our life and our thoughts, words, and deeds. It is a profound, inspiring, life-enhancing tradition based on the teachings of the prophet Micah, who proclaimed more than twenty-five hundred years ago: "O humans, what is good and what does God ask of you: Only to do justly, to love goodness and mercy, and to walk humbly with your God." (Micah 6:8)

The foundations of the spiritual essence of Judaism are threefold. First, as developed in chapter 3, "God: The Focus of Jewish Spirituality," we need to realize and deep down grasp the notion of the Eternal, the Transcendent Force, giving order and meaning to the cosmos. In the midst of our stress-filled lives and the perplexing and seemingly overwhelming dilemmas we face, each of us can appeal to God, as the one Divine Presence in every human heart, for aid and guidance in our personal and interpersonal growth and development and in times of need and distress. Chapter 4, "Finding God and Invoking Divine Aid and Guidance in Our Daily Lives," provides an introduction to spiritual practices, including prayer, meditation, and visualization, offering us a more personal, far less institutional, awareness of the Eternal Who is at the core of our nature. These practices help us attain a better understanding of God, a more intimate connection with the Divine, and a deeper realization of the spiritual depths of our being.

Second, our faith must influence our daily dealings with and conduct toward others, by inspiring and directing us to lovingkindness (chapter 5, "The Importance of Loving and Being Compassionate Toward Others"), forgiveness (chapter 6, "Forgiveness: A Key to Loving Others and Enhancing Inner Peace of Mind"), and truthfulness (chapter 7, "Truthfulness: Another Key to Our Dealings with Others"). Jewish Spirituality points the way to improving our words and deeds in human relationships and, more generally, in our approach to life.

Third, our faith must help us develop our inner lives through the cultivation of certain personal virtues and character traits. Jewish Spirituality provides guideposts for daily living: conquering our tendency to pride and ostentation, eliminating envy and pessimism, and curbing our anger. It points the way to a life marked by humility (chapter 8, "Striking the Balance Between Humility and Positive Self-Esteem"), joy and optimism (chapter 9, "The Importance of Joyfulness and Optimism"), and equanimity and inner peace of mind (chapter 10, "Strive for Equanimity and Inner Peace of Mind to Overcome Stress, Anger, and Envy"). In these three chapters, I draw on modern, empirical evidence from psychology and medicine to reinforce the teachings of Jewish Spirituality.

By thinking in spiritual terms, being more God-conscious, conducting ourselves ethically, and practicing certain personal virtues, spiritually directed Judaism enables us to realize the essence of the Jewish tradition in our daily lives, here and now. Jewish Spirituality helps us grapple with "real life": difficult people, interpersonal conflicts, failures at work and in business, stress that lies at the root of many illnesses, and the immense quandaries raised by death and dying.

The spiritual essence of Judaism thus provides a source of comfort, helping us cope with hardships and tragedies and the critical situations we all encounter in life. Chapter 11, "Facing Serious Illness, Curing Symptoms, and Promoting Healing," deals with the role of faith in healing physical and mental illness, again drawing on concepts and evidence from psychology and medicine to bolster the insights of Jewish Spirituality. One of the most important purposes of Judaism (or any religion, for that matter) is healing, which connotes a wholeness of body, mind, and spirit. Chapters 12 ("Facing Terminal Illness and Death: The Process of Dying") and 13 ("Death, Grieving, and the Soul's Afterlife Journey"), respectively, explore how we can better face death and surmount the grief accompanying the death of a beloved, through the Jewish tradition's insights into the soul's afterlife journey. Living with faith in the afterlife, a keynote of spiritually oriented Judaism, helps us overcome our fear of death.

Although Judaism has long emphasized communal prayer and other group activities, as a work of practical spirituality, chapters 5 through 13 contain individualized, spontaneous prayers, meditations, and visualization—highly personalized expressions of belief, more focused on our inner experiences and less on formality in worship and outward practices, designed to enhance our well-being and peace of mind, particularly in times of worry, fear, and sorrow. These spiritual practices enable us to more personally commune with God and provide a profound reawakening of the Transcendent in every aspect of our lives.

The conclusion (chapter 14, "Placing Jewish Spirituality in an Institutional Context") draws together the strands of Jewish Spirituality, as a faith affirming both the love of God and the love of life, and places them in an institutional context. Suggestions are provided for restructuring communal worship services and improving Jewish supplemental school education.

In short, this book aims to help you live a life embodying the teachings of Jewish Spirituality, a more personalized, individualized form of Judaism than nearly all of us are familiar with. How? By fostering a concept of God to Whom you are deeply devoted, a living God Who can help you deal with and even change your life. By developing a life based on the ethics and virtues of spiritually focused Judaism, you can contribute not only to your own personal growth and development but also to the spiritual advancement of humanity. By being kinder to yourself and others, the spiritual essence of Judaism helps you behave better toward others. By being less fearful of death because of your belief in the soul's immortality, a spiritually attuned Judaism helps you be braver in facing life's seemingly ultimate tragedy— death.

AN OVERVIEW OF JEWISH SOURCES USED IN THIS BOOK

Before beginning our discussion of a spiritually oriented Judaism, it is important to keep in mind that the Jewish tradition relies on four major sources: biblical, rabbinic, medieval, and mystical.[2]

Biblical texts include the Five Books of Moses (Genesis, Exodus, Leviticus, Numbers, and Deuteronomy) as well as the Prophets, and various writings including the Psalms and the Book of Proverbs. These biblical texts were written mainly from the tenth to the fifth centuries B.C.E.

Rabbinic Judaism was born out of the destruction of the Second Jewish Temple in Jerusalem some nineteen hundred years ago. For the next five hundred to nine hundred years of the Common Era, until the medieval period in Europe, a vast body of literature developed, reflecting the creative ferment of the rabbis. The rabbinic literature consists of two parts: the Talmud, mainly a legalistic discourse on all aspects of Jewish life as well as various nonlegal materials; and second, the Midrash, interpretations of Biblical passages using allegories, parables, analogies, and stories to illustrate the meaning of a verse.

The rabbis, consistent with the biblical prophetic tradition, maintained that a new Divine world order, a trans-historical human realm of world peace, social justice, and human unity, would eventually replace the existing socio-political realm. However, the rabbis' teachings focused mainly on how to live in the human community, not on interpreting the mysteries of the cosmos.

For the past two thousand years, the rabbinic tradition has espoused an ethical reward-and-punishment stance. Each of us receives rewards or punishments in this world and the afterlife in accordance with our actions, words, and thoughts, particularly our observing of an array of Jewish laws and rituals.

Medieval Jewish materials consist of two major sources: medieval literature, including interpretative biblical Midrash, and philosophical writings. The medieval legendary narratives written in the tenth to fourteenth centuries of the Common Era explore a wide range of Jewish themes. Along with the medieval biblical Midrash, the period 900 to 1300 C.E. witnessed an outpouring of medieval Jewish philosophical writings, blending rabbinic Judaism with philosophy, particularly Greek philosophic thought and its belief in human immortality.

Mystical Jewish teachings (the Kabbalah) are products of academies of Jewish mysticism in thirteenth-to-fifteenth-century France and Spain and sixteenth-century Palestine. The most important written product of these teachings, the *Zohar* (The Book of Splendor), a mystical interpretation of the Five Books of Moses disguised as a novel, appeared in the late thirteenth century of the Common Era. Even today, the *Zohar* remains the major text of Jewish mysticism.

Several centuries later, Rabbi Isaac Luria, a mystic in Palestine, invented the kabbalistic story of creation. Luria taught that before humanity there was only God. Beginning with the act of creation, God withdrew from the infinite space, leaving a vacuum. Into this vacuum God sent rays of light. As these rays of light channeled through vessels, some of these vessels shattered, creating sparks trapped in the material world. According to Luria, our task centers on identifying the Divine Spark in every human and returning each one of us to his or her divinity, thereby repairing the world and ushering in the Messianic Era.

The mystical literature also encompasses the tales produced by Hasidim, a populist Jewish movement based on the Lurianic Kabbalah, emphasizing ecstasy and joy in prayer and worship, that emerged in the eighteenth century and continues to our own day. The Hasidic movement brought mysticism to the Jewish masses and spawned the Hasidic tale that relates in story form the wondrous life and deeds of various charismatic Hasidic rabbis (rebbes or *zaddikim*—highly evolved, righteous spiritual leaders) beginning with the Baal Shem Tov, the founder of the Hasidic movement, who lived in Poland from 1698 to 1760. In addition to glorifying the life and deeds of deceased rebbes, the Hasidic tales provide a rich source of Jewish teachings about life and death.

Let us begin our exploration of Jewish Spirituality by focusing on the three pillars of Judaism in the twentieth century: the Torah as a Divinely revealed doctrine; victimhood stemming from centuries of anti-Semitism that culminated in the Holocaust; and the secular, political approach of Jewish nationalism, support for the State of Israel. We shall see how these foundations are crumbling, creating the need for the positive replacement provided by a spiritually oriented Judaism.

NOTES

1. Lawrence Grossman, "Jewish Communal Affairs," in *American Jewish Year Book* 1993, ed. David Singer (New York: The American Jewish Committee, 1993), p. 179.

2. For background on rabbinic, medieval, and mystical Judaism, I have drawn on Robert M. Seltzer, *Jewish People, Jewish Thought: The Jewish Experience in History* (New York: Macmillan, 1980), pp. 243–314 and 373–450; and Edward Hoffman, *The Way of Splendor: Jewish Mysticism and Modern Psychology* (Northvale, NJ: Jason Aronson, 1992), pp. 7–40.

CHAPTER TWO

The Crumbling
Foundations of Judaism

In the twentieth century, Jewishness has rested on three pillars: first, adherence to God's law as revealed in the Torah (the Five Books of Moses); second, a collective reaction to anti-Semitism; and third, faith in the restoration of Zion, which for the past fifty years has meant support for the State of Israel. Yet each of these pillars is now under attack.

QUESTIONING THE DIVINELY REVEALED
ORIGIN OF THE TORAH

Rabbinic Judaism, which has regulated Jewish existence for nineteen hundred years, rests on a fairly strict adherence to God's law as revealed in the Torah, as elaborated in the Talmud, and as explicated by rabbis. The written and oral law covers every aspect of Jewish life. The law is perceived as Divinely inspired.

According to traditional Judaism, the commanding voice of God remains paramount, fixed, and constant. Thus Orthodox rabbis proclaim that Jews live in a covenant with God, imposing a multitude of special obligations on them, daily throughout their lives. These obligations cover the entire scope of personal and social behavior.

Jewish fundamentalists believe that God gave the Torah, consisting of both the written Torah (the Pentateuch [Greek] or, more familiarly, the Five Books of Moses) and the oral Torah (the books of the prophets, the Talmud, and all the decisions and explanations of Jewish law by rabbis over the ages) to Moses at Mount Sinai. The belief that the two Torah were given at Mount Sinai, including the answers to all questions that might arise, not only adds to the mystery of what occurred at Mount Sinai but also grants special authority to subsequent rabbinical interpretations.

For the traditionalists, the Torah represents a one-time gift to the Jews. Moses held a direct communication with God and received a Divine revelation. The words found in the Torah were not the creation of Moses' mind. As proof of this claim, the fundamentalists cite the Torah text itself. In the Book of Exodus we read: "God spoke all these words. . ." (Exodus 20:1) Thus the whole Torah, as God-revealed, is unimpeachably true and good throughout.

As the late Rabbi Milton Steinberg wrote in his classic work, *Basic Judaism,*

> To the traditionalists the entire Torah-Book, every word, every letter, was imparted by God either directly to the whole people of Israel at Mount Sinai or indirectly through Moses. The fact of revelation is decisive. It is a guarantee of absolute validity, intellectual and moral.
>
> But revelation, according to the traditionalists, does not exhaust itself in the Torah-Book. It suffuses the writings of the prophets after Moses, overflows into the rest of the Scripture, thence into classical Talmudic literature; thence again, though in diminishing degree, into later rabbinic writings. In other words, the mainstream of the tradition everywhere possesses something of the authority of the Torah-Book.[1]

From the premise that the Torah-Tradition like the Torah-Book is of Divine authority and that Jewish law derives from a God-given mandate, Steinberg offers three significant conclusions. First, for Jewish fundamentalists, since "Judaism was complete and perfect at Sinai," it "cannot be susceptible to consequential changes." Under all the subsequent restatements by prophets, sages, and rabbis, "Judaism has persisted as one and the same from Moses to our day."

Second, even for traditionalists, however, Judaism is not "altogether unbending and eternally immutable." Although "some measure of flexibility" exists as Judaism "is always susceptible to reinterpretation" and a crisis may require the suspension of certain of its provisions, "the free play allowed by reinterpretation is not overly extensive and the right to issue emergency decrees has always been used sparingly." The traditionalist accords the Torah the major characteristic of consistency.

Third, and perhaps most important for Jewish fundamentalists, "the Torah is first, last, and always [the] reliable test of the goodness or truth of anything. Any proposition which contravenes the Tradition must be false, no matter how impressive the argument marshaled in its support. Any moral principle that is out of harmony with the Teaching must be of an imperfect rule, though it give[s] every appearance of being wise and expedient."[2]

For the modernist, in contrast, the Torah did not come into being at one time at Mount Sinai as the work of Moses, a single author. Rather, it achieved its familiar shape as the result of an evolutionary process. It represents a combination of multiple, independent documents.

For the past several hundred years, critical biblical analysis has found: first, numerous duplications and repetitions in the Pentateuch; second, variations in the name of the Divine; and third, a broad diversity of language and style as well as contrasting viewpoints in the text. The discovery of duplication extending across a considerable body of text led to the claim, going back to the seventeenth century, that the Torah had its own history of composition. Specifically, that it had been compiled from a number of documents.

There are two creation stories in the Book of Genesis (Genesis 1:1–2:4a and 2:4b–2:25). According to one commentator, the repetitions and parallelisms in the first story give way to a freer narrative style, richer in vocabulary and unencumbered by repeated refrains. The perfectly created world no longer exists and creation starts all over again. Did the narrator suffer amnesia? As one commentator puts it:

> . . . Not only are there duplications and a change in style, but there also seem to be contradictions between the first story and what follows. In chapter one, animals are created *before* mankind. In chapter two, animals are created as a kind of afterthought, to give the man company and assistance. Woman, who is created along with man in the first chapter, is now formed separately. God also seems to have changed the way of creating: living things no longer come into being

by [Divine] command but are fashioned from the ground. In other
words, the second telling of creation is not just a fleshed-out repetition
of the first, but conceives of creation in a different way.[3]

Other notable duplications exist. There are two flood stories
(Genesis 7:7–10 and 7:13–16). Abraham makes two covenants with
God (Genesis 15 and 17). God reveals the Divine name to Moses twice
(Exodus 3:13–15 and 6:2–3). There are slightly different versions of
the Ten Commandments (Exodus 20:1–14 and Deuteronomy 5:6–18).
Variation in Divine names Elohim and Yahweh, in the Book of Genesis
and the first few chapters of the Book of Exodus, represents further
evidence of the different sources.

Three parallel sources—J (for Jahwist or Yahwist), E (for Elohist),
and P (for Priestly)—and the addition of a fourth source, D (for
Deuteronomist), gave rise to the four-source hypothesis. Although
dates and the exact nature of the four sources have been and continue
to be disputed, the view that four sources underpin the Torah holds
the field among nearly all contemporary biblical scholars. Let me try
to summarize these scholarly insights, known as the Documentary
Hypothesis.[4]

The best scholarship indicates that J, so named because in the
narratives in Genesis God is called Yahweh, came from the southern
Kingdom of Judah. J refers to God as Yahweh, the personal name of
God. J endows the Divine with an anthropomorphic quality. In other
words, God has human attributes.

J's work is a narrative of some of the Torah's best stories, sparsely
told with wonderful wordplays, puns, and ironic uses of speech. J did
not have the slightest interest in priestly rules. Also, J was not too
interested in laws.

J, as an advocate of the Davidic royal house, focuses on God's
covenant with Abraham. As to the future, J offers the promise of
blessings by God for the ancient Hebrews. J had faith in a worldwide
future for Israel. Abraham's descendants would be blessed throughout
the world.

E, a priest who came from the northern Kingdom of Israel, refers
to God as Elohim until Moses meets God at the burning bush, when
God becomes Yahweh (Exodus 6:2–3). Like J, God, for E, has an
anthropomorphic quality. By picturing God in personal ways, J and
E emphasize the Divine aspects of mercy and compassion.

As an advocate of the priestly family of Shiloh, perhaps a Shiloh
Levite, E focuses on Moses and denigrates Aaron.

J and E maximize the use of dramatic storytelling: creation and flood, the covenant with Abraham, the plagues, and the Exodus of the Jews from Egypt. Both J and E portray, in somewhat different versions, the covenant between God and the people of Israel at Mount Sinai. In contrast, P, who knew and used the J and E sources, has relatively few stories of this type.

P, a priestly work written by a descendant of Aaron, is distinguished for its interest in the priesthood and ritual laws. P offers laws about priests, rituals, and sacrifices that flow through the Books of Genesis, Exodus, Leviticus, and Numbers. The observance of these laws will ensure, according to P, God's enduring presence among the Israelites, on which their national existence depends.

For P, God is the Transcendent Controller of the universe, a more cosmic, less personal force. P emphasizes the Divine aspect of justice, rewarding human obedience and punishing transgressions.

What concerns P at Sinai was not the original covenant with Abraham, but the bringing of the Jewish people under God's domination and the building of a tentlike tabernacle, a portable Divine residence with its own priesthood. The tabernacle, where the laws were given, the worship of God took place, and the priestly class held sway, looks forward to the eventual Temple and the ascendancy of the priesthood in Jerusalem. For P, a priest, these were Sinai's great events.

D is an independent, fourth source. D is an advocate of the priesthood, particularly the priests of Shiloh. D, probably a Shiloh Levite, perhaps the prophet Jeremiah (who lived in the last part of the seventh century B.C.E. and the first part of the sixth century B.C.E.), writes a history that flows from Moses—both the laws "given" at Mount Sinai and the laws God "gave" to Moses at the end of the forty years of travel by the Israelites in the wilderness—to the writer's own historical moment.

D shares the outlook of Jews who held fast to the Book of the Law. D preaches the Torah as the Book of the Law.

D foresees the future misfortunes of the Jews who would be driven from Israel as the result of their disobedience to God's laws. Looking to the future with hope, if God's people turn to the Eternal again, repentance might assure them of something good from God. D uses long speeches—in modern terms, sermons—to reinforce these themes in the historical narrative.

These four hands, J, E, P, and D, joined in writing the Five Books of Moses together with the hand of a main, but rather unskilled, editor—a redactor, who combined and organized the separate documents into a single work. Scholars are unable to agree on the interrelationship of the four separate documents, namely, J, E, P, and D. Many experts suggest that the various strands were combined into one document at about the time of the return of the Jews from the Babylonian Exile and the rebuilding of the Second Temple in Jerusalem during the sixth century B.C.E.

Under this interpretation, Ezra, a sixth-century B.C.E. priest, who sought to strengthen Jewish religious identity and prevent the dissolution of biblical monotheism, may be the scribe responsible for the redaction. Ezra assembled the Jews in Jerusalem and read and explained the Torah to them. A leading historian of Jewish thought writes, "Many modern historians feel that it was at this moment when the Torah book, the Pentateuch in close to its final form, became the unchallenged norm of Israel's religion and when Judaism took its single most important step to becoming a religion of Scripture. . . ."[5]

Stepping back from this brief overview, we realize that modern critical scholarship has undermined the traditional understanding of the Torah as Divinely revealed to Moses. Biblical scholarship calls into question two bedrock doctrines: first, a literal revelation by God to Moses; and second, the covenant between God and the Jews on which traditional Jewish rituals and laws are based.

The authors of the Bible wove together various source materials, a collection of semihistorical yarns and sheer fantasies, originating at different times in ancient Israel. The Bible, as a human work, was authored by many humans and was subject to editing and re-editing over long periods of time.

Let me be very clear about this: The Torah was not communicated by God to Moses. God was not the direct source of the Torah. At best, a belief in the Eternal inspired the ancient Jews to write the Five Books of Moses.

Although the Torah has special significance for the Jewish people, these writings are not uniquely true or a superior form of Divine revelation. Jews do not possess ultimate truth through the Torah. Rather, I see the Torah as a record of the spiritual life of the Jewish people and as evidence of their religious quest.

Viewing the Bible as a product of humans, an unverifiable mix of myth and historical fantasy, not the commanding voice of God, Jews need not accept either the authority of the Torah or the nearly two thousand years of rabbinic tradition interpreting the Torah. Thus

Jewish law, as formulated by men in a patriarchal culture, no longer provides a basic consensus for the essence of Judaism.

Furthermore, God did not choose the Jewish people to be the recipients of the Torah. For nearly two thousand years, especially in the Middle Ages, the concept of chosenness supplied Jews "with self-respect, purposefulness, and confidence at a time when the whole world conspired to dispirit them and break their strength."[6] However, the myth of chosenness has outlived its usefulness. Because the Torah is a human product, there is no need for Jews to dedicate themselves to the observance of supposedly Divinely revealed law and to separate themselves from other peoples so as to facilitate the observance of these "God-given" rules.

In the twenty-first century, we can therefore de-emphasize the study of the Torah and turn Judaism away from being a religion of scripture. We need not live in accordance with all of the supposed 613 Divine commands designed to take Jews through all the aspects of living and dying, as embodied in a multitude of harsh, rigid, and often archaic legalisms codified by Rabbi Yosef Karo in the sixteenth century C.E. in *The Code of Jewish Law* (the *Shulchon Oruch* in Hebrew)—notably, observing dietary (kosher) laws, respecting the Sabbath, and praying three times each day.

Viewing the Five Books of Moses as a force for humanity to gain deeper insights and be led to nobler conduct, the spirit of the Torah does, however, provide a source of guidance and inspiration for us today. Although the Hebrew Bible retains its spiritual vitality, particularly in the teachings of the prophets and the guidance provided by the Psalms and the Book of Proverbs, each of us is free to make his or her own decisions as to what laws and rituals he or she wishes (or does not wish) to observe and with what degree of rigor. From the perspective of Jewish Spirituality, you need observe only those Jewish religious activities handed down by tradition that you personally find meaningful.

In the wake of the reinterpretation and the downplaying of the role of the Torah, and more generally Jewish law, in the life of Jews for the past 150 years or so, various forms of "liberal" Judaism made ritual more simple and observance more flexible, but did not succeed in filling the spiritual vacuum. A spiritual malaise continued to exist. The vacuum was filled temporarily by the fear of anti-Semitism and support for the State of Israel.

FEAR OF ANTI-SEMITISM AND ITS DECLINE
AS A KEY TO JEWISH IDENTITY

Judaism has long been defined by Jewish enemies through persecution and inequality. For centuries, throughout the world, Jews have protected and defended Judaism against its external enemies, seeking survival in the face of threats to their safety. However, in the early twenty-first century, anti-Semitism and inequality for Jews have basically disappeared as key issues, at least in the United States.

Fear of anti-Semitism has played a critical role in the formulation of Jewish identity. The fight against anti-Semitism remained at the heart of Jewishness not only in the twentieth century but also for the past two thousand years. Anti-Semitism has comprised a fairly constant reality for the past two millennia of Jewish existence, serving as a major source of Jewish identity and group solidarity.

However, vigilance against anti-Semitism represents a negative definition of Judaism. More broadly, Jewish identity has been based on a suspicion of and a hostility toward Christianity. Jews simply don't want to be Christian and have been fearful about Christian attitudes toward them.

For the past fifty years, Jews have been preoccupied with the ultimate nightmare of anti-Semitism, the Holocaust. The contemporary discomfort with and perceptions of anti-Semitism among Jews must be viewed through the lens of the Holocaust.

By the 1980s, Jews had turned the remembrance of the Holocaust into a civil religion. The Holocaust came to symbolize the culmination of nearly two thousand years of the degradation and persecution of Jews at the hands of Christians.

"Remember" became the watchword of Jews—as Frida Michelson, a concentration camp survivor, begins her memoirs: "I hear your cries and screams, the thousands-strong thunder of your feet running to the grave, your last word: 'Remember!'" [7] Thus, the Holocaust came to form the defining moment in Jewish history and the symbol of Jewish identity. In the death camps, God revealed the 614th commandment, to be added to the 613 commandments fundamentalists see as contained in the Torah, directed to post-Holocaust Jews. Rabbi Emil L. Fackenheim explains this new decree mandating that Jews not lose their identity and assimilate into society as follows:

> Jews are forbidden to hand Hitler posthumous victories. They are commanded to survive as Jews, lest the Jewish people perish. They

are commanded to remember the victims of Auschwitz lest their memory perish. . . . A Jew may not respond to Hitler's attempt to destroy Judaism by himself co-operating in its destruction. In ancient times, the unthinkable Jewish sin was idolatry. Today, it is to respond to Hitler by doing his work.[8]

For Fackenheim and many others, Jews have a sacred duty to remember the Holocaust. The Voice of Auschwitz demands that those who perished must not be forgotten.

The obsession with anti-Semitism and the Holocaust has turned into a Jewish cult of victimhood. Jewish history is seen as one of continuing victimization: anti-Semitic decrees, religious persecution, and pogroms—culminating in the Holocaust. A history of persecution and collective suffering shaped a sense of Jewish identity and a feeling of isolation and separation among Jews.

However, at the beginning of the twenty-first century, Jews, at least in the United States, face external friendship, characterized by inclusion, wealth, and political power. American Jews are accepted. They are affluent and influential. Anti-Semitism will not boil over and place American Jews in another Holocaust.[9]

The obstacles facing Jews in the United States eroded markedly after World War II. In contrast to the hostility of fifty years ago, the ability of American Jews to be educated, to work, or to live is no longer restricted or in any way limited. Jews are no longer systematically excluded from neighborhoods, country clubs, universities, businesses, or law firms. Business, governmental units, and universities embrace Jews. Younger Jews do not see themselves as victims of anti-Semitism.

Institutional, particularly church-supported, anti-Semitism has basically ended. To take but several examples, in 1994 the Roman Catholic Church entered into diplomatic relations with Israel. In March 1998, Pope John Paul II issued "We Remember: A Reflection on the Shoah" seeking forgiveness for the failure of Catholics to stop the mass deportations and the killings of Jews during the Holocaust. Also, the Lutheran Church in the United States has explicitly rejected Martin Luther's anti-Semitic teachings.

In short, Christian denominations, influenced by the Holocaust, have called off their long-standing war against the Jews. They have rewritten texts to take a more positive view of Judaism. In addition to admitting their direct connection to anti-Semitism through their past words and conduct, Christian denominations generally have come to reject hostile attitudes toward Judaism and Jews. Condemning anti-

Semitism, they increasingly strive to reaffirm the historic role Judaism played in the Christian tradition.

With the profound post–World War II changes in Christian attitudes to Judaism and Jews, external victimization lies in the past for American Jews. Although experts estimate that somewhat over 10 percent of the U.S. population holds some anti-Semitic beliefs, hard-core anti-Semites comprise only about 5 percent.[10] Today's anti-Semites form the dregs of society. These low-status individuals exist on the margins of American society and are relatively powerless. These private bigots do not significantly impact the lives of American Jews.

The United States is not a land filled with anti-Semitism. We are not on the verge of an anti-Semitic rampage. Instead, anti-Semitism in twenty-first-century America will likely be nonexistent. According to one scholar, who wrote the first comprehensive scholarly survey of anti-Semitism in the United States,

> Today, antisemitism in the United States is neither virulent nor growing. It is not a powerful social or political force. . . . Much less prejudice exists in our own time than in any other period in the history of this nation. . . .
>
> There is no reason to suspect that antisemitism will not continue to decline in the United States even though there will always be sporadic outbursts and temporary flare-ups. . . . By comparing the strength of antisemitism in the United States today with what it had been in previous decades or centuries, the obvious conclusion is that it has declined in potency and will continue to do so for the foreseeable future.[11]

With the decrease in prejudice, particularly church-sponsored hatred, anti-Semitism, one of the historic pillars of Jewishness, is collapsing. Younger Jews perceive this reality, even if their elders, who grew up in a far different era, do not. With the death of more and more Holocaust survivors, the impact of their lives and their personal suffering will diminish. It is unlikely that the emotional impact of the Holocaust, which became a central focus of the Jewishness of many American Jews, can maintain Jewish identity and continuity. Victimhood—namely, the suffering and death experienced by European Jews during World War II—cannot sustain and renew Judaism. The Jewish tradition cannot flourish by looking back to past discrimination and persecution, no matter how vicious.

THE RISE AND FALL OF ZIONISM AND THE STATE OF ISRAEL AS A BEACON FOR JUDAISM

Over the past fifty years, support for Israel has become a key element in the Jewishness of most American Jews, who have staunchly defended the cause of the State of Israel. This strong identification with and feeling of pride for Israel was most pronounced when Israel faced the mortal danger of annihilation by its Arab enemies during repeated times of crisis. For decades, many American Jews linked their Jewish identity with Israel and gave their unquestioned support to Israel. American Jews of all stripes closed ranks when Israel was under siege by Arab hostility in the Six Day War of 1967, the Yom Kippur War of 1973, and the Gulf War of 1991.

Talk about groupthink and peer pressure. For decades, any questioning of Israeli governmental policies was simply not allowed. American Jews gave Israel their blind loyalty and allegiance. Israel became the vehicle, along with remembrance of the Holocaust, through which Jewish identity played out.

In view of the difficulties in bringing the Palestinian-Israeli peace process to fruition and the religious squabbles in Israel, particularly the Orthodox monopoly over religious life, it is now harder and harder for many American Jews to offer their unqualified support for Israel. Along with the fading of anti-Semitism, in the twenty-first century Jews in the United States, particularly the younger generation, may no longer find their Jewishness in an identification with Israel.

Although the quest for a Jewish homeland goes back nearly two thousand years, modern Zionism is only a little more than one hundred years old.[12] Theodor Herzl (1860–1905), the father of political Zionism, argued in the 1890s that unless Jews obtained a homeland they would have no security in the modern world. Zionism in the late nineteenth and early twentieth centuries sought to replace a religious definition of Judaism with a secular, nationalistic one. Herzl and other political Zionists viewed Jews in Europe as a debilitated, powerless people leading a marginal existence, dependent on the goodwill of others, lacking any means for self-defense. A Jewish state, characterized by economic and political independence, would provide a safe haven for Jews to escape from oppression and anti-Semitism, especially in Europe.

Herzl concluded that Jews should take their destiny into their own hands because of endemic anti-Semitism in every nation where substantial numbers of Jews lived. It was dangerous, Herzl maintained, for Jews to live as a minority, usually a small minority, in Christian nations. His answer: political Zionism, a secular nationalism focusing on the creation of an ordinary nation, albeit a secular Jewish state, in Palestine.

Zionism, as a nationalistic movement, used methods common to other nationalistic movements of the time. Zionism focused its quest on the self-determination of a minority ethnic group. Zionists cultivated an association with the historic Jewish homeland, Palestine, and the vision of a secular, utopian future.

Along with other nationalists, Zionists asserted that with a country to call its own, a people would have a voice, would be part of the club of nations. Thus, Jews would even be more accepted in the Diaspora nations if there were a Jewish state.

The appealing vision of the Zionists, namely, providing Jews with a national homeland where they could exercise some political and economic control over their fate, faced one not so small problem. In seeking to move Jews from Europe to Palestine, a land occupied by Arabs, Zionists turned a blind eye to the political, social, and cultural aspirations of the Palestinians, who by the early twentieth century lived in Palestine, the ancestral Jewish homeland.

The Zionist vision of the need to acquire land for Jewish settlement in Palestine as a place of refuge gained increasing credibility in the 1930s and 1940s. The nations of the world had no room for Jews. With Israel, Jews would not be shut out. The Jewish state would safeguard Jews from the vicious jaws of future persecutions. After World War II, the movement for a Jewish state gathered new momentum in the shadow of the greatest catastrophe in Jewish history.

Since the creation of the State of Israel in 1948, marking the fulfillment of the Zionist dream, for many Jews their Jewish identity has to a considerable degree focused on a commitment to Israel, as a safe haven for Jews. Israel served as a means to protect the remnant of European Jews who had survived the Holocaust and increasingly Sephardic (Middle Eastern) and Russian Jews.

Even more than the creation of Israel in 1948, the historic victory in the Six Day War of 1967, which assumed the qualities and proportions of the biblical six days of creation, galvanized millions of American Jews, providing a focus for Jewish belief and action. Israel became an emotional matter, occupying a key place in Jews' hearts and, for many, the source of their Jewish identity. Jews throughout the world were united with Israel. A threat to Israel meant danger to Jews everywhere, including those in the United States.

In the Six Day War, Israel stood defiantly alone. The State of Israel faced a united Arab threat that raised the spectre of another slaughter of Jews, this time in Israel, while the world just closed its eyes. For Jews throughout the world, the Holocaust and the events of the Six Day War were a searing proof that the defense of Israel should serve as the central goal of the Jewish community.

Israel came out of the 1967 war an exalted victor. It had "cachet." With the stunning Israeli victory, American Jews basked in the glow of identification with an Israel that could do no wrong. Israel served as a cause to rally nearly everyone in the American Jewish community. Zionism became the center of Jewishness for American Jews. Israel came to fill the content of Jewishness. According to one commentator, a Zionistic civil religion displaced Judaism as the faith of many American Jews:

> [F]or very many Jews, the experience of the Six Day War had religious significance. Specifically, it was after the Six Day War that Israel came to occupy the center of the Jewish religious consciousness and consensus. In a very precise way, Israel had now become the faith of the American Jew.[13]

As Jewish philanthropy also came to the fore of the modern American Jewish community, funds raised among American Jews for Israel increased each year. Philanthropy, especially for Israel, became a means of expressing Jewishness and achieved a sort of transcendent significance.

After the Six Day War, however, Zionism came under the sway of ultranationalists who pressed for rights to the entire territory west of the Jordan River, the West Bank. Zionism became transformed by Jewish fundamentalists into a land grab. In the late 1960s and throughout the 1970s, these Jewish fundamentalists came to view settling the newly conquered territories as a Divinely ordained task.

By 1982, the politically disastrous Israeli invasion of Lebanon started the first genuine transformation of the perspective of American Jews. Israel appeared to be an aggressor in the Lebanese conflict. With the beginning of the Palestinian uprising (the Intifada) in 1987, world media made the case that Israel was an oppressor. Israel was pilloried for its military occupation and suppression of Palestinian human rights on the West Bank. However, Jewish fundamentalists demanded that land be retained according to biblical dictates.

In the 1990s, the disenchantment within the American Jewish community with Israel came into the open. It is harder and harder for

American Jews to support Israel. Ambivalent and tenuous feelings
toward Israel, especially among younger American Jews, stem from
two factors: dashed hopes for the peace process and rising tensions
between religious and secular Jews in Israel.

Israel has experienced difficulty in arriving at a lasting peace with
the Arab world. The mere giving back of land, whether the Gaza Strip
or, more recently, parts of the West Bank, does not guarantee peace
and a change of heart by the Arab nations. Saying "no" even from a
position of strength and insisting on the importance of maintaining
Israel's security has not led anywhere. Many outside Israel perceive
the Jewish State as the stumbling block to peace.

The hopes of Zionists to build a nation-state around power and
self-defense collapsed. In an era of missile technology and chemical
warfare, security rests on good relations with one's neighbors, not on
the ownership of land and territoriality. The Palestinians and other
Arabs are Israel's partners in the quest for a lasting peace and security.

Sooner or later, the Israeli public and its leaders must face the
need for and the reality of two nations in historic Palestine. Two
nations will emerge, Israel and Palestine, each with its own government.
Coming decades likely will also witness recognition of Jerusalem's
special status as a city holy not only for Jews but also for Christians
and Muslims.

In the 1990s, many American Jews also came to see the Israeli
government as moving toward religious fundamentalism and away
from religious pluralism. This trend has led more American Jews to
publicly criticize Israel for the first time.

With military power and economic prosperity, the old staples of
Israeli life, based on solidarity emerging from anti-Semitism and a
state of permanent war with the Arabs, collapsed. A new war is being
fought between and among Jews. It is a two-front war, focusing on:
What is the nature of the Jewish state? and: What should be the Jewish
character of the State of Israel? A growing polarization has arisen
between secular and ultrareligious Israelis. Mistrust, suspicion, and
often outright contempt separate these two identifiable groups of Jews
in Israel. The ultra-Orthodox in Israel want the Jewish state to be
"Jewish" as they understand Judaism. They press for mandatory public
Sabbath observance—most notably, street closings in Jerusalem—and
adherence to Jewish law in all aspects of life.

Another issue focuses on the delegation of control over life decisions to Orthodox rabbis. More specifically: Who is a Jew and who
should be officially empowered to handle the conversion of Jews in

Israel? Orthodox rabbis, who view Reform and Conservative Judaism as diluting the "Torah true" Jewish tradition, presently control the process of conversion to Judaism in Israel. Only Orthodox-approved converts are accorded full rights to be married and buried as Jews in Israel.

Viewed through the lens of Reform and Conservative Judaism, the Orthodox monopoly over conversion in Israel is seen as delegitimizing these movements, a small minority in Israel but the overwhelming majority of Jews in the United States. The Orthodox monopoly, however, reaches far beyond conversions.

Presently, all Jewish marriages in Israel must be performed by Orthodox rabbis. The Orthodox movement also controls the Chief Rabbinate and one hundred sixty local councils that allot tens of millions of dollars to community groups and synagogues in Israel. Increasingly, Reform and Conservative Jews in the United States, together with their respective movements and organizational structures, have become disturbed and at times outraged at continued Orthodox control over religious matters, including marriage, divorce, and burial, as well as kosher inspections of restaurants and food shops in Israel.

If the Orthodox succeed in pressuring the government of Israel to reject some form of participation by Reform and Conservative movements in conversion (and, ultimately, in lifecycle events such as marriage) in Israel, many American Jews will feel deprived of their spiritual homeland. These Jews will view the continued exclusion of Reform and Conservative movements from their meaningful participation in Israeli religious life as a stigma indicative of second class status, or—even worse—no status at all.

For the past fifty years, American Jews have built their identity on an obsession with anti-Semitism, a Jewish cult of victimhood, and looking to Israel as the anchor and source of their Jewish identity. Anti-Semitism is declining in the United States. Israel resonates less and less. It is increasingly harder for many American Jews to support Israel. They feel alienated from Israel. The central position of Israel to Jewishness will likely diminish as the political and military risks to the Jewish state recede.

―――――――

The beginning of the twenty-first century marks a time of disquiet among many American Jews. A profound sense of disillusionment has set in. This malaise offers an opening for the ethical, virtue-oriented monotheism of a spiritually oriented Judaism. Let us begin by focusing

on God, the One Divine Presence, Who rests at the center of the
Jewish tradition and Jewish Spirituality.

NOTES

1. Milton Steinberg, *Basic Judaism* (New York: Harcourt, Brace, 1947),
p. 24.

2. Steinberg, *Basic Judaism*, pp. 24–26.

3. Victor Hurowitz, "P—Understanding the Priestly Source," *Bible Review*
12:3 (1996): 30–32, 37, 44–47 (quote appears on page 32).

4. I have drawn on Richard Elliott Friedman's lucid explanation, *Who
Wrote the Bible?* (Englewood Cliffs, NJ: Prentice Hall, 1987).

5. Robert M. Seltzer, *Jewish People, Jewish Thought: The Jewish Experience
in History* (New York: Macmillan, 1980), p. 130.

6. Steinberg, *Basic Judaism*, p. 95.

7. Frida Michelson, *I Survived Rumbuli*, trans. Wolf Goodman (New
York: Holocaust Library, 1979), p. 11.

8. Emil L. Fackenheim, *God's Presence in History: Jewish Affirmations and
Philosophical Reflections* (New York: New York University Press, 1970), p. 84.

9. For helpful, popular overviews detailing the decline of anti-Semitism
in the United States see Elliott Abrams, *Faith or Fear: Jews Can Survive in a
Christian America* (New York: Free Press, 1997), pp. 37–97; and Alan M.
Dershowitz, *The Vanishing American Jew: In Search of Jewish Identity for the
Next Century* (Boston: Little, Brown, 1997), pp. 69–142.

10. Seymour Martin Lipset and Earl Raab, *Jews and the New American
Scene* (Cambridge, Mass: Harvard University Press, 1995), p. 87.

11. Leonard Dinnerstein, *Anti-Semitism in America* (New York: Oxford
University Press, 1994), pp. 243 and 250.

12. Jerold S. Auerbach, "Are We One? American Jews and Israel,"
Midstream 44:1 (January 1998): 20–23 provides a helpful overview.

13. Leonard Fein, *Where Are We? The Inner Life of America's Jews* (New
York: Harper & Row, 1988), p. 19.

PART TWO

MONOTHEISM: THE ONE DIVINE PRESENCE

As we contemplate revitalizing Judaism, we cannot bypass the question of God. I see no alternative but to restore God to our consciousness and take the Eternal seriously into our lives. We need to realize that we are not alone in the world. A loving God exists to Whom we may turn in every difficulty and Who will help, guide, and strengthen us in every aspect of life.

We need to put God back on the agenda and believe in the reality of a living God, but without the traditional rigidity and legalisms. We need to realize the Divine Presence and commune with this Presence Who fills all existence. Although recognizing that God transcends human knowledge, chapter 3 discusses how we might view the Eternal. In chapter 4 we will consider various spiritual practices for connecting with God and bringing the Divine into our daily lives.

CHAPTER THREE

God: The Focus of Jewish Spirituality

The world is far more than visible, material reality. There is a Wisdom, infinite and unfathomable, in the cosmos—because God is the Source of all existence. The Divine Presence is at the very heart of the world. The Eternal is the very substance of the universe, the essence of all that exists.[1]

God encompasses all time and space. There is no time or space to limit God's omnipresence. Because God transcends the limits of time and space, the Eternal always remains unchanging and timeless.

God, as the Universal Intelligence, is manifest in everything in the cosmos. God represents the universal source of goodness.

The everlasting reality is the God within us. We are not separate and apart from God. We need to realize God's Presence, have faith in God's goodness, and be conscious of God's nearness to us and the Eternal's compassion and mercy.

We need to accept and fully live our identity as children of God. We are born of goodness. As God's creatures, humans are not depraved beings. We do not exist in an inherent state of sinfulness, requiring extraction depending on acceptance of a human savior or Divine good grace. Sin is not an ineradicable stain on our soul. Humans were not created flawed. We are an extension of God, sharing the Divine attributes. We are loving, joyous, whole, and creative beings.

Because Jewish Spirituality looks at God as a living entity Who can change one's life, not merely as an abstract concept, let us start at the beginning with God the Creator. Then we'll examine God the Continuing Creator and our Loving God, the Sustainer.

GOD THE CREATOR

God is not merely an historic figure, a clockmaker Who wound up the world to let it run, but a present and ongoing reality. God is the Creator of everything and Sustainer of all. God, the essence of all that exists, is an all-pervading presence in the universe. Everything in the cosmos is filled with God. God is in every being.

God, Who gave and continues to give life and existence to every being, guides the world. God is the origin of all things: past, present, and future. God called all reality into existence. The stream of life, in its many shapes and forms, flows from God.

How did existence come into being? Who is the ultimate cause of existence, the source of all light and energy, the originator and the designer of all? Who gave the cosmos and human existence its initial impulse?

Accepting the Big Bang theory, which posits that the universe exploded into being about fifteen billion years ago in a flash of light and energy, creation represents God in action.[2] A guiding hand— God—was at work in the formation of the universe and the evolution of humankind. The cosmos and human life did not result from blind chance, randomness, fortuitous mutations, or natural selection, the struggle among individual organisms to promote their own reproductive success. I do not accept the mechanistic explanation of the universe offered by evolutionary biology that there is no design in nature nor an intelligent, caring purpose at work. Human life did not come about by accident as a result of random, material forces. Randomness cannot lead to order.

According to the Anthropic Principle, our purposeful universe was expressly designed by God for the emergence of human life. By mysterious coincidence, fundamental constants such as the value of gravity and electromagnetism exist for the creation of the universe and for the growth and development of all life, particularly human existence. These fundamental laws of nature, the twenty or so parameters including the numbers governing the strength of gravity and the ratio of the size of a proton to the size of a neutron, were fine-tuned so that conscious organisms could appear. God, the Grand Designer, set these twenty different control knobs at precisely the right values so that the full array of life could appear on earth. The Eternal One chose these laws of nature that permit the evolution of intelligent, self-reflective beings.

Living organisms and the universe are so complex that only an Omniscient Creator could design it all on purpose. Life could not and did not happen without God, a Preexisting Intelligence. Nature and the cosmos are so wonderfully fashioned that they must have been the handiwork of God, the Divine Creator.

Thus, the laws and values of physics fit perfectly with Jewish Spirituality's concept of the Eternal Being as the Creator of a universe capable of producing human life. The cosmos, as designed by God, represents a process to achieve the Divine goal of creating human life and perfecting the world.

GOD THE CONTINUING CREATOR

God is a present and ongoing reality, not merely an historic figure. God remains continually creative. The universe, from the highest to the lowest, from the visible to the invisible, is testimony to the Divine creativeness. God continues to plan and direct the ongoing work of creation.

God, our Life Source, is constantly and continually creative. God's creativeness exercises itself through the advancement and unfolding of each being in existence.

Through the repeated process of creation over the ages, God expresses the Eternal's own essence. Every new being is a new phase of the Divine manifestation. Our existence constitutes a partial realization of the Divine plan.

God continually creates the world, unfolding it, constantly expressing the Divine nature in the form of a never-ending creation. Daily, God renews the work of creation, refreshing all the forces of nature, replenishing all of the powers of the universe, giving rebirth to all of us. God's creativeness is an ever-flowing, everlasting stream. God's creative activity and the continuing outpouring of love and compassion express the Divine abundance.

God, as the Infinite Creator, fashioned the power and beauty of the sun; the quiet, perpetual light of the stars; the unfathomable oceans; and the beauty of the flowers. All existence emanates from God. All life flows from God. All reality expresses the Eternal's presence.

Our powers of thought, imagination, and judgment come from God. We receive our love and compassion from the Divine Source.

THE ONE AND ONLY GOD

One God brought all things into existence. One God formulated the plan by which all beings come into existence. One God directs it all: the world as an indivisible, harmonious whole.

The deep order governing all existence speaks of One Divine Presence Who controls the entire cosmos. The universe is one, its constituent bodies and elements are in harmony one with another, its Creator is One. Recognizing that the universe is one harmonious whole, the Supreme Being, God, Who accounts for the presence of the universe, is also One.

God is the One Who maintains order in nature and is the Source of all wisdom and power. God's wisdom transcends all human wisdom and understanding. God's power is superior to all human power. The Eternal's will is infinite in its creativeness and achievement.

One God saturates all reality, from which all beings and life itself emanate. God is the Divine Source of all phenomena in nature, the eternally creative Mind, and the Infinite Power Who encompasses all reality and sustains all that exists. The One Divine Presence accounts for all things. God remains responsible for all creation and is the Source of all life, the Essence of all existence. All beings emanate from God and by God are all beings sustained.

As the One Divine Presence for all humanity, a universal concept of the Eternal, accessible to all, God is the source of the ethical imperatives for all of humanity. Despite our ethnic, cultural, economic, and racial diversity, we need to recognize our oneness with God and all humanity. We are all children of one Eternal Being, the endless One, Who is without beginning or end. Recognizing our unity and our interconnectedness helps us to overcome our separation and alienation from God and from one another.

GOD THE SUSTAINER

God is the Source and the Creator of all reality and the Sustainer of all life. As the Sustainer of all, God's love and care makes all existence possible. All that God has called into being is sustained by the Eternal. God is present and dwells in all things. The Divine Essence gives them existence.

God sustains everything. God, who granted us life, will supply our needs and guide our steps in life. As our friend, God is here to help those the Eternal created, to give them new strength every day, and to satisfy their desires.

God is omnipresent, filling the universe. God is present in the cosmos, charging the atmosphere with vital elements and life-sustaining energy. God is present in the heavenly bodies, directing their courses, and supplying them with substance. God is present in every living being. God is a vitalizing force, the Life Principle of all that exists. All forms of reality are manifestations of the Divine Reality.

God is both transcendent—vast, infinite, and eternal, dwelling in Heaven—and immanent—the Divine Essence dwelling in every human heart, participating in everyone's life, filling the earth with the Divine Presence.

We encounter God in all phases and aspects of life. God abides in everyone. All humans have a spark of the Divine within them. The God within us is our very essence. Each of us is an expression of the Divine.

Because the Eternal One is not separate or remote from us, God is close to us. The psalmist, the prophets, and the rabbis felt the power of God within them, realizing it with their minds and their hearts.

For the psalmist, God dwells both above creation and within creation. God dwells everywhere and in everything, permeating all reality, as we read in Psalm 139:7–12: "Where shall I go from Your spirit? Where shall I flee from Your presence? If I ascend into heaven, You are there; if I make my bed in the netherworld, You are there, too. If I take wings with the morning and dwell in the uttermost parts of the sea, even there shall Your hand lead me and Your right hand will hold me fast." In Psalm 145:13, the psalmist states: "Your sovereignty embraces all the worlds and your rule extends over all generations."

The prophets were also deeply conscious of God's presence. In Isaiah 66:1–2 God declares: "The heaven is My throne and the earth is My footstool. Where is the house that you built for Me? Where is the place that may be My resting place? For all these things My hand made and all these things came to be." For Isaiah, "the entire Earth is filled with God's glory." (Isaiah 6:3)

In the Talmud we read: For I am God . . . the Holy One Who is in the midst of you. . . . (*Ta'anit* 11b)

Wherever there is life and existence, God is in action. As God is omnipresent, the Divine exists everywhere at the same time, penetrating all things and permeating all worlds. God is at the heart of all beings.

We constantly receive our essence, our health, our vitality and strength, everything that gives us life, from the Eternal Who is within us. This beneficent, personal God dwells everywhere, daily creating and sustaining humanity. We are all manifestations of God. A steady light of the Eternal radiates in and through us. We are inherently Divine beings.

God is deeply concerned not only with the cosmos but also with the life of every single being. God has a beneficent interest in every human.

God is a loving, everpresent Helper, Who cares for everyone. Each of us matters to the Eternal One. Each of us is precious to the Holy One.

The Eternal watches over us, shielding us. God is the Sustainer and Protector to Whom we can turn for guidance and appeal for help. God supplies all our wants and needs and gives comfort to broken hearts and embittered minds.

GOD'S LOVE FOR US

God is inexpressible, indescribable, and incomparable, except in human terms. Many of us have a childish image of the Supreme Sovereign as a grumpy, wrathful, avenging old man with a long, white beard. In contrast to this fear-inspiring vengeful God, the Great Being out there Who rewards or punishes us, giving us what we want or withholding something from us so that we will get back in line, Jewish Spirituality offers the God of lovingkindness, the Eternal Who cares for and loves every human.

God manifests an all-sustaining care for humanity. The Eternal is a compassionate, loving parent (Psalms 103:13 and 116:5) Who desires our happiness.

For spiritually oriented Judaism, the main attribute of God is love: Divine mercy, goodness, compassion, and lovingkindness for humans. God is the source of all love, kindness, and goodness. As the psalmist reminds us, "[O]ur God is compassionate." (Psalm 116:5)

God's will is for love, joy, and our inner peace. We are an extension of God's love and creative energy.

Through love, God called things into existence. The Eternal's love sustains the world. God offers hope and happiness for everyone. When we step back and consider the world, we discover God's all-encompassing love.

We should realize that we live in the midst of beneficent, merciful God. We need to realize that the Eternal is a gentle, forgiving Presence Who awaits us in love and compassion, restoring our inner peace of mind. We need to have faith in the Divine goodness at the core of every living being. Everything and everyone is an expression of God's goodness, kindness, and mercy.

The Hebrew prophets saw God's goodness and mercy. According to Ezekiel, "Have I any pleasure at all that the wicked should die?" says God. "It is rather he should return from his ways and live." (Ezekiel 18:23) Hosea perceives God's mercy as follows: "I will heal them freely, generously will I take them back in love; for My anger is turned away from them." (Hosea 14:5)

When God, the Eternal goodness, answers the psalmist's prayers, his difficulties vanish, his sorrows and sufferings leave him. In Psalm 30:12, we read that God is the source of goodness and the fountain of all joy: "You did turn for me my mourning into dancing, You did loose my sackcloth and gird me with gladness. . . ." In Psalm 106:1, the psalmist declares: "God is good, the Eternal's love and mercy endures forever." The same message is repeated in Psalm 136:25, where the psalmist states: "God's mercy endures forever" and in Psalm 100:5: "For God is good, the Eternal's mercy endures forever, God is faithful until all generations."

God is the Source of goodness. Because of God's goodness, the Eternal called all human beings into existence. God created humans to lavish goodness and love on them.

God's beneficence for humanity perhaps best expresses God's goodness. We exist in the midst of plenty and abundance. God supplies sustenance to all humans. We are endowed with the intelligence to reach out and harvest this abundance. We have the capacity for work and self-expression, enhancing our powers and increasing our rewards and happiness in life. We have aspirations, ambitions, and ideals propelling our desire to use our powers. We have a reservoir of health and a spring of happiness, so that our earthly journey may be one of ever-flowing vitality and steadfast joy.

ROSH HASHANAH: CELEBRATING GOD, CREATION, AND OUR RELATIONSHIP WITH THE ETERNAL

For just about all Jews the High Holidays, Rosh Hashanah (the Jewish New Year) and Yom Kippur (the Day of Atonement), mark the high point of observance and ritual. These holidays, as public ceremonies, reinforce community bonds and give Jews, who fill sanctuaries to capacity, a meaningful experience of group solidarity. Let us briefly consider the role of Rosh Hashanah for Jewish Spirituality, leaving our discussion of Yom Kippur to chapter 6.

Rosh Hashanah, falling in September or October on the first day of the seventh Hebrew month of Tishri, celebrates the anniversary of the world's creation. For spiritually oriented Jews, Rosh Hashanah enables us to remember and reflect on God, the Eternal's role in the initial creation of the world, and our role as partners with God in the ongoing work of creation and the perfection of the world. We celebrate God and a purposefully created universe. We express our gratitude for life and focus on establishing and maintaining our personal relationship with God, our Creator and Sustainer. We rejoice in our living and loving God. The Rosh Hashanah communal worship services aid us in turning these abstractions into something more concrete and vivid.

Rosh Hashanah also marks the start of the ten-day period of self-reflection and personal change culminating in Yom Kippur. Engaging in self-examination, we begin to remember our forgotten self as well as others whom we have hurt. We will return to the topic of forgiveness in chapter 6.

FACING THE REALITY OF EVIL, PAIN AND SUFFERING, AND OUR DOUBTS ABOUT GOD

Some find it difficult to accept the notion of any God, or of a living beneficent God, in the face of evil and suffering—so much of which the Jewish people have witnessed in the twentieth century. Some Holocaust survivors and other Jews have lost their belief in God, who seemingly went into hiding, abandoning the Jewish people. Let us take three examples.

Rudolf Vrba, who was imprisoned in Auschwitz from June 1942 until his escape in April 1944, describes the devout Moses Sonenschein, the son of a Polish rabbi and a sincerely religious man, who murmured,

"It is the will of God," in the face of one horror after another. Then one day, overwhelmed by the unworldly screams of a group of women on their way to a gas chamber, Sonenschein muttered, "There is no God. . . ." Then his voice rose to a shout, *"There is no God! And if there is, curse [God], curse [God], curse [God]!"*[3]

In his emotionally charged autobiographical memoir, *Night*,[4] Nobel laureate Elie Wiesel, who was born in Romania in 1928, recounts his 1944 deportation with his family first to Auschwitz, where his mother and sister died, and then to Buchenwald. He tells how his family was placed on a cattle car, how he was separated from his mother and sisters, and how he watched his father fall ill and die shortly before Buchenwald's liberation in January 1945. Although a student of Talmud and mystical (kabbalistic) lore while growing up, Wiesel's loss of faith began at Auschwitz, which he describes in detail.

His religious rebellion flared as Wiesel was shocked by the disparity between Jewish prayers praising God and the events of the camp indicting God. Dismayed by new camp arrivals who recited the mourner's *Kaddish* prayer (which we will consider in chapter 13) when they recognized their plight, Wiesel's anger welled up. "Why should I bless [God's] name?" he asked. "The Eternal, [Sovereign] of the Universe, the All-Powerful and Terrible was silent. What had I to thank [God] for?"[5]

Wiesel continued to question God as follows: "Some talked of God, of the [Eternal's] mysterious ways, of the sins of the Jewish people, and of their future deliverance. But I had ceased to pray. How I sympathized with Job! I did not deny God's existence but I doubted the [the Divine's] Absolute Justice."[6]

Wiesel's anger intensified. At a Rosh Hashanah service in 1944, he refused to bless God and praise a world consumed by mass murder. He states: "This day I had ceased to plead. I was no longer capable of lamentation. On the contrary, I felt very strong. I was the accuser, God the accused. My eyes were opened and I was alone—terribly alone in a world without God and without man. Without love or mercy, I had ceased to be anything but ashes, yet I felt myself stronger than the Almighty, to whom my life had been tied so long. I stood amid that praying congregation, observing it like a stranger."[7]

Ten days later, on Yom Kippur (the Day of Atonement), Wiesel decide not to fast, noting: "[T]here was no longer any reason why I should fast. I no longer accepted God's silence. As I swallowed my bowl of soup, I saw in the gesture an act of rebellion and protest against [God]. . . . In the depths of my heart, I felt a great void,"[8] the loss of faith, an acknowledgment that God betrayed the Jewish people by allowing horrible mass deaths in the gas chambers and disposal in crematoria.

Focusing on the loss of God's benevolence, another survivor of Auschwitz, Wieslaw Kielar, cries out to us, "If [God] existed—and it is in this belief that I was brought up—how could [the Eternal] allow these murders of helpless beings, carried out by other human beings whose soldiers wore on the buckle of their belts the words 'God with us'?" [9]

More recently, Rabbi Harold Kushner, whose son died in his teens of a rare disease, wrote a bestselling book, *When Bad Things Happen to Good People.* [10] For Kushner, God is sometimes impotent. God cannot do anything to prevent suffering, whether caused by the Nazis during World War II or by cancer cells today.

In his book, Kushner distinguishes between the evil perpetrated by humans—social evil—and the evil of natural catastrophes or diseases—natural evil. For Kushner, human pain and suffering does not result from God rewarding or punishing, but (partly) from humans harming one another. Kushner puts it this way: "When people ask 'Where was God in Auschwitz' . . . my response is that it was not God Who caused it. It was caused by human beings choosing to be cruel to their fellow man." [11] For Kushner, God suffers with us and consoles us.

In answer to the question about the sickness of innocent people, Kushner sees their pain and suffering resulting from the laws of nature, which apply equally to each of us. The laws of nature, for Kushner, decree that we are subject to accidents, to sickness, and to disease. Kushner writes: "I don't believe that God causes mental retardation in children, or chooses who should suffer from muscular dystrophy. The God I believe in does not send us the problem; [God] gives us the strength to cope with the problem." [12]

Many of us have difficulties with Kushner's answers to the perplexing riddle of evil and the pervasiveness of pain and suffering in human existence. We question the notion of God's limited powers—that things happen outside of God's will—or the large role assigned to the laws of nature, bad luck, or randomness. Kushner's view also defies our desire for universal order and purpose.

As we continue to struggle for an explanation of the pain and suffering encountered by seemingly good, innocent people, we recall the biblical Job, a good man who faced calamity—the loss of his family, his wealth, his status, and his health. Job never received any reply to his charge that God was "cruel" to him. The only answer Job received was God's appearance and nearness to him. We are told that Job came to "know" God (Job 42:2) and that the Eternal was aware of Job's plight. Job was shown the magnificence of God's universe extending far beyond human understanding. Job saw that our world is but a tiny part of the cosmos, too vast and magnificent to be grasped by human minds. Realizing his own small place in the glorious universe, Job found his consolidation. Reasons exist for our pain and suffering that humans cannot understand. Job had to be satisfied with that, and he arrived at an implicit faith and trust in God's goodness.

Thus, we need to surrender to God, recognizing that we cannot understand the mysterious ways in which the Divine operates. God's reasons, known only to the Eternal, are hidden from us. Much is beyond our scope. The bigger picture may become apparent over time— however, there is a core of mystery in evil.

If we live life joyfully and if we appreciate that God's ways are not our ways and the Eternal's knowledge is not our knowledge, then perhaps we will find evil, pain, suffering, and tragedy somewhat more bearable. As developed later in this book, we are left with our faith in God's ultimate justice and mercy, which get worked out in the afterlife; our love for and our forgiveness of our fellow human beings; our humility; our joyfulness; and our optimism.

Remember also that God suffers along with the sufferers. Human suffering represents a source of Divine agony. As the prophet Second Isaiah writes, "In all their troubles God was troubled." (Isaiah 63:9) In the Talmud, Rabbi Meir recounts, "When a person is in pain what does the Divine Presence say? My head aches. My arm aches." (*Sanhedrin* 46a) In wondering whether he has been unfair to God, Elie Wiesel on further reflection writes, "After all, Auschwitz was not something that came down ready-made from heaven. It was conceived by men, implemented by men, staffed by men. And their aim was to destroy not only us but you [God] as well. Ought we not to think of your pain, too? Watching your children suffer at the hands of your other children, haven't you also suffered?"[13]

The contrast between good and evil—particularly social evil, the pain and suffering one individual or group causes others—must be set in the context of human free will. We have options and choices in our earthly existence. Humans are morally free. As we read in the book of Deuteronomy: "See, I place before you this day life and prosperity, death and evil." (Deuteronomy 30:15) Every one of us possesses this magnificent privilege of freedom of choice.

The evil humans create—whether war, poverty, oppression, and to some extent disease—is a product of our free will. We can use or abuse this freedom. We have the power to choose between good and evil. Thus evil, which helps us define good, is part of our free will. Without the potential to choose and do evil, we will not have the opportunity to be good. God allows us to be individuals, not robots, possessing free will and responsibility for decision-making, enabling us to make wrong choices and bring pain and suffering on others. The Eternal wants us to help perfect the world by choosing good, but God freely lets us build a world of evil. The Holy One does not shield humanity from its own folly.

In the light of the collective tragedy of the Jewish people in the twentieth century, the traditional passive, rather blind faith and trust in God, a sort of resignation, remains difficult for many Jews to accept. Thus, as we battle against meaninglessness and strive to rebuild our relationship with God, we may need more than faith and trust. We need to couple faith and trust with our moral will and our action. We must strive to do the good and the beautiful. By living in a loving, compassionate, and forgiving manner and by engaging in selfless service to others, we can diminish suffering and eradicate—or at least roll back—social evil. Through selfless deeds and words of goodness, strive to root out the causes of evil from yourself, from others, and from society. Do not ever let evil, as well as human pain and suffering, demoralize you. Focus on the good you can accomplish in the world.

We must always remember that we are God's partners, the Eternal's coworkers, in the ongoing work of creation. We exist in this world for much more than pursuing our own pleasures. We are here to help God, to be the Eternal's feet, hands, and mind here on earth. Through our words and actions, in rooting out social evil from ourselves and others and in building better interpersonal relationships, we can lift the world closer to perfection. As the Eternal expresses the Divine Presence through humanity, we are indispensable to God.[14] We are an essential part of completing the Divine work of creation and repairing the breach so that God and humanity will one day truly be one. Try to honor God with each breath and every action you take.

Let us come back and focus on the pain and suffering we face as individuals, particularly natural (as opposed to social) evil, such as instant crib death or the agony of the last stages of a terminal illness. Overcoming life's adversities offers each of us innumerable opportunities for growth and improvement, particularly for expressing unconditional love and forgiveness. Through your mind and your way of thinking, you can find meaning in life and create your own future, based on your method of facing the present and the future. How you interpret and respond to the pain, suffering, and tragedy you encounter may make you stronger than ever. Naturally, this is quite difficult. Finding meaning, however, is always an option. You can choose your attitude in any situation. See the positive when others perceive only the negative.

Like Job, you probably will not understand the reasons for your pain and suffering. But do not lose your faith in God in a time of despair. You can grow through your experience, commit more fully to your spiritual development, and move to a new understanding and deeper relationship with God. Like Job, you will realize that the answers to your questions cannot easily be attained, if at all. But trust in God, Who holds the key to all wisdom and knowledge. Always remember that you are loved and cared for by God, Who suffers when you do. Your pain and suffering is in some way part of a much greater good.

How then can we find God and invoke the Eternal's aid and guidance in our daily lives and the difficult circumstances we all face sooner or later? Let us examine various spiritual practices designed to help us connect with God.

NOTES

1. I have drawn on Rabbi Morris Lichtenstein, *Judaism: A Presentation of Its Essence and a Suggestion for Its Preservation* (New York: Society of Jewish Science, 1934), pp. 27–34; Rabbi Morris Lichtenstein, *Jewish Science and Health: The Textbook of Jewish Science* (New York: Society of Jewish Science, 1986), pp. 7–20; Rabbi Morris Lichtenstein, *Peace of Mind: Jewish Science Essays* (New York: Society of Jewish Science, 1970), pp. 297–303.

2. Patrick Glynn magnificently summarizes the scientific evidence pointing to God as the Creator in *God: The Evidence: The Reconciliation of Faith and Reason in a Postsecular World* (Rocklin, CA: Forum, 1997), pp. 21–55. Lawrence Troster offers a Jewish perspective in his article "From Big Bang to Omega Point: Jewish Responses to Recent Theories in Modern Cosmology," *Conservative Judaism* 49:4 (Summer 1997): 17–31. A journalistic approach is provided by Sharon Begley in "Science of the Sacred," *Newsweek*, 28 November 1994, 56–57.

3. Rudolf Yrba and Alan Bestic, *I Cannot Forgive* (New York: Bantam, 1964), pp. 160–161.

4. Elie Wiesel, *Night*, trans. Stella Rodoway (New York, Hill and Wang, 1960).

5. *Ibid.*, p. 43.

6. *Ibid.*, p. 53.

7. *Ibid.*, pp. 73–74.

8. *Ibid.*, pp. 74–75.

9. Wieslaw Kielar, *Anus Mondi: 1500 Days in Auschwitz/Birkenau*, trans. Susanne Flatauer (New York: Times Books, 1980), p. 177.

10. Harold S. Kushner, *When Bad Things Happen to Good People* (New York: Avon Books, 1981). See also Rabbi Joshua Loth Liebman, *Peace of Mind* (New York: Simon and Schuster, 1946), pp. 157–165.

11. Kushner, *When Bad Things Happen*, p. 81.

12. *Ibid.*, p. 127.

13. Elie Wiesel, "A Prayer for the Days of Awe," *New York Times*, 2 October 1997, A25.

14. The importance of human beings to God is developed by Dr. Abraham Joshua Heschel in *God in Search of Man: A Philosophy of Judaism* (New York: Meridian, 1959).

CHAPTER FOUR

Finding God and Invoking Divine Aid and Guidance in Our Daily Lives

God is the One to Whom we can appeal for aid and guidance in our daily lives and in difficult times.[1] God, our Sustainer and Helper, is near to us. God is interested in each of us, in our personal growth and development. As the psalmist declares: "God is near to all who call on the Eternal, to all who call on God in truth." (Psalm 145:18)

God will not abandon us. Because we live in the presence of a beneficent God, all will ultimately be well if we trust in the Supreme One. God watches tenderly over the destiny of all whom the Eternal created. The Holy One is our Strength and our Companion in all of our challenges, decisions, and relationships. God's love created and sustains us every moment of our lives.

God's presence and love expends itself on humans and expresses itself through us. Realizing the nearness of God to us, we can draw closer to the Eternal.

We need to live with the realization of God's Presence. We need to understand that there is a Divine Presence that saturates all existence, in Whose Being we have our being, from Whose goodness comes our life, our health, and our sustenance.

There is a loving God to Whom we may turn for strength, guidance, and help in every circumstance of life. The Source of goodness and mercy watches over us, as the psalmist states: "Call upon God in time of trouble. God will be there for you." (Psalm 50:15)

How can we reach out to and come in contact with God? How can we develop an awareness of God? Some find it easy to connect with God; for others it is far more difficult to establish a direct and intimate relationship with the Eternal and to feel God's Presence—to recognize that our oneness with God already exists. Furthermore, many Jews are quite cynical about personal encounters with God.

Traditionally, Judaism has emphasized communal, public prayer three times daily at fixed times from preestablished texts, standard prayerbooks for weekdays, Sabbaths, and holidays. Fixed prayers are said to enable "Jews to speak appropriately with [God], to request the right types of things in the right manner, and to articulate their personal needs in words and tenses that connected them to the praying Jewish community at large."[2]

The formal, uniform, orderly group recitation of a prescribed liturgy, with its proper sequence and structure, need not be the only way for us to establish a connection with and a bridge to God. Indeed, pious Jews recite a number of blessings privately throughout the day, on washing one's hands and face, attending to bodily needs, and before eating. There is a personal prayer for just about every situation: seeing lightning, hearing thunder, glimpsing a rainbow, and hearing good (or bad) news. Ritually observant Jews also privately pray at night before retiring.

Spiritual Judaism, however, emphasizes that you can set up your own personal, daily relationship with God wherever and whenever the spirit moves you. You need not follow any preset formula to open your heart and connect with God. Because the Eternal is not confined to a Jewish house of worship, you need not even be a member of or pray at a synagogue or a temple.

In this chapter, I will discuss several of these personalized, direct, spontaneous approaches. You can appeal to and commune with God, the Source of our life and health, through prayer, meditation, and visualization at all times, particularly in moments of difficulty.

You can also find God in your daily encounters with other humans. God often comes to the fore in your genuine dialogues with others.

In establishing a direct relationship with God, remember that you do not need an intermediary, a spiritual master, or a guru. Empower yourself! As the Hasidic Rabbi Menachem Mendel Morgenstern of Kotzk—the Kotzker Rebbe, who lived from 1787 to 1859—put it: "Do you know where God dwells? The Eternal resides wherever we let God enter."[3]

FINDING GOD THROUGH PRAYER

According to Herbert Benson, M.D., a member of the Harvard Medical School faculty, we are all "wired for God."[4] Because prayer is instinctively seated in us, we sense the Divine Presence. We have an innate craving for God. We yearn for the Supreme-Being—Eternal—and Almighty. We long for the Infinite One, Who encompasses the cosmos; Who transcends our existence; and Who has the power to help, sustain, guide, and restore each of us.

We pray to heal our minds and to reestablish within us the experience of our wholeness, our oneness with God and all of humanity. Through prayer we seek a connectedness with God. Prayer brings us closer to God by linking the human mind and heart with the Divine.

Prayer is instinctive within us when we find ourselves in times of fear, worry, sorrow, or difficulty. The urge to seek help through prayer is deeply implanted in us. Prayer comes to most of us spontaneously in times of affliction.

God has endowed us with the power to pray. By the power of prayer we can talk to the Supreme Sovereign and invoke God's help when our own faculties fail us. It is the means by which we can reach out for that which our other human powers—our physical strength, our mental faculties, or our emotional capabilities—are too inadequate to attain. Prayer strengthens our will and crystallizes our thoughts. Prayer enables us to tap the resources of the Spirit.

God has given to us the power to pray when we find ourselves in distress, especially when human efforts have failed to bring relief. Prayer represents an appeal to God: a call for courage in time of fear, strength in time of helplessness, hope in time of despondency, cheer in time of dejection, health in time of sickness, and solace in time of sorrow. Through prayer we share our lives with God.

We seek God's help in times of trial, perplexity, and difficulty. We seek God when we yearn for the greater realities and deeper truths of existence. We open our hearts to God when facing challenging problems or dire consequences.

When we are perplexed or in distress and we offer prayers to God, our burdens are lightened, our minds grow clearer, and our hearts become happier. As Rabbi Simcha Bunam of Pshis'cha, who lived from 1767 to 1827, used to say: "When a person's heart is heavy and full of anxiety, he or she may lighten it through ardent prayer and a belief in God's mercies."[5]

Because life and health come from God, we can ask the Divine to heal our illnesses and continue our lives, as discussed in detail in chapters 11 and 12. When we pray for healing and for life, often our ailments disappear, our vigor increases, and our strength is replenished. As the Eternal gave you energy on the first day of your existence, God will continue to supply you with health and life.

In the midst of the death of a loved one, when death severs the nearest ties, the human heart prostrates itself before God, in its devastating sense of loss. As developed in chapter 13, we can turn to God for comfort, with the afterlife teachings of the Jewish sages providing solace for a sorrowful spirit.

Our prayers count, especially prayers of authenticity. Because God is concerned with the life of each and every one of us, God manifests a nearness and responsiveness to each of us.

God responds to our prayers if we open ourselves to the Divine Presence and the Eternal's love to sustain and guide us. According to the psalmist: "In my distress I called on God Who answered me and brought me great relief." (Psalm 118:5)

God endows us with the power of prayer so that through it we may find relief from our troubles and ailments. Through prayer we can lift ourselves from difficulty and distress, be healed and restored to happiness, guided at every step, in every enterprise and in every act, to bring out the best in us. We should always remember that God is ready to restore and sustain us and to lavish on us the Eternal's fountain of goodness and love.

VARIOUS TYPES OF PRAYER: PETITIONARY, AFFIRMATIVE, SURRENDER, AND THANKSGIVING AND PRAISE

As God has created and sustains us, the Eternal listens and responds to four basic types of prayers: petitionary, affirmative, surrender, and thanksgiving and praise.

Petitionary Prayers. Through your petitionary prayers you ask God, Who is gracious and merciful, for help and guidance. For instance you can ask God, Who grants you life, for healing, a wholeness of your mind-body-spirit.

A petitionary prayer often takes the form of a personal prayer, a prayer of genuine supplication through which you express what is in your heart. You enter into an intimate conversation with God, asking for the things you alone need. You pray to God to make specific changes in the circumstances of your life.

We are like little children, feeling powerless, dependent, helpless, and vulnerable, unheard by parents. We tug at parents' clothes; we stomp our feet. So, too, through a petitionary prayer we seek God's help when our powers are too weak to struggle with life's problems, when our health is broken, when our spirit is depressed or disillusioned, or when we are frustrated with what life brings us.

A petitionary prayer is best offered with sincerity, passion, and simplicity. You express quietly in thought the things you lack. You ask God for things you need that by human power you cannot seem to obtain.

To offer a petitionary prayer, place yourself in a calm mental state. Do not try to offer a petitionary prayer when your mind is excited, embittered, or filled with gloom. Try to be free from all distressing thoughts and unpleasant feelings. Strive to be serene, which often can be achieved through bodily relaxation. Aim to relax completely, put yourself at ease, breathe deeply, and close your eyes.

You should offer a petitionary prayer with your whole being. You should declare your most heartfelt wish, in silence. Petitionary prayer is often most efficacious if offered in thought, not speech.

An audible prayer, especially if communicated out loud in public, carries with it a sort of self-consciousness. When you are concerned about the impact of your utterances on those around you, you do not always fully express your deepest and most personal thoughts. In offering an audible prayer, you often think about its acceptability before those in whose presence it is uttered.

Be simple and direct. There is no need to be eloquent. However, you need to offer your petitionary prayer with the full concentration of your mind and heart—not mechanically, when your lips sound the words but your heart and mind are at a distance and your thoughts not centered on the prayer. Concentrate your heart and mind on God. Offer your prayer with your whole being.

In asking God for help and guidance in a petitionary prayer, do not lay down specific details. Pray for health, happiness, or whatever from the depths of your heart and mind.

Try to get your heart and mind to call forth the Divine within you. However, realize that God has various ways of aiding each of us.

In offering a petitionary prayer, you do not need to flatter, appease, beg, or plead. God is not insecure. The Eternal is not power hungry. You need not grovel before the Almighty. Remember also that God is not your servant awaiting your orders. The Supreme Sovereign is not some petty bureaucrat.

The Divine does not have a detailed set of rules. If you do not pray in a certain, traditional way, using a specified format and language, do not feel that the Holy One will reject your prayers. God is more concerned with what is in your heart, as we are told: "While humans see what is visible, God looks into the heart." (I Samuel 16:7).

Affirmative Prayers.   You may want to offer an affirmative prayer. In this type of prayer, you affirm in words the state in which you desire to be. For example, in Psalm 23:1, the psalmist states, "God is my shepherd," not "God be my shepherd." "I shall not want," not "Relieve me from want." In other words, you repeat positive messages, aloud or silently, having meaning for you.

In offering an affirmative prayer, attune your heart and mind to God. Keep your mind free from intensity and agitation. Cast out any bitterness, hate, and anxiety. Relax completely, so there is no tension in your mind or body. Close your eyes so that visible surroundings do not claim your attention. Center your mind on the words you utter. It may be necessary to repeat the affirmation with your lips or even out loud.

Offer an affirmative prayer with profound faith and trust in God's goodness and benevolence and that all help, support, and relief ultimately comes only from the Eternal.

Prayer of Surrender to God.   Surrender and place yourself entirely in God's hands. The Eternal will strengthen and help you in situations where you cannot help yourself. By trusting in God's Presence, you can meet and surmount any challenges you face.

When you encounter difficulties that overwhelm you, put everything in Divine hands. Open your heart to God and surrender yourself to the Eternal's care. Trust in God as the source of all goodness, joy, and well-being. God will not fail you.

Rabbi Meshullam Zusya of Hanipol, one of the most beloved of the Hasidic masters, who lived from 1718 to 1800, recounted the following description of one of his wanderings and the spiritual direction he received: "I came to a crossroads and did not know which of the two roads to take. I lifted my eyes and saw the Divine Presence leading the way."[6]

As developed further in chapters 11 and 12, the prayer of surrender typically takes the form of "Your will be done." The prayer of surrender recognizes the existence of a gentle, loving Presence, ready to guide and sustain you. God's will is higher than yours. Remember that sometimes God says "No" to your petitionary or affirmative prayers.

Give yourself over to the Supreme Sovereign and place yourself into God's hands. By realigning your will with God's, trusting the Eternal's abiding love for each of us, you will come to know deep inner peace and true freedom. Recognize that your wisdom, strength, and health represent a gift from God.

It is easy to say that we should give up trying to manipulate and control our environment, our relationships, our experiences, and the future. However, we want to be in control, to be safe. We assume life is unfriendly and unsafe. Many of us believe we are on our own, struggling for happiness and survival.

Fear of surrender is often rooted in a lack of real faith and trust in God's love for us. We fear surrender because we fear God's will. We feel that surrender to the Eternal's will may mean suffering and loss. However, you need to overcome your separation from and your mistrust of God.

Ultimately, you will realize that your efforts at control break down. Contemplate whichever of these situations you find meaningful: an event you cannot do anything to change, a relationship you cannot turn the way you desire, or a person you cannot manipulate the way you want. In a time of crisis, you will discover that you are not totally in control of everything. Trust that you are connected to God, Who will take care of you, leading you to inner peace.

Surrender thus becomes the path to freedom and fulfillment. Open yourself to God's love and support. By becoming open and receptive and making room for God and the Eternal's love and support, you will receive and experience it in whatever way is best suited to your needs. God is truly within you. You can call on the Divine strength and power to assist you.

Place your life under God's direction and care. Turn your life—your concerns, worries, sorrows, and fears—over to God. Invite God into every significant aspect of your life, every major decision, and each key relationship. Learn to rely on the Eternal, Who will help you.

Start each day consciously establishing the right mental framework.

Spend some quiet time with God each and every morning in personalized prayer. Contemplate your spiritual goals for the day: inner peace, equanimity, or whatever you wish to achieve.

Learn to make decisions confronting you with God's help and direction. Begin the day asking for God's direction in all things. Decisions made with Divine guidance will keep your mind and heart at peace. God's deeper wisdom and understanding will dawn in your mind and heart. By turning your thinking over to God, you will find that you are often answered when you call on the Eternal for help and guidance.

Remember the Supreme Sovereign whenever you can throughout the day. Seek guidance and strength from God. Ask for Divine help whenever it is possible for you to do so. Ask the Eternal to be the eyes with which you see; the mind with which you understand what is happening; and the heart with which you express your lovingkindness, compassion, and forgiveness.

You need to accept and fully align your identity as a child of God. You were born of goodness and need to open yourself to experience the Divine Presence within you and in your life. Entrust yourself to God's love and care.

Listen to and trust in your inner voice. It takes patience. As the *Shema* prayer (Hear O Israel, the Eternal Our God is One) says: Listen, really listen to your inner voice, to your God-like nature. However, you must take responsibility for your words and deeds. If a voice says, "Kill someone," don't. In your dealings with others, always follow the dictates of love, forgiveness, and truthfulness, as discussed in chapters 5, 6, and 7.

Over time and through your experiences, losses, disappointments and tragedies, and pain and suffering, your faith and trust in God's love and guiding presence will grow. You will recognize that everything in your life is part of a greater plan—a plan pointing to a reawakening of your wholeness and inner peace. A greater plan is at work leading you to greater fulfillment, joy, and happiness. Although the Eternal's plan for you may not be what you have in mind, trust that God's plan for you is more beneficial than what you desire or expect. Allow yourself to become a vehicle through which the Divine will is done.

Prayers of Thanksgiving and Praise.   Offer prayers of thanksgiving and praise, deliberately and graciously recognizing the Eternal's work in your life. Be grateful that God is supplying your needs, healing your ailments, sustaining and guiding you at every step, and replenishing you with new strength and vigor. Be thankful for the joy and abundance in your life. At night, thank God for Divine guidance and assistance.

As a model for us, the psalmist offered the following prayer of thanksgiving (Psalm 136:1–3):

> O give thanks to God, for the Eternal is good,
>   God's steadfast love endures forever.
> O give thanks to the God of gods,
>   God's steadfast love endures forever.
> O give thanks to the Sovereign of sovereigns,
>   God's steadfast love endures forever.

To begin to experience the blessings in your life, you need to cultivate a sense of gratitude. Recall warm times, close friends, special occasions, moments of insight and forgiveness, and especially the lovingkindness that makes it all worthwhile. The more grateful and optimistic you are, the more you will come to experience the fullness and spiritual richness of blessings in each moment of your life. Because gratitude involves your whole self, when you feel truly grateful you feel more together—more integrated and whole within yourself, your mind-body-spirit, more connected to others and to the Eternal.

If you love God, praising the Divine is uplifting and joyful, drawing you closer to the Eternal. Focus on God's greatness; express your faith and trust in the merciful, loving God. As the psalmist reminds us in a psalm of praise (Psalm 100):

> Raise a shout for God, all the earth;
>   worship God in gladness
>   come into the Divine presence with shouts of joy.
> Acknowledge that God is Sovereign;
>   God made us and we are the Eternal's people,
>   the flock God tends.
> Enter the Eternal's gates with praise,
>   God's courts with acclamation.
> Praise God!
> Bless the Divine name!
> For God is good;
>   God's steadfast love is eternal,
>   God's faithfulness is for all generations.

CONCLUDING THOUGHTS ON PRAYER

Whatever form of prayer you offer—whether petitionary, affirmative, surrender, or thanksgiving and praise—you need to turn inward and be quiet and receptive. Prayer represents a contemplative time of concentrating, directing your thoughts and feeling toward God, and listening.

To emphasize the importance of praying with a deep and profound concentration, the Baal Shem Tov told the following story about a royal palace: A sovereign once built a palace and surrounded it with guards. Many people came to see the sovereign but departed when they saw the guards. Others, after giving presents to the guards, were permitted to enter. However, when they saw the ornaments in the great halls, they stopped to look at them and forgot their mission to the sovereign. Others looked at neither the guards nor the decorations but went straight into the presence of the ruler.

The Baal Shem Tov continued, "Some people who wish to commune with God retreat at the first hindrance. Others bring gifts of charity and kind deeds before they commence their prayers but become engrossed in a wise comment or fine saying in the prayer book. Others, however, concentrate their minds on God and refuse to be diverted by any distraction, however appealing."[7]

As you pray, try to experience God as your very being. Be conscious of God's nearness and the Eternal's immediate presence. You are whole and abundant.

Do not treat prayer as a practice in the absence of God. You are not separate from God and the Holy One's love. Know and realize your union with God, now and eternally. Open yourself to this wholeness and to your happiness and inner peace. Be aware of God's love and realize you are whole and fulfilled in your oneness with the Eternal and all of life.

In short, true prayer changes us. We overcome our separation and isolation. We remember our true identity as children of God. We are cared for and safe.

CRYING OUT TO GOD

The Hasidic followers of Rabbi Nachman of Breslov—who lived from 1772 to 1811, rousing his followers to heights of attachment to God together with sublime joy—intentionally engage in seclusion or isolation every day.[8] Daily, they talk to God in their own language and from their own hearts. They cry out to the Holy One. They speak whatever is on their minds. Uttering words out loud, shouting above their normal voice, they speak to God about everything and anything, transcending their material condition.

Wherever you are alone and will not be interrupted—in a car, at home, or wherever—you can cry out to the Eternal: "Open my heart. Please help me." Talk to God. Express your desires, your concerns, your problems and your needs. Be truthful.

In entering into a personal conversation with God, get comfortable and speak as you would to your best friend or closest relative. Do not be concerned about using formal prayer language. Use the language you are comfortable with. Talk in a tone that is best for you. Speak of everything, wherever your heart and mind lead you.

Trust God to have your best interests at heart. Pour out your heart and mind to God—your fears, your worries, your sorrows, your anger—and ask for God's help.

After pouring out your heart and mind, turn things over to the Supreme Sovereign, making space for the Eternal. By emptying yourself of your mental and emotional clutter, you will become more open and receptive to God. Surrendering yourself to God's care and delivering yourself to the Divine protection, you will be given help in a manner you can accept and understand. Persist in crying out and turning to God.

FINDING GOD THROUGH MEDITATION

Meditation within the Jewish tradition has existed since biblical times. Although obscured for most of the twentieth century, during the past decade or so the centuries-old tradition of meditation has resurfaced within Judaism.[9]

Meditation facilitates our inner journey and enables us to realize our true and authentic being. Meditation represents the act of shifting our consciousness from external to inner awareness. You do this by going within and turning your attention away from the clamor of external reality, quieting and focusing your mind, calming and centering your being, and bringing yourself to a still place. You withdraw from the whirlwind pace of your life, which otherwise draws out your energy and vitality. In this quiet place, you can reveal yourself. By remaining open to the Divine, you can make contact with and listen to God, aligning yourself with the Higher Energy. You attain a space to experience and commune with your Creator and Sustainer. You connect with your God-like nature, often receiving a new openheartedness and a transcendent vision of God's Presence.

Through meditation, you silently turn inward, focusing your mind on the reality of God, the Sustainer of Life. You become receptive to God's presence and experience love in your being.

Relax, silently and tenderly open your heart, and allow the Divine to come in. You will discover the presence of God's love in the depths of your being, in your heart, and in your mind.

Meditation, as an inward spiritual seeking, serves as means of attuning to the Divine Presence at the core of human nature. You affirm the essential goodness of the human personality and your belief that meditation can evoke the Divine Presence.

Meditate on the fact that you are part of God and that Divine life and energy is running through you at all times. By being quiet and turning inward, you will rediscover God's love within you: lifting a burden, providing a flash of insight, or experiencing a sense of inner peace and a union with the deep spiritual reality.

USING VISUALIZATIONS TO DISCOVER GOD

Visualization involves focusing the mind on a visual image, a deliberately constructed wordless thought directed to a desired goal, in order to project a better idea for yourself. A visualization sends a signal to your brain from your imagination or a past memory.

By means of a visualization, you direct your thoughts to what you require and to what you seek from God. In forming a mental image, you visualize what you desire and outline in your mind what you want to achieve. You identify with what you desire to attain.

Visualization can be a powerful goal-setting technique. Making a mental picture of what you want is often the first step to attaining it. Visualization works best when you imagine a specific, favorable experience. One benefit of visualization is that it forces you to identify what you desire to attain. The clearer the goal—for instance, driving out thoughts of fear, anger, worry, or sadness; or the healing you desire to attain—the more reachable it often becomes. A mental picture represents one of the most powerful commands you can send to your mind and body.

In formulating these mental pictures, do not form any negative images. Visualize what you desire, what you seek to attain. Keep the image fresh and alive.

Relax your mind and body with deep breathing and close your eyes to eliminate distractions. Sit, recline, or lie down in a quiet place. Concentrate your attention and thought. Fill your heart with sincerity and devotion. In forming your mental impressions, involve all your senses: sight, hearing, smell, touch, and taste. Repeat your visualization frequently each day during the week, with ever greater clarity. It is helpful to set aside a scheduled time and a special place where you can return to your visualization (or meditation) again and again.

CONCLUDING THOUGHTS ON MEDITATION AND VISUALIZATION

Effective meditation and visualization depend on relaxed receptivity. Do something else when you are tense or preoccupied.

As with prayer, be patient. Try not to get discouraged. The best results from meditation or visualization often come when you do not expect too much or when you are not trying too hard. View your meditation or visualization as pleasurable and relaxing. They are not quick fixes.

FINDING GOD THROUGH ENCOUNTERS WITH OTHER HUMANS

For the eminent twentieth-century philosopher Martin Buber, we meet God (the Eternal Thou) in our encounters with other human beings, here and now on earth. Each person you meet waits for you to enter into a dialogue with him or her. For Buber, all life is an encounter. All real living is meeting.[10]

In Buber's scheme of things, the basic element of the human world is relational; specifically, human interactions consisting of encounters. For Buber, the I–Thou relationship, in contrast to the I–It relationship, comprises a genuine relation of one-person-to-another-person. The I–Thou relation represents a relationship of reciprocity and mutuality, involving a meaningful meeting and a heartfelt encounter.

Our authentic personality emerges from the I–Thou relationship.

Through real contact with other humans you open yourself up, relating to others with your whole being. In encountering other humans, in all presentness and with your total personality, as Thous, Buber asserts, you meet the living God. Thus, in the context of meeting others through a genuine dialogue, entering into reciprocal relationships based on mutual trust, seeing others in a noninstrumental way, you encounter God.

In contrast to the I–Thou relation, the I–It relationship designates the connection of an individual to a thing. It is a relationship of a subject (the I) to an object (the It), involving some type of control or manipulation. The object (the It) is (or becomes) passive. The I–It relationship, for Buber, dehumanizes a person because it means treating the It as an instrument or tool for one's purposes.

However, by opening yourself totally to others, recognizing the Divine in other human beings, and entering into I–Thou relationships, you surrender your instinct to objectification and enter your whole being into a complete and genuine relationship with others. As you overcome the barriers of separation inherent in our I–It attitude, you meet God in the concrete reality and ordinariness of everyday life. Thus every moment, every person, and every event possesses the capacity to open, for each of us, a window to the living presence of God, the Eternal Thou, Who can never become an It. Apart from your prayers, meditations, or visualizations, you can experience God's presence in each and every one of your personal interactions and relationships, according to Buber, by realizing that God is present in all genuine human encounters, underlying them and making them possible.

While hoping for more I–Thou human relationships, Buber, ever the realist, recognized that most worldly Thous would, in time, become Its. However God, the Eternal Thou, is not an object to be used, controlled, or possessed. In the fuller experience of God as the Eternal Thou, you find greater meaning in your own life. For Buber, in our worldly I–Thou relationships, each of us comes to take away knowledge of God's mysteriousness. We realize that we have known and received God. We encounter the living God and grasp, in some way, the Divine as giving each of us life as a gift and sustaining us.

When you meet someone, it is a holy encounter. Anyone you meet represents an opportunity not only to connect with another human being but also to reconnect with God and your deepest essence—your wholeness and your loving nature—entirely lovable, completely loving, totally loved. Thus, you are able to know God through your interactions with others and your hallowing for day-to-day existence.

For Buber, we find God by discovering each other. Through your love of others, you meet God, as Buber explains:

> You think I [God] am far away from you; but in your love for your neighbor you will find Me [God]; not in [the Eternal's] love for you but in yours for [the Divine]. He who loves brings God and the world together.
>
> *You yourself must begin.* Existence will remain meaningless for you if you yourself do not penetrate into it with active love and if you do not in this way discover its meaning for yourself. Everything is waiting to be hallowed by you; it is waiting to be disclosed in its meaning and to be realized by you. . . . Meet the world with the fullness of your being and you shall meet [God]. . . . If you wish to believe, love![11]

In turning to others in the openness of love, forgiveness, and truthfulness, as well as through selfless service, we recognize that each of us is Divine. Train your mind and heart to learn another's divinity and the God-like nature of all things. You will see the divinity in yourself as well as in others and come closer to God.

A short story, "If Not Higher," by the early twentieth-century Yiddish writer Isaac Leib Peretz, illustrates how we can reach God through our love of and service to other humans. Peretz writes about a rabbi who disappears from his synagogue for a few hours every morning during Selihot, the one-week period before Rosh Hashanah (the Jewish New Year). One of his followers, suspecting that he is secretly meeting with God, follows him. He watches as the rabbi puts on coarse peasant clothes and cares for an invalid woman in a cottage, cleaning out her room and preparing food for her. The follower then goes back to the synagogue. When asked, "Did the rabbi ascend to heaven?" the follower replies, "If not higher."[12]

With a greater understanding of our ability to connect with the One Divine Presence, let us turn and focus on the importance Jewish Spirituality places on our conduct toward others. The next three chapters explore three key aspects: lovingkindness, forgiveness, and truthfulness.

NOTES

1. I have drawn on Rabbi Morris Lichtenstein, *Judaism: A Presentation of Its Essence and a Suggestion for Its Preservation* (New York: Society of Jewish Science, 1934), pp. 102–116; and Rabbi Morris Lichtenstein, *Jewish Science and Health: The Textbook of Jewish Science* (New York: Society of Jewish Science, 1986), pp. 20–24 and 43–56.

2. Donniel Hartman, "Judaism: Creating a Faithless People?" *Tikkun* 3:6 (November/December 1988): 39.

3. Adapted from *The Hasidic Anthology: Tales and Teachings of the Hasidim*, trans. Louis I. Newman (Northvale, NJ: Jason Aronson, 1987), p. 419.

4. Herbert Benson, M.D., with Marg Stark, *Timeless Healing: The Power and Biology of Belief* (New York: Scribner, 1996), pp. 195–217.

5. Adapted from *The Hasidic Anthology*, p. 341.

6. Adapted from Martin Buber, *Tales of the Hasidim: The Early Masters*, trans. Olga Marx (New York: Schocken, 1975), p. 248.

7. Adapted from *The Hasidic Anthology*, pp. 422–423.

8. Rabbi Nathan of Breslov, *Rabbi Nachman: Advice*, trans. Abraham Greenbaum (Brooklyn: The Breslov Research Institute, 1983), pp. 80–87; Chaim Kramer, *Crossing the Narrow Bridge: A Practical Guide to Rebbe Nachman's Teachings*, ed. Moshe Mykoff (New York: Breslov Research Institute, 1989), pp. 137–165.

9. Avram Davis provides a helpful introduction to Jewish meditation in *The Way of Flame: A Guide to the Forgotten Mystical Tradition of Jewish Meditation* (San Francisco: HarperSan Francisco, 1996). Davis's anthology, *Meditation From the Heart of Judaism: Today's Teachers Share Their Practices, Techniques, and Faith*, ed. Avram Davis (Woodstock, VT: Jewish Lights, 1997), presents views on meditation from a number of contemporary rabbis, scholars, psychologists, and teachers.

10. Martin Buber's classic work is *I and Thou*, trans. Walter Kaufmann (New York: Charles Scribner's Sons, 1970). Helpful introductions to Buber's thinking include Samuel H. Bergman, "Martin Buber: Life as Dialogue," in *Faith and Reason: An Introduction to Modern Jewish Thought*, trans. and ed. Alfred Jospe (Washington, D.C.: B'Nai B'rith Hillel Foundations, 1961), pp. 81–97; and *Great Twentieth Century Jewish Philosophers: Shestov, Rosenzweig, Buber*, ed. Bernard Martin (New York: Macmillan, 1970), pp. 238–265.

11. Martin Buber, *At the Turning: Three Addresses on Judaism* (New York: Farrar, Straus, and Young, 1952), pp. 43–44.

12. *The J. L. Peretz Reader*, ed. Ruth R. Wisse (New York: Schocken, 1990), p. 181.

PART THREE

HOW TO TREAT OTHERS WITH WHOM YOU COME IN CONTACT: ETHICAL DEEDS AND WORDS

The teachings of Judaism remain vital and helpful for the twenty-first century. The prophets' dream of a more perfect world is within our reach. However, we must do our part.

The next three chapters deal with the words we express and our conduct toward others. Jewish Spirituality rests, in part, on bringing us into an ideal relationship with others in a day-to-day way. A spiritually-oriented Judaism influences our relations with others, making us more loving, more forgiving, and more honest with ourselves and with others. In addition to being just and truthful in all of our human interactions, we are asked by Jewish Spirituality to speak kind words and perform good deeds, by living in a loving, compassionate, and forgiving manner.

As we saw in chapter 4, the concrete reality of everyday life and real contact with other humans offers the possibility for genuine encounters and meaningful relationships. God speaks to us through other humans. Each person with whom you come in contact offers you the possibility of extending to him or her your sense of that individual's special value. Your encounters with others leave lasting impressions. Open yourself and relate to others with your whole being. Turn to others in the openness of love, forgiveness, and truth—considered, respectively, in chapters 5, 6, and 7.

The following midrashic story, interpreting a verse in the Book of Psalms, "I will show you the protection of God to one who blazes a path of righteousness," (Psalm 50:23) illustrates the importance of our upright, righteous ethical interactions and of promoting social harmony with others:

> It happened with Rabbi Yannai (second century C.E.) that he was walking along the way when he came on a man who appeared very distinguished and saintly. Said Rabbi Yannai: "Will the rabbi consider accepting an invitation?" Said the man to him: "Yes." Rabbi Yannai took him into his home and served him food and drink. Then he examined the man's knowledge of the written tradition, but the man knew nothing. He examined him in the oral tradition, but he knew nothing; in the exegetical tradition, but he knew nothing; in the interpretive tradition, but he knew nothing. Then he said to him: "Take up [the wine cup] and recite [the blessing]." Said he: "Let Yannai recite the blessing in his own home." Rabbi Yannai lifted his cup and said: "Can you at least repeat after me?" Said he: "Yes." Said Rabbi Yannai: "Then say this: 'A dog has eaten of Yannai's bread.'" The man jumped to his feet and grabbed hold of Rabbi Yannai, saying: "My inheritance is in your hands, and you dare to withhold it from me?" Asked Rabbi Yannai: "How does your inheritance come to be my responsibility?" Said he: "The tradition belongs not to you alone just because you are so religious and more learned than I, but it belongs to all of us, whether we are observant or not and whether we are learned or not." Said Rabbi Yannai: "Tell me how it is that you who know nothing and practice nothing yet appear so saintly that I took you for a distinguished rabbi." Said he: "In all my days I have never, after hearing gossip, repeated it to the person spoken of, and I never passed by two people who were quarreling without trying to make peace between them." Said Rabbi Yannai: "You have so much decency and good breeding, and I call you a dog!"*

*Adapted from Leviticus IX:3, *Midrash Rabbah*, ed. Rabbi Dr. H. Freedman and Maurice Simon, trans. J. Israelstam (London: Soncino, 1939).

CHAPTER FIVE

The Importance of Loving and Being Compassionate toward Others

We are here to express love, which draws people together. We are here to be the presence of love, the vehicle through which our lives express even more love in the world. See yourself as a complete, whole being ready to give of your abundance of love to others.

Each day be loving and compassionate.[1] Love implies warmheartedness and kindness. Recognize that we love best when we have as much regard for others as we have for ourselves. In other words, only in giving love will we receive it in return.

We are endowed with the power of love by God. Love is inherent in us. God's Presence within us causes us to love. As discussed in chapter 3, our love flows from the love of God; the Eternal is love.

Love resides in the depths of our hearts. It is intertwined with the roots of our being. Everyone has within him or her a spark of God's love. Everyone we meet is a part of ourselves.

Love of humanity represents an all-embracing, transcendent expression of the Divine. The highest and noblest manner in which love finds expression is our love for others. Because we were born to love, a love of humanity exists in everyone.

Let us contrast love with hatred.

Love is that power that makes for harmony and happiness. Love brings people together; it holds the world together. Hatred makes for separation. Hatred divides us one from another, contributing to human misery.

Love heals and soothes. It generates new strength through the birth of kind and tender feelings. Hatred brings agony. It makes a person angry. Hatred consumes the mind and the spirit. Hatred destroys the heart in which it dwells, contributing to mental and physical illness. It keeps an individual in a state of bitterness and irritability. It often leads, in our society, to litigation as a means to unleash our hatred.

Notice when you use the word "love," to what things you attach the word "love" and what do you feel when you "love?" For most of us, the experience of love is immediate. It pulls our attention out of both the past and the future. Love focuses us on the present. It is pleasurable and expansive. It is a feeling of connectedness with others and the world around us. It is a feeling of happiness and joy in the present moment.

LOVE IN THE JEWISH TRADITION

The basic principle of Judaism is universal lovingkindness. We are told: "Love your neighbor as yourself. . . ." (Leviticus 19:18) The phrase refers to a neighbor or a fellow human being, not to your blood relatives or friends.

Natural love ties us to our blood relatives. This love is inborn. We are inseparably united with our relatives. The lives of parents and children are invisibly cemented. An innate love springs from this blood union. Children naturally love their parents; parents naturally love their children.

Our love for friends develops. It is not innate. Love among friends grows through the expression of mutual tenderness and courtesy, through the congruent sympathy, attention, and loyalty that we give one another.

However, you do not have any blood kinship or relationship with your neighbor or a fellow human being. He or she may not contribute to your happiness or well-being. You may not know him or her at all. Nevertheless, you do not need kinship or friendship to feel near to others. Having our humanity in common is sufficient for our love of others to blossom.

Loving your neighbor means feeling and expressing a deep

compassion for others. Feel and act toward others as you would have them feel and act toward you. Feel and act toward your neighbor or another human with the same feeling, with the same unselfishness, with the same devotion that you would want him or her to have toward you if the circumstances were reversed.

As Hillel, who lived in the first century of the Common Era, put it in the Talmud: "What is discomforting for you do not do to another." In other words, "Do not do unto others as you would not want them to do unto you." (*Shabbat* 31a) Hasidic Rabbi Shmuel Shmelke Horowitz of Nikolsburg, who lived between 1726 and 1778, paraphrased Hillel's notion of the Golden Rule as follows: "What is hateful to you in your neighbor, do not do."[2]

If you love your neighbor, you will not harm others. You will not kill, steal, covet, deceive or take advantage of others. You will sustain others in distress or want.

We can all learn how to truly love our neighbors, as did Rabbi Moshe Leib of Sassov, the Sassover Rebbe, the most prominent disciple of Rabbi Shmelke of Nikolsburg, who lived between 1745 and 1807, when he went to an inn and overheard the following conversation between two peasants:

First Peasant: "Tell me, do you love me?"

Second Peasant: "Certainly, I love you. I love you like a brother."

First Peasant (shaking his head): "You do not love me. You do not know what I lack. You do not know what I need."

As the Sassover Rebbe so well understood, "To know the need of others and to bear the burden of their sorrow, that is true love."[3]

Love precludes malice and bitterness. We are instructed in the Book of Leviticus: "You shall not hate your kinfolk [relatives] in your heart. . . . You shall not take vengeance or bear a grudge. . . ." (Leviticus 19:17–18)

Love also precludes prejudice and intolerance with respect to all peoples, all races, all religions, all nationalities, all personalities and temperaments, and all economic classes. Become conscious of the unity of all human beings. The authors of the Book of Leviticus advise us: "When a stranger resides with you in your land, you shall not wrong him or her. The stranger who resides with you shall be to you as one of your citizens; you shall love him or her as yourself. . . ." (Leviticus 19:33–34)

Love involves a deep consideration for others, even those whom we know little or not at all, or people not like us. Welcome the stranger, extend hospitality to one who comes from another land, who speaks with a strange tongue, and who has quite different manners. But why should you welcome and love someone who does not "fit in"?

We all have the same heart, the same feelings, and the same aspirations. We all have the same Divine Presence in us. We are more like others than we are unlike them. Thus, act and speak kindly even to others who are strangers, even to those who hate you.

Love in the Hebrew Bible even precludes unkindness toward an enemy. In the Book of Proverbs we read: "If your enemy falls, do not rejoice. If he or she stumbles, do not let your heart be glad." (Proverbs 24:17) Also, "If your enemy is hungry, give him bread to eat; if she is thirsty, give her water to drink." (Proverbs 25:21)

The authors of the Five Books of Moses advise us not to do less for our enemies than for our neighbors. We are told: "If you encounter your enemy's ox or donkey wandering, you must take it back to him or her. If you see the donkey of someone who hates you lying under its burden, do not pass the donkey by; you must release it. . . ." (Exodus 23:4–5)

When you love your enemy, he or she ceases to be your enemy. Thus, come to the aid of anyone in distress—within, of course, the limits of your resources: financial, mental, emotional, and physical—just as if you were in trouble and prayed that another would aid you.

The Jewish tradition teaches us to love others and thereby unite all of humanity. In raising human consciousness toward the goal of lovingkindness and compassion, restore the gap separating you from others that results from the distance, or even the hatred, you have carried inside you. Although this is extraordinarily difficult, helping others—even your enemy—will forge a healing and restore the wholeness of the cosmos.

Always remember that the same God is present in each of us. We are all one; unity is our natural state. As the prophet Malachi, who lived in the fifth century B.C.E., observed: "Have we not all one Divine parent? Has not one God created us all?" (Malachi 2:10) There is a place for each of us in the Eternal's purpose.

If we neglect words and deeds of lovingkindness, the Jewish sages concluded, we betray God. Stated positively, if you love everyone, you are loving God. Furthermore, as the author of Proverbs put it: "One who strives to do good and kind deeds attains life, success, and honor." (Proverbs 21:21) True and lasting love is universal.

MEETING THE CHALLENGE OF DEALING
WITH DIFFICULT PEOPLE

The challenge of loving others is a difficult one. It does not take a great deal of effort to love "good" people; the real test is loving those who may not be as "good" in our eyes—people who leave us "cold," or those we perceive as "bad" or even "evil."

In learning how to conduct yourself toward others, love and fear must be contrasted. Love represents a giving and a sharing with others. Fear cripples our capacity for giving and sharing by draining our energies from positive efforts to assist others into negative efforts to serve ourselves. Love thus represents an infinite, all-encompassing energy pattern that should replace fear in our lives, particularly in dealing with "difficult" people. If we let go of our fear, by opening our hearts to others, then love remains.

Building on your own love of self—your self-esteem, as developed in chapter 8—let love for others serve as your priority in every situation. Because your generous love for others is dynamic, not static—in that this type of love evolves, grows, and matures—let your unconditional, selfless love for others represent one of your key lifelong goals. Daily perform small acts of gentleness, patience, and kindness, one building upon another.

Try to be a love finder, not a fault finder. Do not focus on what is wrong or lacking in your life or in others. Do not discover only shortcomings or see only errors or deficiencies in others. Whenever you engage in fault finding, whether in its subtle forms like complaining or worrying, or in its more overt forms such as overtly attacking others or being judgmental or critical, you feel isolated, separated from other humans and from the goodness of life.

You harvest what you sow. There is an iron law of fault finding: The more you complain, the more you seem to have to complain about.

People who go through life with the sting of criticism, of judgment, or of complaint on their lips are often very lonely. If you see others' wrong deeds, shortcomings, and weaknesses; if you find fault with others' opinions and judgments; or if you see others' stupidity, meanness, and vulgarity, you will shut out any space for love.

Being a love finder means opening your heart, your mind, and your eyes to see the wonder that is around you. There is something good and beautiful in everyone. There is something noble in each soul, some tenderness in each heart, some wholesomeness in every mind.

See others' goodness and reflect on the beneficial reaches of their essence.

We are all God's children ready to do the Eternal's will. We are all expressions of the same Fountain of Life. There is a Divine Spark in each of us. Sometimes the spark is difficult to find, but it is there.

Make an effort to penetrate into the Divine depths of others. See the beauty and the potential each human soul possesses. If you see others as the children of God, you will come to love others. If you see only the good and the Divine in others, then the good and the Divine will express themselves to you.

THE ATTRIBUTES OF LOVE

Love implies compassion, warmheartedness, and kindness. These attributes link us together.

Nothing brings more cheer than a sympathetic thought. Nothing binds one heart to another heart more closely than an act of kindness. Nothing knits soul to soul more firmly than a tender word.

Be compassionate and sympathetic. Compassion is a matter of feeling with and for others. By acknowledging and opening your heart to others' pain and suffering, you feel your unity with others.

Compassion also implies a kindly, tender interpretation of others' motives, words, and acts. Do not dwell on others' weaknesses; do not focus on others' faults.

A sympathetic interpretation of others' deeds and words will show their better and finer nature. Divine attributes are in each of us. There is goodness in every heart, nobility in every spirit, refinement in every soul. The more you look for the finer traits in others, the finer, in turn, everyone becomes.

To establish and maintain a sympathetic relationship with others, cooperate with and help others. Offer your aid when others are in need, give your courage when others are despondent, provide your succor when others are distressed, and offer your cheer when others are dejected.

Our heart is the cementing power between human souls. We love a person for the qualities of his or heart. The heart is implanted with the Divine qualities of love, kindness, compassion, and goodness. These are qualities that make for understanding and cooperation between and among humans.

Let your heart vibrate in sympathy and unison with others. Let your heart send forth its compassion and tenderness. Open your heart to loving others and, in turn, to being loved by others. The more you love, the more you will be loved. Love stimulates love. We love the loving. We will always remember the impression of a great heart.

Keep your heart warm and open. Give it the opportunity for self-expression. A warm and gentle heart expresses itself in kindness and compassion. A warm and good heart seeks out others on whom to lavish helpfulness. Assist others with your encouragement, your advice, and your prayers.

Do not harbor bitterness or hatred in your heart. Do not erect barriers isolating your heart from others. Do not close your heart in fear, judgment, criticism, anger, or worry. When your heart is closed, you are cut off from the flow of love. If the flow of love is blocked, you experience pain.

Kindness and goodness are inherent in each of us. They are in the depths of each human heart. Do not let bitterness, anger, or indifference cloud the natural kindness in your heart.

You have a spark of the Divine goodness and kindness in you. Consciously cultivate kindness and bring it into your thoughts, your words, and your deeds. Kindness is a Divine substance possessing the power to cement humanity and make all of us kin. We appear Divine when we give expression to kindness. Kindness represents a deep sympathy and compassion for others regardless of their circumstances. Kindness reaches the heart and stimulates love. We love those who are kind.

It is important for each of us to develop kindness through actual practice. Nothing binds one heart to another heart more closely than a kind act. Nothing knits soul to soul more firmly than a kind word. Nothing brings more cheer than a kind thought.

As the contemporary saying goes, "What goes around, comes around." Give and receive. If you give kindness, you will receive kindness. If you give love, you will be rewarded with love. Every stream of compassion flowing from the heart brings back joy.

HOW SPIRITUAL SEEKERS CAN STRENGTHEN THEIR LOVE AND COMPASSION FOR OTHERS

Practice choosing love throughout the day. Be love's instrument, minute by minute, day by day. Doing and speaking the good and the beautiful represents the highest ideal of Jewish Spirituality. Express your love in every situation.

Begin your day with love for everyone. Remember that you and humanity are one. Each of us has the same life flow. There is the same Divine Presence in each of us. Because we are one, we must feel one. Begin the day filling your heart with love, with goodness, with kindness, and with compassion for everyone. Let this natural unity between humans assert itself. Do not obstruct its way. Keep as open a heart as possible. Let invisible rays of love radiate from your heart and soul, reaching out to others.

Begin each day with thoughts of goodness and kindness for others. In return, you will receive goodness and kindness from others. Others will treat you as you treat them. The world will give you love for your love.

Many have found the Lovingkindness Meditation helpful in facilitating compassionate interactions with others. By generating lovingkindness you will be able to deal with your feelings regarding difficult people at work or school, in your own family, or among those with whom you have disagreements, and plant the seeds of love and compassion. The Lovingkindness Meditation will open your heart to the love that transforms every experience, whether painful or pleasurable.

The next time you meet someone to whom your heart does not incline, offer the Lovingkindness Meditation (or say a blessing for him or her) for ten to fifteen minutes daily for one to two weeks, to turn your heart to love him or her. Follow up with words or acts of kindness to someone you have wronged (or who has wronged you) in the past.

Lovingkindness Meditation. Introduction: Create a warm, welcoming atmosphere. Lower the lights. Close your eyes, sit quietly, calm and relax your body, breathe in and out normally, feeling where the breath flows into and out of your body. Adjust the breaths so that the in and out breaths are the same length, thereby bringing about both a relaxation of the body and an alertness of the mind.

Recall to mind someone toward whom you feel tremendous gratitude. Then recall a friend. Next recall a difficult person, someone toward whom you feel anger or hatred, or someone you fear. Ultimately, focus on the person who has hurt you the most. To each of those, express the following:

As I wish to be free from danger and achieve safety,
  so may you be free from danger and achieve safety.
As I wish to have happiness, so may you have happiness.
As I wish to have good health and be free from physical or mental
    pain,
  so may you have good health and be free from physical or mental
    pain.
As I wish inner peace of mind, so may you have inner peace of mind.

Feel yourself surrounded by warmth. Allow any anger or hatred you feel to dissolve into the warmth and patience. Breathe in patience and feel the spaciousness that patience creates within you. Gently open your heart.

Give yourself time. Wish yourself well. Let your heart fill with lovingkindness toward yourself.

May you be: healed; at peace; happy; free from pain and suffering; free from anger, hatred, and fear; filled with joy and love.

Toward someone for whom you feel great love may you be: healed; at peace; happy; free from pain and suffering; free from anger, hatred, and fear; filled with joy and love.

Let your love expand. Let your lovingkindess radiate to all human beings. May they be: healed; at peace; happy; free from pain and suffering; free from anger, hatred, and fear; filled with joy and love.

May all of our hearts open. May we all be healed by the power of love for each other.

Concluding Instructions: Now come back to the here and now. Take time to ease yourself back. Slowly bring your awareness back into your body. Feel yourself back in the room and open your eyes.

Manifest lovingkindness and compassion each day in your words and in your deeds. When you bring happiness to others, the emotions of kindness and goodness will grow strong until they become the deepest part of your being. Kind words are not lost; kind acts are not forgotten.

Words are very powerful. Use them carefully. Pay attention to what you say about people. During the day do not speak ill of anyone for any reason. Try to minimize (or, hopefully, eliminate) negative talk about others. Avoid passing on anything negative you have heard about another, even if it is true.

If a friend introduces a mutual acquaintance into a conversation with you by way of gossip, try, if possible, to steer the conversation in a different direction rather than asking for more details. Avoid the company of individuals who gain pleasure in disparaging others.

Do not embarrass or put another to shame, especially in public. Do not wrong another with words that cause pain or distress—for instance, by bringing up unpleasant memories, failures, or past misdeeds.

Train your tongue to speak kind words. Speak kindly to people; speak kindly of people. Speak kind words: words that encourage, that bring out the best in others, that inspire others to higher achievements and better conduct, that offer expressions of appreciation—not words that hurt, humiliate, cause anxiety, make life's burdens grow heavier, or keep our capabilities imprisoned.

Speaking a kind word kindles hope in the despondent, lifts up downtrodden spirits, creates friendship in enemies' hearts, and transforms enmity to love. A kind word leaves a lasting, positive impression. You will encourage others; you will give them strength; you will gain their respect.

Express your honest, sincere appreciation and gratitude. Overlook the weaknesses in others. Try to see only the good that exists in others. Speak only of the good in others.

Let your deeds demonstrate your lovingkindness. Strive to generate love between yourself and others as well as among people. Through your conduct, your compassion, your kindness, and your warmheartedness, be a helper to all and an enemy to none. Extend love to everyone you touch in any way. Let love's healing power flow through you in every human interaction.

Although there are innumerable possibilities, let me offer a few concrete suggestions. Extend your hospitality to others. Bring peace between people. Do not injure, exploit, or oppress others through your deeds. Do not deprive others of anything to which they are entitled. Do not withhold from others any of the freedoms you claim for yourself. Facilitate others' self-fulfillment by helping them discover and realize their special talents, abilities, and gifts. Give others the attention they seek.

Through your words and deeds bring out the best and the highest in others, elevate others, and encourage and inspire others in their efforts. Give others dignity and respect. Help make others feel better and achieve their potential. Do not put your desires before the needs of anyone else.

During the day, ask yourself whether there are important people in your life whom you have not told how much you love and value them? Perhaps you have told them, but not recently or sufficiently? If so, call, write a note, or send an e-mail expressing your appreciation to each of them.

Each evening think of one or more words or deeds of lovingkindness and compassion you performed during the day. You may want to keep a journal of your words and acts of lovingkindness and compassion, perhaps organized by various categories.

Each evening ask yourself: Did you genuinely love others today? Contemplate your missed opportunities for expressing lovingkindness and compassion, in speech or conduct. Cultivate your awareness of missed opportunities, the needs of others, and the possibilities for being of service to others. Always remember to strive to facilitate love and compassion through your speech and conduct.

THE IMPORTANCE OF EXPRESSING YOUR LOVE AND COMPASSION FOR OTHERS THROUGH SELFLESS SERVICE

Each day, remember that you live to serve others and benefit humanity. Dedicate part of your daily existence to helping perfect the world through your selfless service to others. Turn outward and identify with and feel for others. Do for others.

Each day reach out to those around you by being of service to others. Ask yourself: What can you best do for others to help relieve their pain and suffering, to make their life easier, and to aid them in experiencing happiness? Through your service to others, you cheer the depressed, provide hope to the discouraged, lighten some of the burdens of others, comfort those in pain, console the sorrowful, and kindle hope in human hearts.

Even if you cannot take a job directly helping others—such as social worker, teacher, or health care professional—you can serve others in numerous ways. Acts of lovingkindness and compassion need not be on a grand scale. You can assist individuals and organizations with your compassion and concern, your humor, your prayers, your counsel and advice, your talents, or your money. Give of yourself to others through whatever means is appropriate for you. However, things or money cannot substitute for time. Try to volunteer your time for even a few hours a month. Open your heart to bring joy to people suffering from the pain of loneliness, homelessness, hunger, or sickness.

Be present for others—to listen, to talk, to care for, to love. In a world in which everyone is jabbering but few are listening, focus on what someone else really needs. See the world through another's eyes. Put another first.

Offering others your genuine yet humble help through your love and compassion for them, you evoke in others the qualities that benefit humanity. As you radiate love, those with whom you come in contact are positively affected.

In making decisions about how to allocate your time and your abilities, reflect on the goals of unconditional love and rendering selfless service to others. Each day ask: "How much love am I giving others? How much service am I rendering others?" Remember that you can give your love and compassion and not be diminished through your gifts of love and compassion.

By considering and devoting yourself to others, you not only demonstrate your oneness and solidarity with all of humanity but you also affirm that each person is part of the ongoing process of planetary creation and healing. By recognizing our common humanity, we can help create a better world. Each of us, in performing beneficent deeds and speaking kind words, brings nearer the healing of the world—the tradition of *Tikkun Olam* in Hebrew.

As Jewish sages taught, when we stand before our Creator at the end of our lives, more than anything else it is about our deeds on behalf of others that we will be asked. In interpreting the phrase "Open to me the gates of the righteous" (Psalm 118:19), the Midrash, Jewish interpretative literature, states:

> When a man is asked in the World to Come: "What was your work?" and he answers: "I fed the hungry," it will be said to him: "This is the gate of the Eternal (Psalm 118:20). Enter into it, O you who did feed the hungry."
>
> When a woman answers: "I gave drink to the thirsty," it will be said to her: "This is the gate of the Eternal. Enter into it, O you who did give drink to the thirsty."
>
> When a man answers, "I clothed the naked," it will be said to him: "This is the gate of the Eternal. Enter into it, O you who did clothe the naked."
>
> This will also be said to her that brought up the orphan and to them that gave charity or performed deeds of lovingkindness.

And David said: "I have done all these things. Therefore, let all the gates be opened for me."[4]

Ask yourself: What am I here to give to others? What is my unique talent and the means of expressing this talent? How can I best help others? In short, combine your ability to express your unique talent, something in which you can lose yourself for a period of time, with your selfless service to humanity.

In serving others, however, do not become a self-sacrificing martyr. Finding an appropriate balance is not easy. In striving to perform selfless services, do not neglect your family, your friends, or yourself. There is a time to say, "Enough." Sometimes in giving to others we avoid facing our own emptiness or loneliness. The following talmudic story illustrates the need to balance our concerns for the welfare of others with more personal concerns, the emotional and material needs of our family.

One year there was a drought in the Land of Israel and the High Court in Jerusalem sent a delegation of rabbis to ask Abba Helkiah (first century B.C.E.) to pray for rain.

When the delegation arrived, they found Abba Helkiah laboring in the fields. They greeted him with greetings of peace, but he ignored them and did not reply. The rabbis were puzzled at his silence and waited. When he had finished his labor, the rabbis observed in amazement as he removed his work cloak and draped it over one shoulder and then carried his tools upon his bare shoulder. They followed him. When they came to a stream, the rabbis removed their sandals but Abba Helkiah, who had been walking barefoot, now put his on. Reaching the other side, they walked through thorny bushes. The rabbis lowered their cloaks to protect their legs but Abba Helkiah lifted his. When they arrived at his home, his wife was waiting at the door to greet him. The rabbis prepared to enter first, as was customary, but Abba Helkiah blocked their way allowing his wife to enter first instead, followed by him and the rabbis. Though seated around the table, Abba Helkiah did not invite the rabbis to eat, and they observed in puzzlement that he gave double servings to his youngest son and but a single serving to his eldest. He then whispered to his wife: "They have come to ask us to pray for rain," and the two ascended into the attic. The rabbis watched how the two took up separate stations on the roof and began to pray for rain. To their amazement clouds began to appear, but they first appeared from the direction his wife was praying, and only after that cloud had burst did other clouds appear in the direction he was praying. The couple then rejoined the others and Abba Helkiah finally greeted the rabbis with words of peace and bid them to eat.

But the rabbis, overcome with curiosity about his strange behavior, asked him to explain. He explained thus: "When you greeted me, I did not feel it right to respond because I am a laborer, and I am paid wages for the time I work and did not wish to waste any of my employer's money socializing. I removed my work cloak rather than place the tools upon it over my shoulder because the cloak is borrowed, and the lender let me have it for the express purpose of wearing, not for laying tools upon it. I put on my sandals when we crossed the creek for I know not what lies at the bottom of the creek, but I can see what lies in the grass on dry land. I lifted my robes in the thorny bramble for it is well known that while scratched flesh heals, ripped garments do not. When we arrived at my home my wife entered first and then I did, for I do not know you, and though one must welcome strangers, one need not, however, risk leaving strangers alone in the house with one's family. I did not invite you to eat right away because I wanted to make sure there was enough food for my family first. I fed the younger one more than I did the elder for the elder is home most of the day and has access to the kitchen, whereas the younger is away at school and does not have access to food whenever he wants. Now that I have answered your questions, what is the purpose of your visit?"

The rabbis replied that they had come to ask him to pray for rain. Abba Helkiah smiled and pointed at the rain that was falling outside the window. "There is obviously no need for that now, is there?" he said. Said they: "But we know that it is raining in the merit of your prayer and your wife's prayer, yet we are curious why the prayer of your wife was answered before yours." Said he to them: "For she provides for the needy." Said they: "And you do not?" Said he: "I give indirectly and she gives directly. I give coins that the needy then must take to the market and exchange for flour that they must then bring home and toil over for hours before they can finally have bread from it with which to satisfy their hunger. My wife, however, bakes extra loaves each day and has always bread prepared for the hungry so they could eat of it immediately, and thus, in turn, are her prayers answered more immediately than are mine." (*Ta'anit* 23a–23b)

A WORD FOR PARENTS

Teach your children to give expression to their inherent love, kindness, and compassion. Instill in them the lessons of love, kindness, and compassion. Instruct your children to put themselves in the place of others, to identify with others, to do for others what they expect others to do for them. Draw forth this inherent potentiality for love, kindness, and compassion so that it becomes a part of each child's consciousness—so that it becomes a habit.

In teaching your children to express love, kindness, and compassion in words and deeds, in turn seek love, kindness, and compassion from your children. Expect your children to perform acts of compassion and speak words of lovingkindness. One kind word, one compassionate deed will spark your children to speak another kind word, to perform another compassionate deed.

Through speaking kind words and performing acts of love and compassion, the habit of love will become the deepest part of your being, replacing the habits of fear, criticism, and suspicion. As you fill your heart with love for everyone, implementing your feelings through your words and your conduct, others will respond with love. You will find yourself linked to the hearts of others. You are doing your part to create a new era of human relationships.

Kindness reaches the heart and stimulates love. The more you love, in turn the more you will be loved. You will find yourself linked to the hearts of others.

As the Baal Shem Tov put it: "If your desire is to be loved, then love others."[5] In response to the question, "How can I have people love me?" the Hasidic Rabbi Levi Yitzchak of Berditchev, who lived from 1740 to 1810 in Poland, the Berditchever Rebbe, known for his consuming love of God and the Jewish people, answered: "Love them first."[6]

Always give others your love and compassion—but do not expect any reward in return. Sometimes your love and compassion is not returned. It is not a matter of striking a bargain. Love without any expectation of another's positive response or any type of compensation from others. In other words, your love should be a selfless love.

Always remember that love opens your heart, your mind, and your soul to life's myriad possibilities. Loving others will enable you to see the richness and fullness of life.

Making an effort to love your neighbor will bring you happiness. You are happier when you love than when you are hateful or fearful. Your vision will be enriched, your heart ennobled.

As important as love and compassion are in our interactions with others, we must also strive to be more forgiving. While not ignoring others' difficult qualitites, see the goodness in others.

NOTES

1. I have drawn on Rabbi Morris Lichtenstein, *Judaism: A Presentation of Its Essence and a Suggestion for Its Preservation* (New York: Society of Jewish Science, 1934), pp. 64–71; Rabbi Morris Lichtenstein, *Jewish Science and Health: The Textbook of Jewish Science* (New York: Society of Jewish Science, 1986), pp. 25–42 and 127–134; Rabbi Morris Lichtenstein, *How to Live: Jewish Science Essays* (New York: Society of Jewish Science, 1957), pp. 181–188; Rabbi Morris Lichtenstein, *Peace of Mind: Jewish Science Essays* (New York: Society of Jewish Science, 1970), pp. 259–266.

2. Adapted from *The Hasidic Anthology: Tales and Teachings of the Hasidim*, trans. Louis I. Newman (Northvale, NJ: Jason Aronson, 1987), p. 222.

3. Adapted from Maurice Friedman, Ph.D., *A Dialogue with Hasidic Tales: Hallowing the Everyday* (New York: Insight Books, 1988), p. 86; and *The Hasidic Anthology*, p. 221.

4. Adapted from *The Midrash on Psalms*, vol. 2, trans. William G. Braude (New Haven: Yale University Press, 1959), p. 243.

5. Simcha Raz, *Hasidic Wisdom: Sayings from the Jewish Sages*, trans. Dov Peretz Elkins and Jonathan Elkins (Northvale, NJ: Jason Aronson, 1997), p. 17.

6. Adapted from *The Hasidic Anthology*, p. 220.

CHAPTER SIX

Forgiveness: A Key to Loving Others and Enhancing Inner Peace of Mind

Love and forgiveness are interrelated. You experience love by extending forgiveness to others. By forgiving others, you will open your heart and rediscover the capacity to love within you. Each of us is here to express forgiveness and unconditional love.

Every situation offers us the chance to reunite with the love within us that is our true nature and the true source of our joy and fulfillment. Every human has the same need and longing for love, the essence of our being. We should see in others their pure spiritual soul, which is inherently good. Open your eyes and your heart to the spark of the Divine in others who are calling out for love from you.

We are all united with and connected to God, the Divine Realm linking all of us. We all want to experience happiness, avoid suffering, and make a worthwhile contribution to life.

You experience love by extending forgiveness to others, by accepting others, and by letting go of the past. By forgiving, you invite love to replace fear, anger, rejection, humiliation, judgment, blame, disappointment, and resentment—any of which constrict your heart and narrow your world.[1] You also will not add to the fires of bitterness consuming humanity.

FORGIVENESS IN THE JEWISH TRADITION

The notion of forgiving[2] and forgetting, of turning the other cheek, goes back to the sixth-century B.C.E. prophet Second Isaiah, who advises, "I gave my back to the smiters and my cheeks to them who tore out my hair. I did not hide my face when they shamed and spat at me. For God will help me; therefore I feel no disgrace; therefore, I have set my face like a flint, and I know that I shall not be ashamed." (Isaiah 50:6–7) In the Book of Lamentations we read: "Let him give his cheek to her who smites him." (Lamentations 3:30)

In the Talmud, Jewish sages emphasized forgiveness. Mar Zutra (fifth century C.E.) used to say daily, "If anyone has hurt or wronged me, they are forgiven." (*Megilah* 28a) Just as God is forgiving, so we are supposed to be forgiving: "Only if you forgive others will God forgive you." (*Rosh Hashanah* 17a) Others commented, "One who is merciful and compassionate toward others, God will be merciful to him." (*Shabbat* 151b)

This easy type of forgiveness works for most of us if, for instance, we are only monetarily or otherwise slightly inconvenienced. It is a lot more difficult if we are physically or emotionally hurt or injured.

In tolerating others' frailties, offer your forbearance and peacefulness. However, there are limits to forgiveness. Do not endure or acquiesce in injustice or another's harmful words or deeds.

The Jewish tradition clearly permits self-defense to prevent physical or emotional harm. In the Talmud, our sages instruct us: "If someone comes at you to kill you, rise [to your self-defense] and kill him first." (*Yoma* 85b) You need not remain passive when others try, in any way, to harm you. Resist evil, otherwise you will encourage humanity's evil nature: The strong would rule the weak; the selfish and envious would readily satiate their desires; the mean and base would freely plunder at their pleasure. You need not meekly offer the left cheek to someone who strikes you on the right cheek.

Whether or not you have taken appropriate self-defense measures, the author of the Book of Leviticus tells us, "Do not hate your relative in your heart, rather rebuke him or her. . . ." (Leviticus 19:17) In other words, express your discomfort to the perpetrator, air out your feelings for the benefit of another—privately, with kind and gentle words and without anger or attack. Do not retaliate or embarrass another publicly, because shaming another in public is equivalent to shedding blood. Be open to hearing the other side of the story—what led another to speak or behave the way he or she did? Try to talk it out with the offender, if he or she is prepared to be open-minded and to listen. However, do not waste your time if the injuring party will not listen to you. As the Book of Proverbs reminds us, "Do not rebuke a fool for he or she will hate you. . . ." (Proverbs 9:8)

THE IMPORTANCE OF FORGIVENESS

Forgiveness represents a key to your cultivating inner peace of mind and to experiencing wholeness and well-being. Forgiveness helps you forget past, often painful, experiences that otherwise continue to allow the offender to maintain control over you.

Forgiveness often is not easy. It is hard to forgive, especially if you have been hurt badly by a major breach of trust and loyalty, a betrayal that tears people apart, particularly where its effects are irreversible— for instance, murder; adultery; incest; child, spousal, or parental abuse; child, spousal, or parental abandonment; discrimination because of race, gender, or age; or severe alcoholism. The harm caused by people you are close to can be overwhelming.

Forgiveness often demands courage and a strong sense of self to overcome the pain you have experienced. You do not know in advance how things will turn out.

To make the concept of forgiveness more concrete, contemplate an interpersonal problem, situation, interaction, or relationship you currently face (or have encountered in the past). Think of striving to choose forgiveness in the face of being tempted to perceive another's thoughtless deeds and hurtful words as an attack on you and to respond with your own counterattack.

We have all experienced this kind of physical or emotional discomfort. We have felt the pain of another's unkind deeds and words—to take several job-related examples: when you are overlooked for a promotion, when you are hastily and impersonally evaluated at work, or when a coworker takes all the credit for a shared project. It is like being kicked in the groin. The body grows tense, the mind becomes tight, and the heart closes. We are tempted to become bitter, to hold a grudge, to dislike someone, to desire revenge or vengeance.

Before you retaliate, keep in mind the consequences of your words and deeds as well as the bigger picture. According to Rabbi Shmuel Shmelke Horowitz of Nikolsburg, "It may sometimes happen that your own hand inadvertently strikes you. You will not take a stick and hit your hand for its heedlessness, thereby adding to your pain. So with another human, whose soul is one with yours, who, because of insufficient understanding, harms you. If you retaliate, only you would suffer." The rebbe's disciples asked him, "But if I see a person who is wicked before God, how can I love her?" "Don't you know," the rebbe responded, "that the original soul came out of the essence of God, and that every human soul is a part of God? And will you have no mercy on her, when you see that one of the Eternal's holy sparks has been lost in a maze, and is almost stifled?"[3]

In forgiving others, you cannot pretend that you are not affected by someone's hurtful conduct or speech. Forgiveness is not permissiveness: It is not an expression of "anything goes." By forgiving, you do not pronounce as acceptable someone's cruelty, thoughtlessness, inhumanity, or dishonesty.

Others utter words or do things that are unkind and unloving, whether intentionally or negligently, out of ignorance or forgetfulness, or even out of fear. They may do cruel or violent things. These actions or statements bring suffering not only to the actors or speakers, but also to others—to you. Forgiveness does not mean condoning, accepting, or justifying another's actions or statements. Forgiveness does not excuse someone else's behavior. You cannot ignore another's difficult qualities or his or her insensitive, hurtful, or unloving acts or words.

Consider two situations: All of us can see that it is one thing to forgive a blind person who trips over you or steps on your foot. If a blind person stands on your foot and hurts you, you would naturally ask him or her to step off your foot. You would make your request calmly and quietly, without malice.

But let us take a much more difficult situation: Victims of child abuse—whether emotional, physical, verbal, or sexual—often indicate that forgiveness, in the sense of letting go of their focus on the past and another's guilt, enables them to find inner peace. Realizing that their parents, among other abusers, did the best they could, lets child abuse victims be at peace in their hearts.

Forgiveness by child abuse victims, as for many others, takes time. It is a lengthy, difficult process. They need to be gentle with themselves to allow the layers of grief, pain, and vengefulness to develop into an awareness and a healing transformation. They need to rediscover the humanity of the abuser who hurt them even if that person shows no remorse.

Ultimately, some child abuse victims arrive at an understanding about what their parents or others did to them and their feelings about it. They need to cultivate their awareness and recognize the need to move beyond it. Forgiveness validates their capacity to move beyond, unburdened by the past. Forgiveness brings closure and inner peace of mind to the victim.

Through forgiveness, you can accept people who have disappointed you by not being perfect. You judge others far less severely. You become more accepting of human frailty, more ready to give the benefit of the doubt. You show that you are willing to let go of your focus on another's "guilt" deserving of punishment and of the way you have been looking at a situation, an interpersonal problem, or a relationship, and not hold on to the past. You become remarkably less hostile and more open-hearted and tolerant.

Do not let your anger and your hate continue to poison you. Do not carry a grudge, seek to punish or take revenge, or blame another. Letting go of your resentment and relinquishing your goal of retribution lifts the weight of hate and anger from your shoulders, easing your pain and helping you forget how you were wronged. By forgiving, you release the offender's hold on you.

You would be amazed if you saw your unforgiving face in a mirror. The ugliness and hatred would shock you. You would recognize the price you are paying for your unwillingness to let go of the past. Holding onto your feelings of anger and vengeance is self-defeating. It is an ever festering wound that will not bring you any happiness, and indeed may contribute to your health problems. However, you need not be bound by the negativities created by another.

Through forgiveness, you shift your perspective and strive to see things differently by looking beyond another's body, behavior, words, or personality. This shift in perception dissolves your fears, restoring your inner peace of mind and reducing depression, anxiety, and unhealthy hostile anger.[4] Your feelings of isolation and alienation drop away.

Reframing, as we shall see in detail in chapter 9, facilitates your understanding. Go beneath the surface differences in appearance or behavior that seem to separate you from another to the more profound reality, to the deeper truth of the love each of us shares with our fellow human beings. Perceive another human being in the light of love. See another's true essence, his or her essential innocence, wholeness, and fundamental worth; deserving of your compassion, understanding, and lovingkindness. There is beauty in every soul, tenderness in every heart.

Look at others for who they really are. See others, whether physicians and business executives or thieves and murderers, as the children of the God within all of us. Because everyone is basically the same, focus on what is good in others, forging a sense of connection with them. You are not separate from others. We are all in this world together.

Love is something we are and that we share with others. As Rabbi Aharon Perlow of Karlin, who lived from 1808 to 1872 and was said to be endowed with the spirit of holiness, put it: "Love is hidden in the recesses of everyone's heart. There is no one who has not had at least an hour of love and yearning."[5] By focusing on the loving nature of others, the suffering experienced by others, and the innocence of others, you will have the chance to more fully experience your own inner peace of mind. Reflect on how it feels to give up your grudge and let go of the hurt. Recognize the emotional relief.

A summer camp story I once heard illustrates the importance of change in perception as a key to forgiveness. An eight-year-old boy received in the mail a box of home-baked cookies from his parents. After eating a few of them, he put the rest under his bed. The next day when he went to get a cookie, the box was gone. All the camp counselors were told of the theft.

That afternoon, one of the camp counselors saw another boy eating the stolen cookies. He sought out the boy whose cookies had been stolen and told him, "I know who took your cookies, but will you help me teach him a lesson?" The boy replied, "OK, but won't you punish him?" The counselor explained, "Punishment will only make him hate you and resent me. Call home and ask your parents to send you another box of cookies."

The boy phoned home and in a few days received a second box of cookies. The counselor said, "Now, the boy who took your cookies is sitting near the baseball diamond. Go over there and share your cookies with him."

The boy protested. "But try it," the counselor stated, "and see what happens."

Later that afternoon, the counselor saw the two boys walking arm-in-arm. The boy who took the cookies was trying to get the other to accept his pocketknife in repayment for the stolen cookies. The other refused the gift from his new friend, indicating that a few cookies were not that significant.

Although difficult, realize that others' hurtful deeds and words, their anger, cruelty, jealousy, lust, fear, pride, anxiety, thoughtlessness, or selfishness, may deep down be a plea for love. As another calls out, meet their cries as the expression of a desire to be healed, not to be blamed, attacked, or judged harshly.

Each of us has the same need and longing for love, inner peace, and happiness. We all want to release our potential for love. There is something unique and valuable in every human life. See another human being through the eyes of love and compassion, not with the mindset of judgmentalism, punishment, or moral superiority. Do not forgive by reinforcing another's guilt or dwelling on another's negatives. Perceiving the holiness in others, answer another's acts and words with love and compassion; let go of the rest—your fears, your hatred, and your anger—so that they are no longer present for you, consciously or unconsciously.

PATHWAYS SPIRITUAL SEEKERS CAN USE IN FORGIVING OTHERS AND ASKING FOR FORGIVENESS

As you contemplate how to forgive and reopen your heart to love, give up the way you have been looking at a situation, an interpersonal relationship, or human interaction. Let go of your painful, fearful attitudes about your lifetime of experiences. Forgiveness represents the capacity to love when your mind resists love, insisting on a closed, fearful heart.

Forgiveness begins with self-forgiveness. Overcome any lingering beliefs of your unworthiness, including recollections of the ways you have been unloving or harmful, past mistakes you have made, or your past misdeeds. Let go of your feelings of self-doubt. By giving others the right to make mistakes, you become more willing to do that for yourself. We will come back to the importance of self-forgiveness when we discuss self-esteem in chapter 8.

I wish I could offer a magic approach you could use in forgiving others or asking others for their forgiveness. However, there is simply no formula to put forgiveness into practice. It is difficult, if not impossible, to figure out how to accomplish or express forgiveness in any situation or relationship.

Start by acknowledging your hurt to yourself, admitting that someone did something seriously harmful to you. Then decide to forgive, even if you do not know how exactly you are going to forgive.

Begin by focusing on and striving to actualize some of the basic concepts of Jewish Spirituality. Sincerely ask God to guide and direct your thoughts, perceptions, and understanding. Turn it over to the Holy One. Trust that the Eternal will show you the way to forgiveness. Recognizing that you are not fully in charge, surrender and align yourself with the Divine will. Realize that closing your heart to love results in pain; choosing to forgive will release you from this pain. Have faith in another's spiritual identity and essence as a child of a loving God.

The following prayer may be useful in stimulating your thoughts, words, and deeds of forgiveness: O God, help me see ——— through Your eyes of love, not through the eyes of judgment, guilt, or sin.

If you ask God with sincerity, you will receive a new vision of another human being. A shift in perception will dissolve your fears, your hatred, and your anger, engendering your love and compassion for another. Your new perception represents a transforming healing, replacing pain with an inner peace of mind. Relinquish to the Supreme Sovereign any of your remaining anger, hatred, or resentment against the offender.

Many have found the Forgiveness Meditation helpful in forgiving someone they dislike or hold a grievance toward, or someone to whom their heart has been closed, or in asking another for his or her forgiveness. Remember we are all connected to God and therefore to each other.

Use the Forgiveness Meditation for ten to fifteen minutes, once or twice daily, for at least three weeks. Be patient. Forgiveness is often a lengthy process.

Forgiveness Meditation. Introduction: Try to create a warm, welcoming atmosphere, an environment of serenity and spaciousness for the journey within. Lower the lights in your room. Close your eyes, sit quietly, calm and relax your body by sitting, reclining, or lying down. Breathe in and out normally, feeling where your breath flows into and out of your body. Adjust your breaths so that the in and out breaths are the same length, thereby bringing about both a relaxation of your body and an alertness of your mind.

Feel yourself surrounded by warmth and patience.

Allow any anger or hatred you feel toward others to dissolve into the warmth and patience.

With each breath, breathe in warmth.

Feel the warmth nourishing you.

Breathe in patience and feel the spaciousness and the opening of your heart that patience creates within.

Allow the warmth and patience to give rise to forgiveness.

The power of forgiveness is great.

Release yourself from any tension or tightness you feel inside, caused by resentment.

Let go of the pride that holds on to resentment.

Allow the pain of old hurts to fade away.

Reflect on ———; someone who has caused you pain and suffering; someone who has made you angry, hateful, or fearful, intentionally or unintentionally; and send him/her forgiveness. Say: I forgive you.

Forgive him/her as best you can.

Allow the power of forgiveness to grow.

Out of compassion for yourself, allow the resentment to fade away.

Let go of your judgment of another, and replace it with understanding and compassion.

Ask that no harm come to ——— because of what he or she has done to you.

For ———, another whom you have caused pain, anger, hatred, fear, and suffering, intentionally or unintentionally, ask for his/her forgiveness. Say: I ask you for forgiveness.

Forgive yourself for anyone's pain and suffering to which you have contributed.

Also forgive yourself for having harmed yourself, not loved yourself, not lived up to your expectations. Say: For every way I have harmed myself, I offer forgiveness.

Concluding Instructions: Come back to the here and now. Take time to ease yourself back. Slowly bring your awareness back into your body. Feel yourself back in the room and open your eyes.

When you think of someone you have harmed in the past, consider writing a note of apology requesting his or her forgiveness. Say that you are sorry. You need not send the letter: The important thing is expressing your thoughts in writing.

When the spirit of forgiveness moves you, remember that forgiving another means saying "no more" from a calm, quiet place. Do not dismiss or condone another's hurtful, negative deeds or words.

Although quite difficult, forgiveness often means confronting the offender (even if he or she does not seek forgiveness) face-to-face, sharing your issues, making explicit your concerns, and discussing what you see as the transgressor's "shortcomings." Hear the other's explanation for his or her behavior, his or her side of things, his or her feelings. Think about his or her vulnerabilities. Walk in his or her shoes. Develop a degree of empathy for the "offender." See things from his or her viewpoint.

Offer your support and your constructive suggestions for improvement, without judgment, blame, or attack. Speak sincerely from your heart. Taking a nonjudgmental stance, however hard it may be for you, is especially important. As Hillel reminds us in the Talmud, "Do not judge your fellow until you have been in her place." (Avot 2:4) Always see others as the children of a loving God.

Through an honest exchange, share your feelings, lovingly and truthfully, with the other about his or her "shortcomings." Make it a positive sharing, not a destructive attack. Keep in mind Rabbi Nattan, who lived in the second century C.E., and taught: "Do not rebuke your friend for faults that are really your own." (Baba Metzia 59b) Rabbi Shmuel, who lived in the third century C.E., put it this way: "One who is always condemning others probably sees in them his own faults." (Kiddushin 70a)

In a relationship based on mutual trust and open communication, you can gently point out another's errors, weaknesses, mistakes, his or her shadow or darkness, without fear of withdrawal, attack, retaliation, defensiveness, or denial.

In a relationship where you take the initiative in forgiving another but the offender has not sought your forgiveness, the reality often departs from the ideal. Be patient. Be prepared for the injuring party's negative, often defensive, reaction, which may culminate in an intense, painful verbal attack on you, in response to your expression of forgiveness. Regardless of the nature of your relationship or another's response to your efforts, honor the injuring party's process of growth and change, however difficult this may be for you. Always treat the other person with the utmost respect.

If you anticipate an ongoing relationship, you will probably need to set some boundaries on your future interactions. You will need to learn to say "No," calmly but firmly, to another's preferences, demands, or behavior. Stand fast. Back up your words with action.

Also, know when to be silent and hold your peace though in the heat of the moment you may be very tempted to "have it out" with an offender. As Rabbi Akiva, who lived in the second century C.E., taught: "The key to wisdom is silence." (*Avot* 3:13)

If your heart does not allow you to love someone you have forgiven, try to think of some great goodness concerning him or her, find one good quality, or hope for something good for that person, so that you may come to perceive his or her inner worth. Seeing good in or for another often allows you to begin to relate better to him or her.

What about someone who will not forgive you, despite your efforts to seek forgiveness? In addition to working through the Forgiveness Meditation, you may want to express your remorse in some tangible way. Perform some concrete act that, (for instance) given your financial situation, may be quite extravagant, such as sending flowers, for a person who will not forgive you despite your genuine efforts.

YOM KIPPUR: FROM FORGIVENESS TO RECONCILIATION

The most sacred day of the Jewish year, Yom Kippur (the Day of Atonement), plays a key role in the process of forgiveness. Yom Kippur falls in the autumn on the tenth day of the Hebrew month of Tishri, bringing to an end the ten days of self-examination and repentance that begin with Rosh Hashanah.

On Yom Kippur, Jews throughout the world seek a spiritual regeneration, a reconnecting with our Divine essence. We seek to reunite with God, the loving and compassionate Divine Presence, Who, as the authors of the Hebrew Bible repeatedly pointed out, will forgive us, collectively and individually. We read: "God! Slow to anger and abounding in kindness, forgiving iniquity and transgression . . ." (Exodus 34:6–7; Numbers 14:18; Nehemiah 9:17)

The prophetic writings contain numerous affirmations of Divine forgiveness. Jeremiah proclaims that God declares: "Return, O faithless Israel. I will not look on you in anger, for I am merciful. I do not bear a grudge for all time." (Jeremiah 3:12) The Second Isaiah recounts God, as the Redeemer of Israel, declaring: "In slight anger, for a moment, I hid My face from you, but with everlasting love I will have compassion on you." (Isaiah 54:8) The psalmist tells us: "God is compassionate and gracious, slow to anger, abounding in steadfast love." (Psalm 103:8) As God is merciful and forgiving, so we should forgive ourselves and others, and ask others to forgive us.

The ten days between Rosh Hashanah and Yom Kippur, culminating with the Day of Atonement, represent a time for self-reflection and personal transformation. We pause to reevaluate our personal lives and our interactions with others. The process of introspection hopefully leads us to change, to turn away from the negative, and to take positive steps. We can and should turn our lives around.

Because we have free will and personal responsibility, we can choose goodness, behaving positively and treating others with care, over evil, behaving negatively and treating others with contempt. We are neither damned nor doomed. On Yom Kippur, we celebrate our capacity for change and turning (*teshuvah* in Hebrew), which are always possible. We recognize that all human lives can be given new beginnings and that in our dealings with others we can be more loving, forgiving, and truthful. Through our past mistakes, we can learn to make good choices and remove the obstacles separating us from God and each other. The Day of Atonement frees us from the past and opens up for us a bright future of inner peace, joy, and serenity.

As we turn, forgiving others and asking others whom we have harmed or hurt to forgive us, we go beyond forgiveness to reconciliation, making our amends and rebuilding relationships with the participation of others. We enter into a dialogue, person-to-person, one-on-one, with actual parents, siblings, spouses, ex-spouses, children, friends, colleagues, and others.

Be inspired to be bold enough to speak directly to those whom you have wronged in your deeds or words, even if they do not know it. This is excruciatingly difficult for most of us. Realizing we have hurt others can be intolerable for some. Apologize and sincerely ask others for their forgiveness. Remember that the act of apologizing is not a sign of weakness. Offer to make amends or restitution. Strive to repair the relationship.

Grant forgiveness to anyone who genuinely seeks it from you by confessing that he or she did something wrong and promising not to repeat the offense. If a victim refuses to forgive and the offender apologizes three times, then the transgressor is absolved. (*Yoma* 87b) Judaism seeks to liberate an offender who undergoes a profound change from his or her past mistakes, and allows for redemption. Thus the ideal of reconciliation promotes interpersonal healing, not merely the inner healing of the victim provided by forgiveness.

Cause and effect, which has an important role in our existence and in the universe, comes into play regarding forgiveness. Everything you think, speak, and do represents a productive cause, impacting on you and those around you. As you forgive others, so, in turn, you will be forgiven. Thus, in every situation, remain open to the wholeness and the inner peace of mind that forgiveness offers you. Through giving others the gift of mercy, love, and compassion, you will be healed, able to go forward in life, to grow and to love.

Open your heart to others. Be open to loving and being loved. Ask God to see another through the eyes of love, not the eyes of judgment.

Forgiving starts and ends with truthfulness, the genuine expression of your feelings and emotions. With truthfulness, you can make a new start. Let us then explore the importance of truthfulness in our interactions with others.

NOTES

1. I have drawn on various articles on forgiveness in *On Course* magazine by Rev. Dr. Diane Burke and Rev. Jon Mundy, two of my instructors at The New Seminary; and on Berton H. Kaplan, Heather Munroe-Blum, and Dan G. Blazer, "Religion, Health, and Forgiveness: Traditions and Challenges," in *Religion in Aging and Health: Theoretical Foundations and Methodological Frontiers*, ed. Jeffrey S. Levin (Thousand Oaks, CA: Sage Publications, 1994), pp. 52–77.

2. Louis E. Newman, "The Quality of Mercy: On the Duty to Forgive in the Judaic Tradition," *Journal of Religious Ethics*, 15:2 (Fall 1987): 155–172; Elliott N. Dorff, "The Elements of Forgiveness: A Jewish Approach," in *Dimensions of Forgiveness: Psychological Research & Theological Perspectives*, ed. Everett L. Worthington, Jr. (Philadelphia: Templeton Foundation, 1998); and Elliott N. Dorff, "Individual and Communal Forgiveness," in *Autonomy and Judaism: The Individual and the Community in Jewish Philosophical Thought*, ed. Daniel H. Frank (Albany, NY: State University of New York, 1992), discuss forgiveness as expounded in classical Jewish sources.

3. Adapted from *The Hasidic Anthology: Tales and Teachings of the Hasidim*, trans. Louis I. Newman (Northvale, NJ: Jason Aronson, 1987), pp.

221–222; Martin Buber, *The Tales of the Hasidim: The Early Masters*, trans. Olga Marx (New York: Schocken, 1947), p. 190.

4. Robert D. Enright, Suzanne Freedman, and Julio Rique, "The Psychology of Interpersonal Forgiveness," in *Exploring Forgiveness*, ed. Robert D. Enright and Joanna North (Madison, WI: University of Wisconsin, 1998), pp. 58–59; Michael E. McCulloch, Everett L. Worthington Jr., and Kenneth C. Rachal, "Interpersonal Forgiving in Close Relationships," *Journal of Personality and Social Psychology* 73:2 (1997): 321–336; Suzanne R. Freedman and Robert D. Enright, "Forgiveness as an Intervention Goal with Incest Survivors," *Journal of Consulting and Clinical Psychology* 64:5 (1996): 983–992; Berton H. Kaplan, "Social Health and the Forgiving Heart: The Type B Story," *Journal of Behavioral Medicine* 15:1 (1992): 3–14.

5. Simcha Raz, *Hasidic Wisdom: Sayings from the Jewish Sages*, trans. Dov Peretz Elkins and Jonathan Elkins (Northvale, NJ: Jason Aronson, 1979), p. 18.

CHAPTER SEVEN

Truthfulness: Another Key to Our Dealings with Others

Truthfulness represents a key to our character and our dealings with others.[1] A person of truth is an ideal individual.

Truthful people are trusted without reservation. They are boundlessly honored. Honesty is the foundation upon which interpersonal relationships are based. Conversely, habitual liars lose the confidence of others. They are doubted even when they tell the truth.

Jews should stand out as a group who serve as the exponent of truth in dealings between and among humans. Jews must be distinguished for their righteousness and integrity. They must live lives of righteousness and integrity even in the midst of unrighteousness. They must fortify themselves against the influences of evil and corruption. In the most complex moments of life, immovable integrity must direct the lives of Jews.

Be true to yourself and to others. Say what you mean and mean what you say. A yes should mean a yes; a no should mean a no. (*Baba Bathra* 49b) Do what you promise to do.

TRUTHFULNESS IN THE JEWISH TRADITION

Judaism stresses the virtues of truthfulness and honesty. God loves an honest person. A truthful person is the pride of humanity. Honesty and trustworthiness may be the world's only true wealth.

The Jewish tradition exalts truth and condemns falsehood. You should think the truth, seek the truth, speak the truth, live the truth. Your word should be as good as gold, in both personal and business matters. The psalmist notes: "God . . . who may dwell in Your holy mountain? He who lives without blame, who does what is right and in his heart acknowledges the truth." (Psalm 15:1–2) It is also written: "You will support me because of my integrity and let me abide in Your presence forever." (Psalm 41:13) In the Book of Proverbs, we read: "Truthful speech abides forever, a lying tongue for but a moment." (Proverbs 12:19)

The Jewish tradition warns us against lying. Lies separate us from God. When you forsake honesty, the spirit of wisdom leaves your soul. The writers of the Hebrew Bible tell us: "Keep far from falsehood. . . ." (Exodus 23:7) The psalmist admonishes us: "Guard your tongue from evil and your lips from deceitful speech." (Psalm 34:14) According to the psalmist: "One who deals deceitfully shall not live in God's house; one who speaks falsely shall not stand before God's eyes." (Psalm 101:7) The author of Proverbs reminds us: "Lying speech is an abomination to God. . . ." (Proverbs 12:22) Also: "Acquire truth and do not dispense with it. . . ." (Proverbs 23:23)

The prophets of old condemned the deceitful, whom they viewed as stepping outside God's protective love. Isaiah mocks those who boast of the fact that they can take refuge behind a screen of lies: They "have made falsehood [their] refuge." (Isaiah 28:15) Jeremiah criticizes the people of Judah because "[t]hey deceive everyone" and "[t]hey have trained their tongues to speak falsely." (Jeremiah 9:4)

Leading Hasidic rabbis also warned against deceit. According to Rabbi Pinchas Shapiro of Koretz, who lived from 1728 to 1790 striving for uncompromising truthfulness: "It is better that one's soul departs from the body than a false word departs from the mouth."[2]

A Hasidic story points to the importance of being truthful. Reb Elimelech of Lizhensk, a leading Hasidic rabbi and a person of unrivaled greatness, who lived from 1717 to 1786, once said: "When I stand before the Heavenly Tribunal and they ask me: 'Have you studied all you should?' I will answer 'No!' Then they will inquire: 'Have you prayed all you should?' Again, I will respond: 'No!' I will also answer

'No' to their third question: 'Have you done all the good you should?'
They will pronounce the verdict: 'You told the truth. Therefore, you
merit a share in the World to Come.'" [3]

Jewish sages have long praised and extolled truth as the lasting
order of things. They recognized that at times truth is perverted and
sometimes it is denied—but in the end truth emerges triumphant:
"Truth springs up from the earth. . . ." (Psalms 85:12) "Truthful
speech abides forever. . . ." (Proverbs 12:19) Zephaniah, who lived in
the last part of the seventh century B.C.E., prophesied that the remnant
of Israel that God will save "shall do no wrong and speak no falsehood,
a deceitful tongue shall not be found in their mouths." (Zephaniah
3:13)

When we lie we violate the very nature of our being. Lying severs
the unity of each of us. It represents a division between our hearts
and our tongues; between each of us, our fellow human beings, and
God. Liars absent themselves from contact with the Divine Presence;
they are left in a profound state of loneliness.

THE REALITY: THE PERVASIVENESS
OF FALSEHOODS IN OUR SOCIETY

Despite the Jewish tradition's adoration of truth and its contempt for
falsehood, we continue to lie. Lying is at epidemic levels. In a survey
of forty thousand Americans, ninety-one percent admitted they lied
regularly and habitually at work.[4] A majority of job résumés, on the
magnitude of fifty to seventy-five percent, contain major distortions.
In job interviews, employers misrepresent themselves as often as do
job applicants. Workers make false excuses for being late to or absent
from work or being behind on scheduled assignments.[5] One out of
four "major" deceptions centers on extramarital affairs.[6]

In a pioneering empirical study, researchers asked seventy-seven
college students and seventy community members to keep a diary, for
one week, detailing each "lie" they told in any conversation lasting
more than ten minutes. The students admitted to lying an average of
twice a day, while local residents lied half as often. Community members
lied in one-fifth of their social interactions; students, one-third. One-
tenth of the lies represented mere exaggerations, designed to make the
teller kinder, smarter, or more gregarious; sixty percent were outright
deceptions. Most of the rest were subtle lies, often of omission.[7]

How do we lie? Obviously, we lie directly in our actual words, through our speech. But we also may lie implicitly or indirectly by insinuation, by a gesture or through our silence, or by being purposely ambiguous—that is, by any acts or other channels of human expression that mislead, convey a false impression, or deflect from the truth.

We can distinguish five basic types of lies: of malice, for business, for our defense, to gain the esteem of others, and to facilitate social relationships.

Through a lie of malice, you degrade another individual in the eyes of the world. Lies of malice, designed to besmirch a person's reputation by creating rumors that may ruin a person's standing in his or her community, among his or her colleagues, or within a circle of friends or relatives, are simply outrageous transgressions. To give another a bad name represents a form of murder—character assassination.

We can also lie for the sake of business and profit-making. Deceit in business is the equivalent of stealing. By seizing something to which you have no claim, business deceit deprives another of his or her possessions.

A person may tell a lie to save or defend him or herself. For instance, if you are caught in an act of wrongdoing, such as a minor traffic violation, you may lie to save yourself from the consequences of your act or from punishment: You claim you were doing 55 mph when you were pulled over for exceeding 75 mph.

Lies of malice, deceit in business, and falsehoods to save oneself are legally punishable in our society, but these untruths also have spiritual consequences. For example, inventing and speaking evil of another disrupts the harmony between people, generating animosity and bitterness in an ever widening circle.

These three types of deceptions also constitute a deception to God, a misrepresentation before the Eternal. As Jewish sages noted in the Talmud, when you go before the final judgment (discussed in detail in chapter 13), you will be asked: "Have you conducted your business with integrity?" (*Shabbat* 31a) If words contain sparks of Divinity, then their misuse represents an abuse of the Eternal's Sanctity.

Other types of falsehoods, although seemingly harmless and not illegal, must also be avoided. For example, you may lie about yourself to attain the esteem of others, or you may indulge in flattery to ingratiate yourself with others. In Proverbs we read: "A flattering mouth works ruin." (Proverbs 26: 28) Flattery, a manipulative, self-serving action, tends toward deception or malicious speech. All of these falsehoods corrode a person's nature and diminish his or her holiness. The Talmud records Rabbi Jeremiah ben Abba's statement, "Four kinds of people are not permitted to greet the Divine Presence: mockers, flatterers, liars, and slanderers." (*Satah* 42a)

WHITE LIES: FALSEHOODS FOR THE SAKE OF PEACE AND SOCIAL HARMONY

There are also lies for the sake of peace and social harmony. These lies, so-called white lies, may be necessary for the sake of promoting greater harmony among people and preventing unfriendliness, bitterness, or misunderstanding between or among individuals.

Let us take several concrete examples that illustrate how white lies perform important interpersonal functions, serving as social lubricants. There may be relatives or neighbors whom you do not like, yet toward whom you act in a friendly manner so as to spare them pain and protect their feelings. You tell a neighbor you have an appointment rather than saying that you do not care for his or her company because he or she is a bore.

You may tell someone he or she looks good or is smart, even if you do not think so. Is it a "lie" when you help another gain confidence in himself or herself? Telling the complete truth to someone who is ugly or dumb may not be the best way to enhance that person's self-esteem. In these situations, truth inflicts a hurt that is incompatible with lovingkindness and compassion. By shading the truth to express your lovingkindness and compassion, you may protect another's fragile self-esteem and save his or her heart from needless hurt.

The intention or motivation behind what you say is important. Lying to harm someone is wrong, as is not speaking out in the face of injustice, while white lies are the lubricants of society. Lying to make someone feel better, to spare them embarrassment, or to preserve interpersonal peace often is the right thing to do.

When you visit someone who is in the hospital suffering from lung cancer, after smoking three packs of cigarettes daily for years, do not tell him or her: "You brought this illness on yourself. Now your family has to suffer." In the midst of a patient's fears, pain, and suffering, it is cruel to blame him or her.

In giving advice that another might find painful to hear or difficult to bear, try to be gentle. Cruelty cloaked as truth is not right. Be careful and thoughtful in your pursuit of the virtue of lovingkindness and compassion.

In the perfect world, if love and compassion were potent, if kindness and sympathy were strong, white lies would be unnecessary. Ideally, an individual would have nothing to hide from others. His or her lovingkindness would be genuine. However, when genuineness of feeling is lacking, white lies take their place for the sake of peace and social harmony. According to the Talmud, peace is exalted over truth, at least where an important principle is not at stake (*Yebamot* 65b). White lies often promote the dignity of others.

HOW SPIRITUAL·SEEKERS CAN ENHANCE THEIR TRUTHFULNESS

Try to be honest with yourself, with others, and with God. Being honest means concealing nothing, disguising nothing, and living out what you actually are. Resolve to stop lying.

It is not easy. As the Rabbi Pinchas Shapiro of Koretz, the Koretzer Rebbe, put it: "Nothing has been as difficult as my effort to rid my spirit of falsehoods. It took me twenty-one years to discover the truth: seven years to recognize what truth is, seven years to drive out falsehood, and seven years to fill my inner self with truth."[8]

To help you on your spiritual quest for truthfulness, you may want to offer the Koretzer Rebbe's daily prayer: "O God, lead me in the path of truth."[9]

Admit your falsehoods. As Rabbi Mordecai of Chernobyl stated: "If you wish to acquire the habit of truthfulness, make it a point when you catch yourself telling a falsehood, of saying: 'I have just been guilty of a lie.' In this manner you will quickly discipline your tongue."[10] If you find yourself lying, stop!

Begin by being honest with yourself. If you are honest with yourself, then you are honest with the world. Do not deceive yourself. Do not blame others, your family members, friends, neighbors, or colleagues, for your shortcomings or misdoings. Locate your faults within yourself. Acknowledge your deficiencies and be ready to correct them. If you are honest with yourself, you will take life more seriously and live in accordance with the highest principles and virtues of Jewish Spirituality: through your lovingkindness for and forgiveness of others; by developing your humility, optimism, and equanimity.

Do not deceive others. Honesty is a principle expressed in each and every one of our relationships with others. Speak your thoughts, express your feelings, and perform your tasks in a genuine and loving manner.

When you tell people the truth, whether in business dealings or any other interactions, others will trust and respect you. They will look at you as a friend on whose word they can rely. People who are truthful are trusted without reservation and are boundlessly honored. Stand out in the eyes of others as an exponent of truth in your dealings with everyone.

Finally, be honest with God. As discussed in chapter 4, surrender and offer yourself to God, holding nothing back. Pour out your heart to God. You cannot fool God, Who knows the secrets of every mind and heart. God knows your innermost motivations even if on the surface you say and do the "right" things.

Demonstrate to humanity that the prophets' vision of a loving and just world is within the reach and practice of everyone. Each and every day, through your thoughts, words, and deeds, practice lovingkindness, forgiveness, and truthfulness in all your interpersonal dealings. In short, one of the most important keys to the Jewish ideal rests on our ethical interactions with others. Place truth at the center of your heart, mind and soul. According to Rabbi Nachman of Breslov, the great-grandson of the Baal Shem Tov: "When there is no truth, there is neither faith nor lovingkindness."[11] When you are truthful, burdens will be lifted from your shoulders and your spirits will soar.

Strengthening your conduct toward others through your lovingkindness, forgiveness, and truthfulness rests on cultivating your personal virtues. Let us examine three personal attributes: humility, joy, and equanimity.

NOTES

1. I have drawn on Rabbi Morris Lichtenstein, *Judaism: A Presentation of Its Essence and a Suggestion for Its Preservation* (New York: Society of Jewish Science, 1934), pp. 95–98 and 172–173; Rabbi Morris Lichtenstein, *Joy of Life: Jewish Science Essays* (New York: Society of Jewish Science, 1938), pp. 276–292; Byron L. Sherwin and Seymour J. Cohen, *How to Be a Jew: Ethical Teachings of Judaism* (Northvale, NJ: Jason Aronson, 1992), pp. 196–199; and Louis Jacobs, *Jewish Values* (Hartford: Hartmore House, 1960), pp. 145–160. In *Lying: Moral Choice in Public and Private Life* (New York: Pantheon, 1983)

Sissela Bok condemns lying and offers its negative impact on human relationships and trust as the rationale for her condemnation.

2. Simcha Raz, *Hasidic Wisdom: Sayings from the Jewish Sages*, trans. Dov Peretz Elkins and Jonathan Elkins (Northvale, NJ: Jason Aronson, 1997), p. 47.

3. Adapted from Martin Buber, *Tales of Hasidim: The Early Masters*, trans. Olga Marx (New York: Schocken, 1975), p. 253.

4. James Patterson and Peter Kim, *The Day America Told the Truth: What People Really Believe about Everything that Matters* (New York: Prentice Hall, 1991), p. 45; Don Oldenberg, "The Truth About Deception," *Washington Post*, 14 April 1998, D4.

5. Lynne G. Vance, "Liar, Liar, Pants on Fire," *Washington Post*, 14 April 1998, D4.

6. Janny Scott, "Bright, Shining, or Dark: American Way of Lying," *New York Times*, 16 August 1998, Week in Review, 3.

7. Bella M. DePaulo and Deborah A. Kashy, "Everyday Lies in Close and Casual Relationships," *Journal of Personality and Social Psychology* 74:1 (1998): 63–79; Allison Kornet, "The Truth About Lying," *Psychology Today* 30:3 (May/June 1997): 53–57.

8. Adapted from Raz, *Hasidic Wisdom*, p. 44.

9. Adapted from *The Hasidic Anthology: Tales and Teachings of the Hasidim*, trans. Louis I. Newman (Northvale, NJ: Jason Aronson, 1987), p. 491.

10. Adapted from *The Hasidic Anthology*, pp. 490–491.

11. Raz, *Hasidic Wisdom*, p. 42.

PART FOUR

PERSONAL VIRTUES: BRINGING PEACE and HARMONY to OUR INNER LIVES

You need to practice certain personal virtues in your daily life. Humility when coupled with positive self-esteem, as well as optimism and equanimity, bring peace and harmony to your inner life.

You should incorporate these virtues into your daily life. The care and support you give yourself provides you with the strength to love and forgive others. Only by first loving and accepting yourself can you love, accept, and forgive others.

As we begin our inquiry into these personal character traits, it is useful to reflect on one of Rabbi Nachman's most memorable stories, "The Sophisticate and the Simpleton."*

In the story, the Simpleton has very little formal education and is very limited in his abilities. He sews triangular shoes for a living, has nothing but bread and water for sustenance, and is so poor that he must share a tattered sheepskin coat with his wife. Yet, for him, this coat serves as "exquisite finery" for every occasion. His daily rations taste like the "finest wines and delicacies." Although with his limited skills the Simpleton earns far less than his fellow shoemakers, his self-confidence and joy are such that he feels absolutely no jealousy or want. "Why must we speak about others," he tells his wife when she criticizes his inability to charge as much as others for his work. "What do I care about that? That is their work, and this is my work!"

When some of the townspeople engaged him in conversation so that they could make fun of him, the Simpleton had but one request: "Just without mockery." If they assured him of their sincerity, he would never probe their motives more deeply. Being a simple person, he never engaged in the sophisticated speculation that would suggest that this in itself might be a means of mocking him.

Indeed, the Simpleton never questions or tries to second-guess anything. He just conducts himself simply and honestly, feeling only a great deal of satisfaction with his lot. No matter what happens, he is always very happy. Because of his simplicity he never feels any lack, and due to his simplicity he is eventually named the prime minister of the land, becoming even wiser than his friend, the Sophisticate.

The Sophisticate, on the other hand, has advanced education and training. He is truly a worldly person. He has experience in business, various crafts, and even medicine, and has broadened his outlook through travel. Despite all this, the Sophisticate is never satisfied with what he has; he is always looking for something better over the horizon.

The Sophisticate is also very exacting and very stringent in everything he does. When his work as a master goldsmith is not appreciated by others he feels rejected, yet when minute imperfections in his diamond engraving go unnoticed he chastises himself for what he sees as his flawed skills. In contrast to the Simpleton, the Sophisticate needs public approval, and when his expertise as a physician goes unrecognized, he rejects this profession as well. Furthermore, because his strict standards allow for no flexibility, it is impossible for him to appreciate the work of others. His clothing, his accommodations, and his life have to be just so, or else he is upset and becomes depressed. He is unable to appreciate simplicity or the simple way of life. In fact, he has no life.

The Sophisticate's lack of self-confidence does not allow him to speak with those whom he considers his inferiors, because this would tend to reduce his own status, something he feels he must protect at any cost. As a result, he can unburden himself to no one, and is, therefore, always miserable. His sophistication not only makes him arrogant, but also skeptical and unable to trust anyone. Never satisfied with the obvious meaning of things, he always probes and analyzes for the "true" meaning. This often leads him to wrong conclusions and eventually causes him to lose both his stature and wisdom.

Moral: You do not need to be perfect. Rather, just try to do your best; live simply; be satisfied with your portion in the world; see and accept things as they are; and cultivate your humility, joyfulness, and equanimity.

*Chaim Kramer, *Crossing the Narrow Bridge: A Practical Guide to Rebbe Nachman's Teachings*, ed. Moshe Mykoff (New York: Breslov Research Institute, 1989), pp. 21–22; *Rabbi Nachman's Stories*, trans. Rabbi Aryeh Kaplan (Brooklyn: Breslov Research Institute, 1983), pp. 160–196; Adin Steinsaltz, *The Tales of Rabbi Nachman of Bratslav* (Northvale, NJ: Jason Aronson, 1993), pp. 165–194; Martin Buber, *The Tales of Rabbi Nachman*, trans. Maurice Friedman (Atlantic Highlands, NJ: Humanities Press International, 1988), pp. 71–94.

CHAPTER 8

Striking the Balance between Humility and Positive Self-Esteem

Humility forms the basis on which the virtues of optimism and equanimity rest. This is the key virtue, not chutzpah, or brashness, as many of us think.

Yet, you need to balance your humility and your self-esteem.[1] You need to think well of yourself and maintain not only your self-respect, but also your space for God and for others. As Rabbi Simcha Bunam of Pshis'cha, who lived from 1767 to 1827 developing an approach to Hasidim accentuating introspection and self-searching, stated: Every person should have two pockets as the occasion demands. In one of which are the words, "For my sake the world was created." In the other, the words, "I am earth and ashes."[2] Your inner peace comes from keeping the pockets separate. Do not mix up the pockets. Let us first begin by considering humility; then we shall take up self-esteem.

HUMILITY IN THE JEWISH TRADITION

Judaism decries conceit and arrogance, the egotist's preoccupation with self that leaves little or no room for the Holy One and others.

The more that you think you are, the less room you have for the
Eternal and for others. Conversely, the less you think you are, the
more room there is for God and others.

The Book of Proverbs contains much reproof of the proud, who
have a falsely elevated view of themselves. Pride is equated with
foolishness (Proverbs 14:3). A fool fails to notice fine qualities in
others, while always conscious of these attributes in himself or herself.

The Wisdom Literature emphasizes what awaits prideful, arrogant
individuals. The proud will be humbled and humiliated (Proverbs
29:23). "Pride goes before ruin, arrogance before failure." (Proverbs
16:18) The psalmist reminds us that God despises the arrogant and
the proud (Psalm 101:5). The author of Proverbs asserts that God will
punish the proud (Proverbs 15:25).

In contrast, Judaism celebrates humility. The psalmist declares,
"[M]y heart is not proud nor my look arrogant. . . . " (Psalms 131:1)
Humility represents a special virtue of the Jewish leaders and sages
throughout the ages.

The legendary Moses, despite all of his extraordinary talents
and achievements—his defense of the Jewish people in repeatedly
arguing their case before God, his organizational skills, his formulation of monotheism, and his political leadership—is aware of
his inadequacy for the task he must accomplish. Perhaps Moses'
most important characteristic is his humility. Moses is described as
"a very humble man, more humble than anyone else on earth."
(Numbers 12:3)

Throughout his career, Moses manifests his humility. At the
Burning Bush, Moses asked God, "I am nobody. How can I go to
Pharaoh and bring the Israelites out of Egypt?" According to the
author of the Book of Exodus, God responded, "I will be with you."
(Exodus 3:11–12)

Moses was still unsatisfied and asked for proof. After God told
him what to say to the Jewish people, Moses still had his doubts.
"What if they do not believe me and do not listen to me?" Moses asked.
(Exodus 4:1) Even after God showed Moses signs and gave him a
staff with which to perform magical wonders, Moses still hesitated.
He offered excuses indicative of his feelings of inadequacy: "I
have never been a man of words. . . . I am slow of speech and
slow of tongue," (Exodus 4:10) hoping God would choose someone
else.

When facing the complaints of the Jewish people in the wilderness,

Moses cried out to God in a prayer: "I cannot be responsible for all these people by myself, it is too much for me!" (Numbers 11:14)

Moses' hesitation to take on the task of leading his people is similar to the reluctance later expressed by many of the great Hebrew prophets, for instance, Isaiah (Isaiah 6:5), Jeremiah (Jeremiah 1:6), and Amos (Amos 7:14). They doubted their abilities and asked God to find others. These towering prophets feared that they were incapable of doing what God asked of them. Their hesitation arose out of genuine humility. However, their humility was proof of their real strength and their loyalty to God. It requires a great deal of humility to realize that you are not fully in control.

Jewish kings also demonstrated their humility. Perhaps King Saul's most memorable moment was when he hid himself among the baggage so as not to be called to the throne of Israel (I Samuel 10:22). The author of the Book of Deuteronomy cautioned rulers: A person must not permit his or her heart to rise above others even if he or she is the sovereign (Deuteronomy 17:20). Why? All of us are the children of God.

Those who are humble will be rewarded for this character trait. God loves the humble. The Eternal shows them grace (Proverbs 3:34) and victory (Psalm 149:4). The Divine will cause them to inherit the land and delight in abundant well-being (Psalm 37:11). They will have cause to rejoice in God (Isaiah 29:19). Honor will come to those who are humble (Proverbs 29:23).

As Rabbi Elimelech of Lizhensk, one of the leading figures in the Hasidic movement, put it: "The top of the ladder leading to perfection is humility. She who has it, has everything else."[3]

HUMILITY, NOT TIMIDITY

In the Jewish tradition, "humility" connotes the absence of pride, a diminished sense of self-importance or self-orientation, and is marked by the consideration of the perspective and needs of others. It does not connote timidity or meekness. Humility is not self-debilitating.

Timidity represents a great hindrance in life. It creates a barrier between an individual and others. It also thwarts one's achievements.

Do not confuse timidity or meekness with modesty. A modest person does not fear facing the world. A humble individual expresses his or her thoughts, participating in a range of human activities. He or she is not a pushover and is not taken advantage of. A humble individual sees the good qualities of others and appreciates what others do or say.

A timid person often does not cherish a high opinion of others. He or she may consider himself or herself superior to others, fearing, however, the notice of others, particularly dreading their criticism and ridicule.

A meek person mistrusts himself or herself, fearing being unable to create a favorable impression, being misunderstood, possibly violating the rules of etiquette.

A timid person often distorts and exaggerates every situation in which he or she takes part, assuming that everyone is watching him or her, scrutinizing every gesture, expression, and word. Such a person assumes a retiring position, shrinking before others.

Timidity interferes with both a person's happiness and achievement. It locks up an individual's powers by preventing the best that is in him or her from being brought forward. His or her whole life, in essence, becomes repressed. A meek person becomes limited in thought, interests, outlook, and reach—anything that involves fearless self-expression.

THE NEED TO BALANCE HUMILITY AND POSITIVE SELF-ESTEEM

Strive to achieve a balance between being self-effacing and developing and maintaining a positive self-image. In other words, honor yourself and foster your self-actualization, yet provide space for God and others.

True humility means neither affirming nor denying yourself absolutely. You should value that God gave you your own ground on which to stand and from which to move to meet others in a genuine dialogue.

Rabbi Jonathan Omer-Man, the founder of Metivta, the Los Angeles Center for Contemplative Judaism, tells the following story of Erev (the evening before) Yom Kippur, as illustrative of the elusiveness of humility and how easily any practitioner of humility can be deflated:

> The rabbi comes into the synagogue by the open ark and says, "O God, I am nothing." Then the *gabbai* (a synagogue official; in modern terms, the executive director) comes in and says, "O God, I am nothing." Finally, the *shamash* (the doorman) comes in and also

says, "O God, I am nothing." The *gabbai* turns to the rabbi and says, "Look who thinks he's nothing."[4]

Some of us are prone to underestimate ourselves through ignorance of our true capabilities, powers, and creative energies, which are hidden in the depths of our consciousness. However, self-esteem represents the key to achievement. As discussed later in this chapter, self-reliance, self-confidence, and courage, the manifestations of a positive self-image, represent the pathways to greatness.

HUMILITY, NOT PRIDE OR ARROGANCE

Pride must be contrasted with humility. Prideful individuals boast of what they can do. Not believing in themselves, arrogant individuals want others to believe in them.

Conceited people seek the admiration of others. In their manner, speech, clothes, residence, autos, and other consumer goods, they subject themselves to the opinions of others. So enamored of the need for recognition, they become enslaved to the opinion of society. They act and spend in order to satisfy the opinions of others. In becoming more pretentious, ever more boastful, they lose their simple self, their genuine dimension. They make their lives uneasy and restless. They are deprived of their tranquillity and inner peace of mind.

Detesting the haughtiness, the aloofness, and the self-absorbed attitude of the prideful, humanity loves the humble. Others adore those who are humble, as does God.

A person who is modest and sympathetic to everyone, not depending on others' affirmations, receives, in turn, praise from everyone. Neighbors and colleagues respect those who act unassumingly, making no effort to evoke envy or admiration.

In contrast, a person who is proud and indifferent to the world becomes the object of disdain. A vain individual often assumes an air of superiority, claiming more for himself or herself than is warranted. As a result of their self-centeredness and the barriers they build between themselves and the rest of humanity through their arrogant responses and their scowling faces, the proud, who have few friends, often find themselves alone.

Let us now examine some spiritual practices designed to help you purify yourself of pride and vanity while building a positive self-image, so that you can attain the highest expression of yourself.

HOW SPIRITUAL SEEKERS CAN PURSUE
THE ELUSIVE QUEST FOR HUMILITY

From a spiritual perspective, constantly remind yourself that your abilities and efforts as well as the fruits of your powers represent a Divine gift. Thus, in focusing on developing your humility you should realize that your pride is based on a deceptive and often quite destructive foundation. As the Baal Shem Tov stated it: "The source of all sadness is pride. The proud person thinks he is entitled to everything."[5]

Those who are obsessed by pride lack a positive perception of others. Their narcissistic vision is self-centered. They are unwilling to see others' needs and desires.

Pride represents self-admiration, self-love. Conceited individuals exaggerate their own value. Because their ego displaces God as the ultimate object of concern, they do not view themselves as the recipients of Divine gifts. They also believe themselves better than what others are. They remain aloof from humanity, manifesting a disregard for others.

However, their assumptions of pride and aloofness are false. God makes no distinction between rich and poor, levels of intelligence, races, genders, religions, or nationalities. In the Eternal's eyes, each of us is neither inferior nor superior to anyone else. Although our skills, talents, and achievements obviously differ, our essence is the same in God's eyes. The Holy One loves each of us equally. Strive to cultivate your sense of equality.

The authors of the Hebrew Bible were well aware that pride often comes with the acquisition of wealth (Deuteronomy 8:12–14). Wealth may lead us to believe that we possess superior abilities and talents and that our riches flow solely from our own power and might (Deuteronomy 8:17). As a result of our wealth, we may become overbearing and treat others in a condescending manner.

The past fifty years of material prosperity and success have fueled an unpleasant ostentatiousness among some Jews. Our wealth may cause us to forget our need to rely on God. The Jewish tradition reminds us: "[I]t is God who gives us the power to acquire wealth." (Deuteronomy 8:18) Always be grateful for all the blessings the Eternal bestows upon you. Remember that money is only valuable when it serves as a vehicle for "good." If a wealth holder's heart swells, money represents an evil, character-destroying weapon. Wealth, like fame, is tenuous. We can never be certain our wealth will last.

Surmounting your pride takes time. It needs to be overcome day by day. Start by admitting your pride, your self-preoccupation.

A certain amount of self-reflection and introspection is in order, if not hourly, then daily or weekly. A man once came to the Lekhivitzer Rebbe and asked the rebbe to teach him humility. At the very moment the man spoke, the clock struck the hour. The rebbe commented: "From the sound of the clock striking the hour, we can receive ample instruction regarding the submission of the heart. Each of us should ask: 'Another hour of my life has departed; have I accomplished any improvement of my soul within it?'"[6] This is good advice to reflect on. Also consider the impermanence and fragility of human existence. As the Talmud notes, "Today we are here and tomorrow in the grave." (*Berakhot* 28b) Each of us is a speck of dust, an insignificant being in a vast cosmos of unlimited space.

To facilitate your mental and spiritual cleansing, the emptying out of your mental and spiritual clutter, including your pride and conceit, many have found the following meditation helpful. Use this self-forgetfulness meditation for ten to fifteen minutes once or twice daily, for at least three weeks. Be patient. It is a lot more difficult than you think.

Cleansing Meditation. Introductions: Try to create a warm, welcoming atmosphere, an environment of serenity and spaciousness for the journey within. Lower the lights in your room. Close your eyes, sit quietly, calm and relax your body, breathe in and out normally, feeling where your breath flows into and out of your body. Adjust your breaths so that the in and out breaths are of the same length.

Come to a place of stillness.

Focus on your breath as it comes and goes. Notice your breath but try not to think about it.

Empty out your projections: your pride, your anger, your aspirations, your perspectives, whatever you have picked up from others.

Continue to empty your mind, letting go of your mental processes, until you are simply present in the moment, neither in the past nor in the future.

Concluding Instructions: Come back to the here and now. Take time to ease yourself back. Slowly bring awareness back to your body. Feel yourself back in the room and open your eyes.

Each day express your humble, true self, not your pretend self, and the world will cherish your thoughts, your words, and your deeds. In your behavior, manifest your natural goodness and your unaffected tenderness. The world will appreciate these qualities. Benefit humanity through your love, your compassion, and your altruism toward others. By being your true self, your natural Divine self, the high opinion of others will be yours without seeking.

Do not struggle to achieve something or relentlessly search for status or rank. At the hint of recognition, deny that you are a person of importance. When you are in a group of people, take the least prominent position. Sit far back in a room or at the end of the table. Be appropriately dressed, but wear the most modest of clothes. Strive to develop your humility and conquer your vanity by living a simple, genuine, modest life; by being true to yourself and the Divine nature within you; and by transcending your selfish concerns. Underscore your own weaknesses; emphasize others' strengths.

As the ancient rabbis taught in the Talmud: "If you pursue greatness, it will elude you. If you flee from greatness, if will pursue you." (*Erubin* 13b) However, even if you run away from greatness and honors, they may not pursue you. "The reason," Rabbi Simcha Bunam of Pshis'cha once explained to a man who complained to him, "is that you keep looking backwards."[7]

As you make space for your true self to be present and assert itself, you will be able to experience others around you. If you do not make room for your true self to be present, then you cannot really experience others around you.

Our lifelong quest for humility represents a difficult, ongoing task, as the following Hasidic tale illustrates: Before the Baal Shem Tov died, his disciples asked him who would replace him as their master. He said, "Whoever can teach you how pride can be broken shall be my successor." After the Baal Shem Tov's death, they first put the question to Rabbi Dov Baer, the great Maggid of Mezritch, who lived from 1704 to 1772: "How can pride be broken?" He replied: "Pride belongs to God, as it is written, 'The Eternal Sovereign reigns Who is clothed in pride.' That is why no counsel can be given on how to break pride. We must struggle with it all the days of our life." Then the disciples knew that it was he who would be the Baal Shem Tov's successor.[8]

ENHANCING YOUR SELF-ESTEEM

Though humility is an important personal virtue, do not neglect your self-esteem, a well-developed sense of self. Ask yourself: Do you feel good about yourself? Do you have the confidence to face life's challenges?

You are only capable of achieving inner peace of mind and extending lovingkindness and forgiveness to others if you love yourself and feel that you are a good, worthwhile person, deserving of joyfulness and happiness. Rabbi Simcha Bunam of Pshis'cha, emphasizing the importance of finding peace within our own selves, put it this way: "When a man has made peace within himself, he will be able to make peace in the whole world."[9]

Self-worth builds on your self-acceptance of both your perfections and imperfections. You must accept who you are. Of particular importance is the notion that your flesh is of no special value to you. As long as the essence of your mind—your intellect, your will, your personality, and your spirit—is not impaired, bodily blemishes or defects cannot prevent achievement. Your mind will find its own way; it will use what it has to make up for what you are otherwise denied.

Do not brood over your physical defects. Do not see yourself as inferior to others because of your shape, weight, height, or physical appearance. Do not keep them constantly before you. Do not tell yourself, "I'm physically unattractive"; otherwise it will become a reality for you.

Do not consider yourself among the inferior because this view will interfere with your personal growth and development. Do not foster within yourself a sense of inferiority, which will limit you to a low level of achievement and happiness. In your mind, do not place yourself among the lower ranks. You need to venture out of any self-imposed circle hindering your mental, emotional, and spiritual growth and development.

In striving to build your self-esteem, avoid any setting that discourages you, as well as people who dishearten you, who pity you, or who bemoan your fate with you. These people dampen your positive spirit of action, weaken your daring, kill your enterprise, and keep you in a state of victimhood.

When you come in contact with toxic people—even a parent, a sibling, or a child—detach gracefully from them. Disengage from noxious people who rob you of your self-esteem, who tell you that you are not good enough or that you will never make it. In your encounters, be civil, state your boundaries, maintain your composure despite provocation by others, and remember you cannot change their behavior. Do not let them "push your button." This too will pass.

Rather, seek people who will encourage you, individuals who express confidence in your abilities and trust in your powers. Associate with people who value your talents, those who like and appreciate you.

As an adult, enhancing your self-esteem rests on an inner self-searching for your positive qualities. Find a good point within yourself. According to Rabbi Nachman of Breslov, you should find and use your good points to draw support for yourself.

> . . . [S]earch until you find that little bit of good within yourself.

> You have to search until you find some modicum of good in yourself to restore your inner vitality and attain happiness.

> And in just the same way you must carry on searching until you find yet another good point.[10]

In your searching, you will discover lots of good qualities within yourself. You have vast, untapped treasures—physical, mental, emotional, and spiritual—within yourself.

To remind yourself of your strengths, combine several of them into an affirmative sentence, for instance, "I am a warm, loving, caring person," that you can repeat to yourself several times throughout the day.

No matter how much support and encouragement you get from others, self-esteem boils down to how much you care about yourself. You also need to develop certain attributes of self-esteem, namely, self-respect, self-confidence, and courage.

POSITIVE SELF-ESTEEM RESTS ON SELF-RESPECT, SELF-CONFIDENCE, AND COURAGE

Self-esteem rests on respecting yourself with all your achievements and shortcomings as well as trusting in yourself—in others words, developing self-respect and self-reliance. Courage represents another important component of a positive self-image.

Self-respect differs from self-pride. A humble person who possesses self-respect recognizes and appreciates his or her Divine self. Such a person realizes the Eternal's gifts that are his or hers. He or she respects himself or herself based on the recognition that something Divine is in each human heart, mind, and soul. His or her whole being emanates from the Infinite Source of Life. Such a person respects the Divine presence not only in himself or herself but also in each and every human being. However, self-respect does not mean regarding oneself as superior to other human beings. Remember, we are all formed in God's image.

Others will come to respect you more if you act in an unassuming manner, not seeking to evoke admiration or recognition. In commenting on the phrase in the Talmud "You shall cherish your neighbor's honor as you do your own," (*Avot* 2:10) Rabbi Shmuel Shmelke Horowitz of Nikolsburg explained its meaning as follows: "You should cherish the respect your neighbor gives you as you cherish your own self-respect. If you have none of the latter, then you shall not have any of the former."[11]

Self-esteem also encompasses self-reliance, which means relying on the God-given gifts in each of us. Self-reliance connotes self-trust, resting on your own inner powers and trust in the Divine that is within you.

Self-reliance does not result from greater intelligence or deeper knowledge. Self-reliance connotes faith in yourself, in your own thoughts, opinions, and feelings. Self-reliant individuals stand their own ground; they let their own powers and abilities express themselves. They trust their own judgment. They rely on their own understanding, seeing the world with their own vision, analyzing it with their own reason. Self-reliance in every aspect of your life will bring forth the greatness of your soul, your heart, and your mind.

The more you rely on your own judgment, the more its resourcefulness will grow. Your judgment will be perceptive enough to discern the difference between benefit and allurement, truth, and its shadow.

Rely on your will, perhaps the greatest asset you possess. Your thoughts and aspirations vanish without the action of your will, which translates your mental plans into reality, giving them form and substance.

Self-reliance implies a love of responsibility, cultivated through the assumption of ever greater degrees of responsibility. By assuming responsibility and beginning to discharge it, you will feel ever greater powers within yourself. You will begin to realize what you can do and what you have the ability for. You will attain what you set out to achieve.

To gain self-reliance, embrace responsibility in all of its aspects, including responsibility for attaining your goals, the choices and decisions you make, the words and deeds you express in your interactions with others, and your joyfulness and inner peace of mind.

Responsibility urges you to do more and more things. The more you do, the more you will be convinced that you can do. With every new responsibility you assume, new powers are brought into action, new plans and new hopes are brought to life, your mind and spirit rise to a higher stature. Thus, do not draw back in the presence of responsibility. Responsibility will bring forth a greater degree of self-reliance as well as enhance your self-confidence.

You can discover your inner powers and abilities, as well as your special strengths, through action. Do great and noble things. You need to make an effort to achieve, not merely to contemplate. Through your action and hard work, your inner capacities will assert themselves. You will grow and develop. Your powers will unfold; plans will formulate themselves in your mind; visions of achievement will make their appearance. You will reach out and achieve more and higher things, instead of opting for secure but limited gains.

Learn to aim high. Strive for as lofty a realization of your abilities and potential as possible. Constantly try to improve your intellect, the quality of your work, and your lot in life generally.

Rabbi Naftali Tzvi Horowitz of Ropshitz, the Ropshitzer Rebbe, who lived from 1760 to 1827, told this tale of the foolish request, what not to aim for:

> During the siege of Sebastopol, Czar Nicholas I was once riding along one of the walls when an enemy archer took aim at him. A Russian soldier who observed this from far off screamed and startled the czar's horse so that it swerved to the side and the arrow missed its target. The czar told the man to ask for any favor he pleased.
>
> "Our sergeant is so brutal," the soldier faltered, "He is always beating me. If only I could serve under another sergeant."
>
> "Fool," cried Czar Nicholas, "be a sergeant yourself!"
>
> The Ropshitzer Rebbe concluded: "We are like that: We pray for

the petty needs of the hour and do not know how to pray for our redemption."[12]

Self-reliance and self-confidence are intertwined. Approach each task, each action you take, no matter how small, with self-confidence, not listless indifference. By attacking a task with trust in your powers and confidence in yourself, you will work enthusiastically, bent on achievement. Although aiming high, a self-confident person will attain his or her goals. Difficulties will not stop you. You will find a way. Nothing will stand between you and your goals.

Believing in himself or herself, a self-confident person "just does it." He or she is not much concerned with the opinion of others. He or she realizes his or her own inner strength and does not depend on the opinion of others.

Courage represents another aspect of a positive self-image. You need the courage to trust in God's guidance and help. You need the courage to be yourself, to create and build, to achieve, to help others, to actualize your ideals, to be truthful and honest with others (even with those who are less than forthright with you), and to use your knowledge and skills for the benefit of humanity. It takes courage to live life; it is not easy.

Our nature is intended for growth and development through surmounting obstacles. If you refuse to dive into life for fear of encountering troublesome waves, you miss the true exhilaration of life.

Courage enables you to overcome life's difficulties, dangers, and hardships, what is unpalatable or unknown. Courage lets you deal constructively with life's complexities, ambiguities, and contradictions. It enables you to surmount your fears and worries and to defy obstacles. Armed with courage, nothing is too difficult or too high for you to each. Courage is critical to developing your self-love.

Courage is essential in attaining your emotional and spiritual growth. Ask yourself: Do you have the courage to leave a job you hate, to open yourself to love, to acknowledge how you have hurt another, to think for yourself, to speak up for and act on what you believe?

You need courage to be yourself and abide by principles you consider right and just, to sustain and defend them, and to spread these principles even if in so doing you may be isolated from others.

You need courage to express God's perfection and live a God-inspired life in the midst of an "anything goes" world; to cherish lovingkindness, compassion, and forgiveness in the midst of hatred; and to be truthful in an atmosphere of deception. Use your courage to rise above unwholesome influences and always act in accordance with God's guidance.

If you are conscious that the Supreme Sovereign is with you all the days of your life, courage will replace timidity, self-doubt, procrastination, and poor self-image. Each of us is endowed with courage, fortitude, determination, tenacity, persistence, and an unwillingness to acknowledge defeat.

Courage comes from the realization that God is within you, that you express Divine powers. Courage depends on your utilizing this Divine endowment, even when you feel your worst: when you lose a relationship, a job, or a beloved; or face business reverses, financial ruin, or a physical or mental crisis.

Let courage stir and awaken, allowing you to engage with life. Plunge into what needs to be done. Do not hesitate; ward off discouraging thoughts and invoke God's assistance. Courage makes the impossible become possible, allows trust to be restored, and enables what seems unendurable to be endured. Remember that nothing is too difficult to achieve with the Eternal's help and guidance.

You manifest your courage not only in dealing with obstacles standing in the way of achieving your goals but also through your assertiveness, which characterizes a courageous, independent person. An assertive person, expressing personal likes and dislikes, disagreeing openly with others, saying "no," wants others to recognize his or her needs, desires, and value. Assertiveness is not an inappropriate or hostile aggressiveness. You need to stand up for and protect yourself when something seems unfair and "go for it," as the following Hasidic tale demonstrates:

Rabbi Elimelech's servant once forgot a spoon for Rabbi Mendel, who was a guest at Rabbi Elimelech's table. Everyone ate except Rabbi Mendel. Rabbi Elimelech observed this and asked: "Why aren't you eating?" "I have no spoon," said Rabbi Mendel. "Look," said Rabbi Elimelech, "one must know enough to ask for a spoon, and a plate too, if need be!" Rabbi Mendel took the word of his teacher to heart. From that day on, his fortunes were on the mend.[13]

Assertiveness helps you attain what you want or need without alienating others. It lets you refuse requests without feeling guilty or selfish. It enables you to be heard, taken seriously, and treated with respect and fairness. Assertive people derive intellectual and emotional satisfaction from exchanging their opinions and feelings with others, thereby enhancing their self-esteem.

HOW SPIRITUAL SEEKERS CAN IMPROVE THEIR SELF-ESTEEM

In your effort to cast off your meekness and timidity and build a positive self-image, characterized by self-reliance, self-confidence, and courage, remember that a loving God is at your side, ready to aid and guide you. High self-esteem, researchers have concluded,[14] relates positively to your possessing an image of a loving, accepting God.

Be ready to ask for the Eternal's help. In so doing, the difficult will become easy; the impossible will become possible. There is nothing to fear as long as you place your faith and trust in the Holy One. God is always near to those who call out with sincerity.

Ask for God's help in strengthening your self-esteem. According to Jewish legend, when God asked Moses to go to Pharaoh and request the emancipation of the Jews, Moses was timid. The task appeared to him so gigantic, so impossible, that he initially refused God's call. God answered, "I will be with you. . . . " (Exodus 3:11–12) Basically, God told Moses, "I will give you courage. I will lend you strength. I will make the task possible."

When Moses realized that God was with him and would be his helper, he cast off his timidity and his low self-esteem. The legend recounts that Moses succeeded, going to Pharaoh, declaring his mission, and freeing the Jews from bondage.

Also according to the biblical legend, when Joshua was about to lead the ancient Jews into Israel, a goal obstructed by numerous barriers, God spoke to him saying, "Be strong and of good courage, do not be afraid or dismayed, for I [God] am with you, wherever you go." (Joshua 1:9) We all have our own promised land before us. Entry, however, requires courage and persistence to overcome the obstacles each of us faces.

Learn to invoke God's assistance to develop your courage and strength. When warriors were sought to challenge Goliath, the Philistine giant, David insightfully said to Saul, "God who saved me from the lion and the bear will save me from that Philistine." (I Samuel 17:37)

In Psalm 23, the psalmist portrays God as a shepherd, at his side ready to supply all his wants and to minister to all his needs. If bitterness, hatred, or danger surround the psalmist, he sees God as a protecting shield around him, warding off evil and suffering.

If you find your powers or your will wanting, appeal to the Eternal for assistance and guidance. At the beginning of each day, relax completely, close your eyes, and sincerely and wholeheartedly offer and slowly repeat one of these affirmative prayers for ten to fifteen minutes:

Affirmative Prayer for Self-Esteem

The God within me finds expression in my self-esteem.

- or -

I am created in the image of God. I am lovable.

Affirmative Prayer for Self-Reliance

The God within me finds expression in my self-reliance.

- or -

God has provided me a path to attain good and useful achievement.

Affirmative Prayer for Self-Confidence

The God within me finds expression in my self-confidence.

- or -

God has provided me a path to attain good and useful achievement.

Affirmative Prayer for Courage

The God within me finds expression in my courage.

- or -

I am expressing Divine courage.

- or -

God is my protector.

- or -

God has provided me a path to attain good and useful achievement.

- or -

God is with me.

In offering one of these affirmative prayers, your faint-heartedness and hesitancy will vanish. You will hear God urging you to do, to achieve, and to manifest your capabilities and powers. Remember that the Eternal is always here to help and guide you.

The following visualizations will help in building your self-esteem and your courage. Sometimes you need to create an additional source of courage and strength—for instance, when you begin or end a relationship or start a new job or business venture. Twice daily, in the morning and the evening, close your eyes and relax completely, as an effective visualization depends on your relaxed receptivity. Use one of these visualizations for ten to fifteen minutes each day, for at least three weeks. Be patient and do not get discouraged. Do not try too hard or expect too much too soon.

Visualizations for Self-Esteem, Courage, and Strength. Introduction: Create a warm, welcoming atmosphere, an environment of serenity and spaciousness for the journey within. Lower the lights in your room. Close your eyes, sit quietly, calm and relax your body, breathe in and out normally, feeling where the breath flows into and out of your body.

For Self-Esteem: Visualize God's love flowing through you, clearing away the dark clouds surrounding you, revealing and enhancing your self-esteem, which was always there.

For Courage and Strength: Visualize successfully performing an act you want to perform but dread performing, or a goal you want to achieve but typically beat yourself up about. Break the act or the goal into small steps. Focus on your behavior and your initial struggles. Conclude with the positive consequences of your masterfully performing the act or achieving your goal.

Or, visualize where, in whom, and with what you have found courage and strength in the past when facing a difficulty. (It may help you to set out a photo, a poem, or whatever you found meaningful or strengthening in the past.)

Visualize yourself in your moment of past need. Focus on a situation exemplifying the quality of courage and strength. Visualize your newfound courage and strength coming not only from your past source(s) but also from God.

Ask God for the kind of courage and strength you now need. Imagine God preceding you, clearing away all obstacles.

Concluding Instructions: Slowly come back to the here and now. Take time to ease yourself back. Slowly bring awareness back into your body. Feel yourself back in the room and open your eyes.

A WORD FOR PARENTS

Children *acquire* self-esteem; it is not innate. Imparting high self-esteem to your children turns on your possessing good self-esteem and demonstrating it daily. Children model themselves after their parents.

Parents must love and nurture their children. You should give your children love and encouragement so as to build their self-esteem. You need to hold, cuddle, and kiss your children, starting at birth, and tell them that they are loved and valued. A parent (or a parent-like figure) must convey this love out of which self-esteem grows early in life. Until you are ready to do this, do not have a child!

Communicate to your children their worth, competence, desirability, and goodness. Help each of your children believe: "I am a lovable and capable person." Take pride in your children's achievements. Love your children (and make sure your children know you do) whether they win or lose, succeed or fail. Praise them for making an effort and remind them that failure happens to everyone. Because children focus on details, be specific in your praise. Acknowledge their attempts. Tell them they are wonderful just for trying. By your rewarding them verbally for their efforts, they will be less fearful of failure and more willing to try again in the future.

Empower your children. Because even a toddler can help make decisions, ask: Do you want to wear a white or a green shirt? Through empowerment, you send a message that he or she is sufficiently important that you value his or her opinions.

Emphasize the importance of perseverance and of "hanging in there" in the midst of difficulties. Demonstrate to your children that they can find a way around life's obstacles without being overwhelmed or defeated. Help your children learn to cope with life's challenges, frustrations, upsets, and disappointments while maintaining a commitment to their goals and without viewing helplessness as a permanent, unchanging condition.

Encourage your children to see positive qualities, in themselves and in others, explaining and showing them by your actions that no child is inferior. Help your children to overcome their weaknesses or learn to ignore their deficiencies. Every child has the capability to make a contribution to human improvement. Discover and bring out this unique talent and strength but do not demand the impossible or the angelic of them. Encourage them to do their best; it is not necessary to achieve perfection. Do not force them into doing too much. Focus on something the child does well and have him or her get involved with that activity. Let each feel successful at an activity he or she enjoys.

Do not live vicariously through your children. Do not push your children to accomplish what you could not achieve. Treat each child's interests and talent with respect.

Emphasize to each child: You need to become what in your Divinely created uniqueness you can become. In other words, be the special individual you were born to be. Rabbi Meshullam Zusya of Hanipol, who was born in 1718 and died in 1800, posed the question of all questions: "When I get to the World to Come, they will not ask me: Why were you not Moses? But, Why were you not Zusya?"[15]

Encourage each child to fulfill the special earthly task that is only his or hers, by developing his or her interests and talents. According to the late Rabbi Milton Steinberg, each child should learn that:

He owes himself self-respect, a dignity of thought and action befitting one in whom burns a spark of God.

And he is under a duty to express his individuality. For bearing the divine image, he bears it uniquely. No one in the world exactly duplicates him. Therefore he is obliged to discover and develop his uniqueness. Otherwise, to all eternity some aspect of the divine nature shall have been left latent and unfulfilled.[16]

Help your children focus on realistic goals that they can achieve, as well as on how and with whom they spend their time. Encourage your children to change friends from those who dwell on superficial concerns and to avoid print and visual media (films and TV) emphasizing looks over behavior and character.[17]

Last but not least, never ridicule, humiliate, or abuse a child as a means of control or manipulation. If, in the heat of the moment, you display this type of behavior, apologize promptly and sincerely.

The respect that you receive from others is commensurate with the respect you have for yourself. By demonstrating more genuine love and compassion with and forgiveness of others, you will find less self-identity and more humility. You will discover yourself dissolving into an interconnectedness with all humans.

When you couple humility with a positive self-image you start to have a genuine inner life. However, you must also add joy and equanimity before your inner world allows you to connect with others. Let us turn to and explore the importance of being joyful and optimistic.

NOTES

1. I have drawn on Rabbi Morris Lichtenstein, *Judaism: A Presentation of Its Essence and a Suggestion for Its Preservation* (New York: Society of Jewish Science, 1934), pp. 91–95; Rabbi Morris Lichtenstein, *Jewish Science and Health: The Textbook of Jewish Science* (New York: Society of Jewish Science, 1986), pp. 149–160; Rabbi Morris Lichtenstein, *Joy of Life: Jewish Science Essays* (New York: Society of Jewish Science, 1938), pp. 8–15, 45–52, 109–116; Rabbi Morris Lichtenstein, *How to Live: Jewish Science Essays* (New York: Society of Jewish Science, 1957), pp. 67–74, 125–132, 225–233; Rabbi Morris Lichtenstein, *Peace of Mind: Jewish Science Essays* (New York: Society of Jewish Science, 1970), pp. 37–45; Byron L. Sherwin and Seymour J. Cohen, *How to Be a Jew: Ethical Teachings of Judaism* (Northvale, NJ: Jason Aronson, 1992), pp. 81–88; Sol Roth, "Toward A Definition of Humility," *Tradition* 14:1 (1973–1974), 5–22, reprinted in *Contemporary Jewish Ethics and Morality: A Reader*, ed. Elliott N. Dorff and Louis E. Newman (New York: Oxford University, 1995), pp. 259–270; Louis Jacobs, *Jewish Values* (Hartford: Hartmore House, 1960), pp. 108–117.

2. Adapted from Martin Buber, *Tales of the Hasidim: The Later Masters*, trans. Olga Marx (New York: Schocken, 1948), pp. 249–250.

3. *The Hasidic Anthology: Tales and Teachings of the Hasidim*, trans. Louis I. Newman (Northvale, NJ: Jason Aronson, 1987), p. 185.

4. Adapted from Rodger Kamentz, *Stalking Elijah: Adventures with Today's Jewish Mystical Masters* (New York: HarperSan Francisco, 1997), p. 204.

5. Simcha Raz, *Hasidic Wisdom: Sayings from the Jewish Sages*, trans. Dov Peretz Elkins and Jonathan Elkins (Northvale, NJ: Jason Aronson, 1997), p. 237.

6. *The Hasidic Anthology*, p. 189.

7. Ibid., p. 180.

8. Martin Buber, *Tales of the Hasidim—The Early Masters*, trans. Olga Marx (New York: Schocken, 1975), p. 100.

9. Buber, *The Later Masters*, p. 264.

10. Rabbi Nachman, *Azama!* (Jerusalem: The Breslov Research Institute, 1984), pp. 8–9.

11. Raz, *Hasidic Wisdom*, p. 240.

12. Adapted from Buber, *The Later Masters*, p. 194.

13. Ibid., p. 125.

14. Peter L. Benson and Bernard P. Spilka, "God-Image as a Function of Self-Esteem and Locus of Control," *Journal for the Scientific Study of Religion* 12:3 (1973): 297–311, reprinted in *Current Perspectives in the Psychology of Religion*, ed. H. Newton Malony (Grand Rapids, MI: William B. Eerdmans, 1977), pp. 209–233.

15. Adapted from Buber, *The Early Masters*, p. 251.

16. Milton Steinberg, *Basic Judaism* (New York: Harcourt, Brace 1947), p. 70.

17. Jane E. Brody, "Personal Health: Parents Can Bolster Girls' Fragile Self-Esteem," *New York Times*, 11 November 1997, C7.

CHAPTER NINE

The Importance of Joyfulness and Optimism

Joyfulness is a Divine state.[1] The Eternal finds expression in joy. Joy lies in the heart of creation; it is the soul of the universe. God is a vast reservoir of joy. Joy is the Holy One's gift to us. God created each of us to know and attain joy. God called humanity into existence to feel and express this Divine joy. People are not born to pass through life in suffering and in misery, in woe and in tears.

The world is a place of delight. It is charged with hope. The forces of nature are here to test and strengthen us, but not to destroy us. Life is not a source of pain and suffering. We crave joy and happiness, not misery. Our ambitions, hopes, and efforts point to creating joy and happiness for ourselves and for others.

Joyfulness and optimism are within us. They are our natural state. We were created to live in joy and with enthusiasm. Joy and hope fill each human heart; they are the very essence of our being.

Strive to maintain the flow of joy and hope that is part of your Divine disposition. Clothe all of your thoughts, words, and deeds with joy and hope. However, it is not easy to attain and maintain a state of joyfulness and optimism.

This chapter presents both spiritual and practical suggestions to fill your mind with hope to replace fear, with optimism to replace worry, and with cheer to replace sorrow. Strive to shut the gates of your heart (or remove from your heart) fear, worry, and sorrow and free up your natural flow of cheerfulness and joy. The greater your sense of joy and optimism, the greater your ability to cope with hardships and tragedies, the unexpected setbacks and the unforseen hurdles you face in life, as we shall see in chapters 11, 12, and 13. Embrace joy and hope and always try to bring them into your life. Let joyfulness and optimism be of central importance in your life.

JOYFULNESS IN THE JEWISH TRADITION

The Jewish tradition emphasizes the importance of joyfulness. As Ecclesiastes teaches us, we should strive for joy because " . . . the only worthwhile thing then is for [people] to enjoy themselves and do what is good [i.e., eat, drink, and afford themselves enjoyment within their means] in their lifetime . . . " (Ecclesiastes 3:12 and 2:24) Joy represents a Divine gift. (Ecclesiastes 3:13) Strive to attain and enhance your cheerfulness.

When we are joyful we are ourselves. When our spirit is filled with joy we experience and radiate the fullness of life. When we are joyous, the best comes out in us—our highest thoughts, our loveliest feelings, and our utmost achievements. When we are joyful, our mind works with great clarity, our thoughts multiply and flow with ease and depth, our judgment is perceptive, our will asserts itself with energy and enthusiasm, and creation and achievement are made easy.

With a joyful disposition, the world is always bright and sunny. We feel good. As Rabbi Nachman of Breslov teaches: "Joy opens the heart."[2]

Joyfulness also strengthens our well-being and preserves our health. The author of the Book of Proverbs states: "A joyful heart makes for good health. . . . " (Proverbs 17:22)

When we are joyous, our health is sustained—even enhanced. When we are joyful, our mind, body, and spirit are invigorated. Joy strengthens every part of an individual, impeding any physical, mental, or spiritual illness. Every cell is charged with more vitality. When the mind is cheerful, the entire body is charged with hope.

STRIVE FOR OPTIMISM, NOT PESSIMISM

Judaism regards optimism as a virtue and pessimism as a profound weakness. Optimism builds on faith and confidence; pessimism represents discontent and doubt.

A pessimistic viewpoint precludes joyfulness and happiness. Pessimism clouds your countenance, dims your visions, sours your heart, weakens your body, and lowers your vitality. In the Wisdom Literature, we read that pessimism interferes with your well-being; it breaks down your strength and dries up your bones. (Proverbs 17:22) Modern research bears out these admonitions.

Professor Martin E. P. Seligman, in his book *Learned Optimism*,[3] concludes, based on clinical experiments with human subjects, that how an individual interprets events occurring in life as well as future expectations impacts on physical and psychological well-being and job and school performance. Seligman sees clear psychological benefits in optimism. Conversely, Seligman concludes, pessimism leads to greater levels of unhappiness and failure. According to Seligman, negative thinkers have weaker immune systems, encounter more infectious diseases, and after age forty-five face more major health problems. They are far more likely to suffer depression. For Seligman, pessimism represents a prime cause of depression. Other researchers have concluded that our feelings, especially pessimism and depression, influence or cause not only problems with our immune system, but also many serious illnesses, such as heart disease and high blood pressure.[4]

Pessimism also deteriorates your mind, destroying its fine edge. A pessimistic mind cannot think as clearly or judge as accurately.

Pessimism destroys a person's ambition. It causes one to lose interest in the vital aspects of life. Days move sluggishly and colorlessly. Life soon becomes weariness.

Pessimism predisposes you to failure. Pessimism destroys your courage and bends your heart.

A pessimist looks for pessimism—on TV, in the newspapers, or in others' experiences.

Pessimism injures not only the pessimist but also others as well. A pessimist radiates his or her pessimism to others, permeating the atmosphere with his or her dejection. Pessimistic individuals bring discomfort to others by injecting negativity and dejection into them. Pessimism makes people unsociable, dampening their relations with others.

FEAR, WORRY, AND SORROW REPRESENT MANIFESTATIONS OF PESSIMISM

Pessimism often manifests itself in fear, worry, and sorrow. In turn, fear, worry, and sorrow strengthen pessimism's grip on us. A gloomy state of mind has a pernicious impact on an individual's whole system, causing physical and mental suffering. Conversely, without fear, worry, or sorrow, the mind is free; it can think more clearly, plan more accurately, hope, and achieve.

Fear about the here and now, about how our words or deeds (or others' speech or conduct) will result in bad or painful consequences for us, keeps us down; it imprisons us. It fills the atmosphere with gloominess and foreboding. It retards our energies and holds back our creative powers. Fear paralyzes our action, stunting our growth and blocking our development. Anxiety destroys our calmness and our peace of mind. When fear takes hold of our being, we find ourselves depressed. We think despondent thoughts, become hopeless when facing a crisis, and feel lost in the midst of a dilemma.

Many people are enslaved by worry, one of the deadliest foes of the heart, mind, and spirit. As the author of the Book of Proverbs reminds us: "Worry in a human heart makes it stoop." (Proverbs 12:25) Worry, a pernicious influence, is very corrosive. Although the Eternal created us to be cheerful, through worry we destroy the Divine image within ourselves.

Worry fills us with fear about the future, robbing us of our present enjoyment and pleasure. Worry prevents us from enjoying our current blessings by filling us with cares about the future. Not only will worry destroy our joy and happiness, it will also contribute to the ruination of mental and bodily health.

Worry destroys the mind in which it dwells. Worry consumes our mental powers. Worry checks our flow of vitality. It disturbs and retards the stream of our thoughts, it perplexes our minds, and it blinds our reason. Worry distorts our power of judgment and our point of view so that nothing is seen in its true perspective. We are incapable of concentration, clear thinking, or logical reasoning. Events may prove unfavorable, but usually not as unfavorable as the worrier pictures them. As a result of our worrying, we become easily discouraged; we fall into the grasp of pessimism.

The more you worry, the more your mind seeks out the causes for worry. Even if causes do not exist, your mind may imagine one or more causes in order to sustain the habit of worrying.

The mind will magnify things. A worrier typically exaggerates little things manyfold. Worry twists and perverts every small incident in life into a gigantic misfortune, into a harbinger of evil and suffering. Worry makes momentous the most insignificant.

Worry also impacts negatively on our bodies. It disturbs our rest and makes us sleepless and physically exhausted. We tire quickly. It often interferes with our digestive processes. Worry physically weakens and shortens human life.

If worry represents concern about the future, then sorrow represents anxiety about the past and the present. Sorrow, like fear and worry, steals into our hearts, minds, and spirits in order to destroy us. Sorrow casts its shadow on the brightness of life, enshrouding all existence with gloom. Sorrow undermines our mental and physical health. It drives out cheerfulness from our mind; it depresses our spirit.

Do not allow clouds to penetrate your soul or fears, worries, or sorrows to invade your heart and your mind, destroying your hope and joyfulness. Remember that the fountain of life is contained in your power for joy and optimism. If you are joyful, your difficulties will diminish, your fears or worries will lose their grip over you, and you will ward off physical and mental illness. Sorrow will not crush you, suffering will not approach you, and your days will be happy and many on earth.

A negative, pessimistic attitude, manifested in our fears, worries, and sorrows, robs us of our joy and optimism. Let us consider some spiritual and practical techniques designed to help us embrace joy and hope, continually bringing them into our lives.

HOW SPIRITUAL SEEKERS CAN ENHANCE THEIR JOYFULNESS AND OPTIMISM

It is not hard to be joyful and optimistic when things are going well and the future looks bright. It is much more difficult when something unexpected happens, when things go wrong, when illness strikes or calamity is at hand, when the future seems to hold no promise. Where can you turn to prevent or root out your despair?

Optimism in Judaism is intertwined with faith and trust in God that all will be well, that the Eternal's goodness will not fail us. Through your faith and trust in God, you will find joy. Remember that you are part of God's plan for the cosmos. You have a specific role to play in perfecting the world.

People of faith are cheerful and optimistic. Through faith and trust in the Supreme Sovereign, you promote your joyfulness and optimism, virtues that enhance and prolong your life. An optimistic outlook on life is one of the best character traits to foster.

As discussed in chapter 3, you should conceive of God as the essence of all existence, the vitalizing force of all reality. The Divine power within you will aid you in overcoming the perplexities you encounter in life. Trust in the Eternal, Who will satisfy all your needs. God will take care of you.

A genuine, sincere faith in God that all will be well, that the Eternal's tender goodness and compassion will not fail, represents a key teaching of Jewish Spirituality. Faith in the Holy One, Who sustains, helps, and provides, serves as an antidote to pessimism and despair. Faith eliminates the enemies of joy that otherwise invade your mind and overthrow your natural optimism.

Despite many painful experiences, the psalmist, sustained by faith in God's goodness and assistance, never lost hope. Faith and trust repeatedly carry the psalmist safely through danger and affliction. The psalmist tells us that those who take refuge in the Eternal have nothing to fear. God is always with them, watching over them.

Optimism rests on the premise that the Holy One continually watches over your destiny. (Psalm 121:4) According to the psalmist: "God will guard you from all harm; the Eternal will guard your life." (Psalm 121:7)

If you lack faith and trust in God, you often find yourself helpless, easily discouraged, and lacking fortification against life's vicissitudes and hardships. When things go badly, your spirits are saddened, your world turns dark. Lacking faith and trust in the Eternal, you have no one to whom to turn, no one on whom to rely; you bear the burdens of life all by yourself.

With faith and trust in Divine aid and guidance, you pass unharmed through difficult times. Through faith and trust, you realize that God guides, helps, sustains, protects, and strengthens you in every time of difficulty and distress. You are not alone in the world or unprotected. You are under the watchful care of the Eternal, to Whose love you can turn at any moment, at any difficulty in your life. God is ready to shoulder your burdens with and for you. Turn, then, to God, the Source of all good.

Call on the Eternal for help. The Supreme Sovereign is ready to aid and guide you. God watches over you throughout the day, each and every day of your life. Turn to the Holy One and the Eternal Light will shine on you. When facing hardships or challenges, put everything in God's hands. The Divine will not fail you. You will be lifted above any barrier placed in the way of your joy and happiness.

God is your partner in every endeavor. As your partner, the Eternal must have your trust and confidence. If you trust in God, you will see your life in a new light. An apparent stumbling block becomes a stepping stone. An obstacle represents a transient, instructive experience. A potential cause for gloom serves as a force for redoubling your energies. The greater the task, the more difficult the problem, the more devout should be your reliance on God. Realize that the Holy One is at your side; God is with you all the days of your life.

Realize that God created the world to serve as an expression of the Divine essence of joyfulness. When you grasp this, you become filled with joy. Your soul vibrates to the joyful mood of the cosmos. You respond to the joy in the world.

Without faith and trust in God, place is made for fear, worry, and sorrow. Drive out fear, worry, and sorrow by maintaining your faith and trust that God makes everything happen for the best. Trust in God and the Eternal's goodness to shield you against fear. As the psalmist tells us: "God is my light and my help; whom shall I fear? God is the stronghold of my life; of whom shall I be afraid?" (Psalm 27:1)

Facing dire want, the psalmist wards off fear of starvation by confidently affirming: "God is my shepherd; I shall not want." (Psalm 23:1) Confronted by death, the psalmist faithfully exclaims: "Though I walk through the valley of the shadow of death, I will fear no harm, for God is with me." (Psalm 23:4)

The author of the Book of Proverbs, finding that reliance on the Eternal offers the best protection against fear, writes, "Be not afraid of sudden terror . . . for God will be your confidence and will keep your foot from being caught." (Proverbs 3:25–26)

People of faith and trust have no fears about their daily sustenance, their interpersonal relations, or their physical and mental health. Their faith and trust in the Supreme Sovereign provide a shelter against the obstacles presenting themselves on the road of life.

Do not fear anything, especially the fear of failure. Fear of failure represents the beginning of failure. Fear of failure flows from a lack of faith and trust in God. Have confidence in your eventual success. Success rests on faith: faith in yourself and faith in the Holy One. When you have faith in yourself, you have faith in the Divine qualities each of us has. When you have faith in God, you have faith in the powers that the Eternal has given you for success.

Avoid worry by trusting in God at all times and under all circumstances. According to the author of the Book of Proverbs, "Trust in God with all your heart, and do not rely on your own understanding." (Proverbs 3:5) When you have faith in the Eternal, worry will leave you. People of faith do not worry about their futures because God will direct their steps. Inner peace of mind and tranquility will flood their hearts, minds, and spirits; their natural joyfulness will find spontaneous expression.

If you believe in God's goodness, you have no worries. Through faith in the Eternal you know that in the end everything will be well, because God created everything for good.

When difficult events arise, the faithful are not worried. When success does not come as quickly as desired, the faithful are not frightened. Even if their plans fail, the faithful remain unbroken, secure in the knowledge that the Divine will help them out of their difficulties.

Form the habit of turning to God in every moment in your life, in all your joys and sorrows. In times of distress, turn to God for cheer; in moments of sorrow, turn to the Holy One for consolation; in perplexing moments, turn to the Eternal for advice. God will enrich your life with Divine blessings.

In darker moments, when fortune seemingly turns against you, look to God—otherwise distress will confound you and sorrow will crush and embitter you. With faith, you can turn to God for help and guidance. The Eternal will lead you to the success for which you are destined. Trust your burdens to God.

Realizing that you live in the hand of a kindly, merciful, loving God, Who brought you into existence and Who cares for your destiny, will free you from sorrow and grief. Life and destiny are under the Supreme Sovereign's care. The Eternal created the world to give expression to goodness and happiness. God's ways are for the best. Do not brood over the past or drown yourself in sorrow.

People of faith overcome sorrow by realizing, as we shall see in chapter 13, that God not only makes provision for life here on earth but also sustains us in the World to Come. Death does not represent the end of human existence; it is the beginning of a new life, the elevation of the immortal soul to a higher sphere. Loss of a beloved should deepen our vision as to the ultimate reality of life, now and in the hereafter.

Trust in the goodness of the Eternal. Whatever God created is for the sake of growth and happiness, not annihilation. With faith in the Holy One's mercy, and confidence in God's kindness, your sorrows will vanish.

Train yourself in faith and trust. Learn to seek God's help and guidance in difficult times. You can always rely on the Holy One.

Through your confidence in the Divine, you will gain a greater degree of patience.

Cultivate the habit of seeking God's help through prayer, meditation, and visualization in moments of pessimism and when you are fearful, worried, or filled with sorrow. Ask God for help, appeal to the Eternal, who fills nature with sunshine, to fill your heart with rays of hope and joy.

TURN TO GOD IN PRAYER

In each crisis in life, turn to God in prayer for assistance. When you feel perplexed and helpless in the presence of difficulties and obstacles, pray to God for help and guidance. When your spirits are crushed, if you feel unhappy, when you are discouraged, or if you lose all of your desire and power to enjoy life, pray to God for joy and optimism. Appeal to the Maker of the Human Spirit, the Builder of the Mind, the Architect of the Soul.

When you are beaten down with failure, stricken with suffering, visited by misfortune, in the midst of sudden catastrophe, or in the presence of danger, turn to God. Throw yourself on the Holy One's goodness. When confronted with disgrace or overtaken by shame, invoke the aid of your Creator and Sustainer. Offer petitionary or affirmative prayers for the return of your joyfulness and optimism, as well as prayers of surrender or thanksgiving.

Approach God with trust in the Divine wisdom and goodness, with confidence that your prayers will be answered. Even if you are "down," prayers emanating from a cheerful heart are the most readily answered. Do not pray to the Supreme Sovereign with tears in order to bring forth Divine sympathy. Come before God with enthusiasm. Be prepared to receive God's abundance. Pray without doubt or skepticism. Express your prayers to God with confidence and hope, confident that the Eternal will listen and that everything for your good will be answered. As the psalmist reminds us: "Serve God with gladness; come before the Eternal's presence with singing." (Psalm 100:2)

Rabbi Simcha Bunam of Pshis'cha once saw a Jew in danger of drowning while swimming in the sea near Danzig (now Gdansk in Poland). Noting that the man was about to abandon the struggle to save himself, Rabbi Bunam shouted out: "Give my greetings to the Leviathan." The drowning man unwittingly smiled at this levity.

Regaining his mental presence, he was able to hold himself afloat until friends rescued him. In relating this experience, Rabbi Bunam remarked: "We may learn from this that prayer with a joyful heart and a cheerful countenance ascends to God, but prayer with outcries and lamentations may be wasted."[5]

To retain or enhance your joyfulness and optimism, offer one of four types of prayers: petitionary, affirmative, surrender, or thanksgiving.

PETITIONARY PRAYERS FOR
JOYFULNESS AND OPTIMISM

Twice a day, in the morning and the evening, close your eyes, relax completely, and slowly repeat one of the following petitionary prayers for ten to fifteen minutes:

> God supply me with an abundance of joy; or
> God fill my mind, heart, and soul with joyfulness; or
> God remove all the shadows from my being and fill me with optimism.

AFFIRMATIVE PRAYERS FOR
JOYFULNESS AND OPTIMISM

Offer the following affirmative prayers. Again: twice daily, in the morning and the evening, close your eyes, relax completely, and slowly repeat one of the following for ten to fifteen minutes:

> God takes away from me all worries, fears and sorrows and fills me
>   with joy; or
> God removes all gloom from me and fills me with delight; or
> God watches over me and protects me; I fear nothing; or
> I am a Divine being; I am cheerful and happy.

PRAYERS OF SURRENDER

Offer a prayer of surrender. Put everything into God's hands. Feel the Holy One's presence, open your heart to the Eternal, surrender yourself to God's care and protection, and trust in the Divine.

Again: twice daily, in the morning and the evening, close your eyes, relax completely, and repeat the following for ten to fifteen minutes:

I trust in God's help; everything will be for the best.

In the morning when you awake, close your eyes, relax completely, and repeat the following for ten to fifteen minutes:

Into Your hand, O Eternal Sovereign, I commit my spirit. You have redeemed me. I have slept; now I awake, for You sustain me.

Whether you use a petitionary prayer, an affirmative prayer, or a prayer of surrender, do not make your prayer too specific. Do not ask for or focus on a specific thing. Let your heart and your soul express your wish. Even if offering a petitionary prayer, leave it to God's kindness and judgment. The Eternal knows countless ways to benefit you. The Supreme Sovereign will choose the best one for you. Trust that everything is for your best and your prayer will be answered.

PRAYERS OF THANKSGIVING

You may want to offer a prayer of thankfulness. Thank God each day for your blessings and the joys in your life. The expression of your gratitude, especially for the simple things in life that you might take for granted, will increase your joyfulness. Focus on your strengths and your blessings. Express your gratitude to the Eternal for your material bounty, such as food, shelter, and clothing. Be thankful for your physical, mental, emotional, and spiritual well-being. Start with your ability to see, hear, smell, taste, touch, and walk and go from there. Reflect on the wonderful people filling your life. Be thankful for your talents, for your freedom, for all the lessons you have learned.

Each night before you go to sleep, reflect on all the things for which you are thankful. Having so many to enumerate, you will soon drift off to sleep.

MEDITATIONS FOR JOYFULNESS AND OPTIMISM

Meditation can help you attain and maintain your joyfulness and optimism. Train your mind to recall moments of happiness, thereby dispelling negative or pessimistic thoughts. Use the following as a meditation or visualization twice a day, in the morning and evening, for ten to fifteen minutes, for at least three weeks. Be patient.

Happiness Meditation (or Visualization). Introduction: Create a warm, welcoming atmosphere, an environment of serenity and spaciousness for the journey within. Lower the lights in your room. Close your eyes, sit quietly, calm and relax your body, breathe in and out normally, feeling where the breath flows in and out of the body. Adjust your breaths so that the in and out breaths are the same length, thereby bringing about a relaxation of your body and an alertness of your mind.

Choose a word, a phrase, a melody, an event, or a person that evokes for you joyfulness and triumph. Repeat the word, the phrase, the melody, the event, or the person. Or, visualize a moment of past happiness, an event or a person, and reflect on the joyfulness you attained.

Concluding Instructions: Come back to the here and now. Take your time to ease yourself back. Slowly bring awareness back into your body. Feel yourself back in the room and open your eyes.

Visualizations for Joyfulness and Optimism. If you find your capacity for joy and optimism obstructed, you may find the following visualization helpful in facilitating the return of joy and hope. Pick one of several alternatives, focus on the visualization twice daily, in the morning and evening, for ten to fifteen minutes, for three weeks. Again, be patient.

Visualizations for the Return of Joy and Hope. Instructions: Create a warm, welcoming atmosphere, an environment of serenity and spaciousness for the journey within. Lower the lights in the room. Close your eyes, sit quietly, relax your body, breathe in and out normally, feeling where the breath flows into and out of your body.

Wholeheartedly visualize your future in bright, harmonious, pleasing colors.

Visualize rays of joy and hope coming from God and penetrating your heart, your mind, your spirit, your entire body.

Or, with your whole heart, visualize yourself receiving God's abundance. See yourself in the midst of plenty, prospering and thriving under God's aid and guidance.

Or, visualize God's help coming to you in the form of rays of joyfulness, saturating the center of your heart, mind, and spirit.

Concluding Instructions: Slowly come back to the here and now. Take time to ease yourself back. Slowly bring awareness back into your body. Feel yourself back in the room and open your eyes.

You may want to try another visualization exercise. Choose a goal and write it on a piece of paper. Look at it several times during the day. Before you go to sleep at night, focus your mind and your heart on the goal you want to accomplish.

As worrisome, fearful, or sorrowful thoughts pop up during the day, visualize the image of achieving your goal. Visualize God's help coming to you and assisting you in attaining your goal. Act as if it is impossible for you not to succeed.

When you find yourself dejected and despondent, use prayer, meditation, or visualization and your dejection and despondency will disappear; joyfulness will replace depression; and streams of optimism will penetrate your heart, mind, and spirit. You will be transformed. Remember that the Eternal sends consoling currents to the despondent and hope to the downcast. Force your mind and your heart to focus on your faith and trust in God. Concentrate on hope and joy.

If gripped by fear and anxiety when facing a seemingly insoluble problem or a difficult situation, use prayer, meditation, or visualization and your fears and perplexities will melt away. Your dark thoughts will eventually disappear. You will find in yourself (or in others) an abundance of resourcefulness to extricate you from your difficulties. As a new vision enters your mind, illuminating your essence, you will see new horizons and conceive new plans. You will find a path to success, a way out of your distress.

THE ROLE OF LIFE CYCLE CELEBRATIONS AND JEWISH HOLIDAYS IN ENHANCING OUR JOYFULNESS

Life cycle celebrations and Jewish holidays not only reinforce Jewish identity, they also contribute to our joyfulness and happiness. Take advantage of these opportunities to be joyous and happy.

We long to evoke religious expression in joyous life cycle events: the rite of initiation accompanying birth, the rite of passage, and marriage. Let us briefly focus on the rites of initiation and passage.

Ritual circumcision (*brit* in Hebrew) has traditionally served as the rite of initiation for Jewish boys. The *brit*, circumcision and the giving of a Hebrew name, has marked the resealing of the covenant between God and an infant male. However, the legend of Abraham is, one historian puts it, a "romantic fantasy."[6] Because there was no actual, historical covenant between God and Abraham, we are free to reshape this custom, modernizing and making egalitarian the rite of initiation into Judaism.

For the twenty-first century, a home-based or communal naming ceremony can serve as the rite of initiation into Judaism for both boys and girls. The giving of a Hebrew name connects an infant to the Jewish people and affirms his or her membership in the Jewish community. A ritual circumcision may take place for boys, at the parents' option.

The rite of passage, the familiar bar/bat mitzvah, marks the transition from childhood to adolescence. At this ceremony, which traditionally has been tied to the Torah, the boy or girl assumes the obligations of the Jewish tradition. As we have seen in chapter 2, the Torah is not a Divinely revealed document. In the context of Jewish Spirituality, the Torah does not serve as the key symbol of Jewish identity.

For the twenty-first century, a ceremony—whether home-based or community-oriented in a synagogue, temple, or other appropriate public place—marking puberty and the coming of adolescence remains appropriate. The ceremony serves as a source of competence and achievement for thirteen-year-old Jewish boys and girls. In making the ceremony—not the party—the focal point of the day, the child should share a project developed under adult supervision, appropriate to the youngster's talents, skills, and interests—anything from baseball to ballet—with a gathering of family and friends. In addition to giving the coming-of-age much more meaning, such a ceremony also serves the audience, enabling them to reaffirm their Jewish identity.[7]

Two home-based, family-oriented holidays, Passover and Hanukkah, remain vibrant on the American Jewish scene and are worthy of continuation, together with the Jewish High Holidays, Rosh Hashanah and Yom Kippur, previously discussed in chapters 3 and 6 respectively.

Today, the Passover observance for most Jews in the United States occurs at a seder at which family members and friends gather to hear the retelling of the legendary story of the Exodus of the Jews from

Egypt, accompanied by special, symbolic foods, which are presented, explained, and eaten. It is a time for family reunions and for strengthening domestic ties.

We associate the celebration of Passover, occurring in March or April, with the liberation from oppression—and, in the northern hemisphere, from the grasp of winter. Passover speaks of the joy of renewal and rebirth.

Legend teaches that Jewish ancestors left the slavery of Egypt to search for freedom and dignity. However, the Exodus story is a historical fiction. As one noted historian concludes, "[M]ore than one hundred years of determined and immensely expensive historical research and archaeological quest in the Nile Delta have not yielded one single shred of verification to this story that has fueled Jewish . . . imagination through centuries."[8]

We are left with Passover as a celebration of life and human liberation. Death has pursued the Jewish people with relentless fury. However, we have chosen to live. Having endured humiliation, Jews in the United States have thrived, enjoying freedom and equality.

Thus, we should dedicate the seder celebration and the Passover holiday to the dream and hope of freedom and its accompanying responsibilities. As Spiritual Jews, we can recast the message of Passover to emphasize the twin beacons of freedom and responsibility.

Freedom means liberation, individually and collectively, from the enslavements that destroy the mind and the soul while leaving the body alive. Today, we can be enslaved in different ways: When we let stress, anger, and envy sway us to our hurt. Bitterness, negative thinking, and pride can sour our joys and darken our contentment. We can be enslaved to the worship of money and overwork. We can become subservient to the mindless consumption of more and more goods and services and to the ownership of unnecessary material possessions.

Passover continues to call to us to be free from the tyranny of our own selves, from the enslavement of money and consumption, and from the corroding hatred that eats away at the ties uniting all humanity.

As we celebrate our freedom at Passover, we should also acknowledge our responsibilities for ourselves, our families, and our communities. Begin by recognizing that personal responsibility for our choices and actions is a necessary and healthy component of our lives.

As we seek to be free from our personal enslavement to false gods—whether power, fame, wealth, pride, addiction, anger, or hatred—

we must remember that we are not victims, forever chained to an oppressive past or present.

Each of us is responsible for his or her own conduct. Do not blame anyone else for your decisions, actions, or the difficulties we all encounter. Each of us—and no one else—is responsible for what we make of our lives. We have free will marked by the ability to choose.

We also have a broader set of responsibilities, namely, overcoming evil and perfecting the world. These tasks imply a great deal of responsibility on our part, a rather strange thought for the era of irresponsibility. Consciously and tenaciously we must choose to heal and transform ourselves and the world around us, whenever and wherever the opportunity presents itself in our lives. Use your distinctive talents and abilities to perfect the world and create conditions of freedom, liberation, and mutual caring and respect.

Wherever you go, whomever you meet, look for an opportunity to help and inspire. Always remember and affirm through your words and deeds that all humans are made in the image of God and are partners with God in repairing the world.

Another home-based, family-oriented holiday, Hanukkah, the Festival of Lights, is popularly celebrated by lighting candles in a menorah for eight nights. In the northern hemisphere, Hanukkah represents a seasonal holiday, marking the depth of darkness, the Winter Solstice, in November and December.

The days are at their shortest; it is easy to despair. Yet, the days do grow longer, so we should search for the spark of light to keep us going, helping us overcome our despair.

The celebration of Hanukkah affirms within us two other key points: the power of humans and the power of God. We commemorate the victory of the Maccabees, the proponents of traditional, ritualistic Judaism, over the armies of the Hellenistic king of the Syrian branch of Alexander the Great's empire. The Maccabees, a small rebel group led by five sons of Mattathias, a Jewish priest, recaptured Jerusalem in 164 B.C.E. after a three-year struggle. The Maccabees cleaned, rebuilt, and rededicated the Temple. So, too, does each of us today have the power to make a difference in the world.

When the Maccabees were ready to reconsecrate the Temple, they found only one flask of holy oil, used to keep the Temple's Eternal Light burning, that had not been defiled. The oil was sufficient to keep the Eternal Light burning for only one more day. However, legend has it that the oil lasted for eight days until more oil could be obtained.

We therefore celebrate Hanukkah for eight days, marking our remembrance of our faith and trust in God.

We should continue to celebrate Hanukkah as a symbol of both human and Divine power. However, do not expect Divine miracles to contravene the laws of nature. From the perspective of reframing events and people, discussed later in this chapter, perhaps we can best view a miracle, as " . . . the willingness to see the common in an uncommon way."[9]

PRACTICAL SUGGESTIONS FOR CULTIVATING JOYFULNESS AND OPTIMISM: THE POWER OF YOUR MIND

In addition to your prayers, meditations, and visualizations and your participation in life cycle celebrations and recurring Jewish holidays, take advantage of your God-given gift of joyfulness. Cultivate your joyfulness and bring it to fruition through constant development and expression.

Beyond your faith and trust in God, by remembering that God created you to be joyful you can restore or achieve inner peace of mind. You can substitute positive life forces for the negative forces that have entered your mind. You are what you think. Because of the power of the mind, your way of thinking—positive or negative—creates the world you see. You need to maintain a positive "can do" attitude. Let us consider two different approaches: first, forcing an optimistic attitude and second, learning to reframe situations optimistically.

FORCING AN OPTIMISTIC ATTITUDE: THE POWER OF POSITIVE THINKING

Always give full expression to your power for joy in every place and in every situation in your life. Identify yourself with an optimistic, cheerful state of mind. Cultivate the habits that make for joy. Embrace the habits of optimism. Think, speak, and act cheerfully. The illusion of "optimism" facilitates a happy, healthy lifestyle.

Select an optimistic outlook on life and make it your habit. Optimism is one of the best habits to foster. Do not let your spirit droop. Do not let external circumstances adversely affect your spirit.

Rather, make joy your habit. Animated by the will to be cheerful, your facility for joy flourishes. Tell yourself positive things.

Regardless of the weather outside or other external circumstances, start each day by saying out loud: "What a beautiful day!" Begin each day anew; start afresh. By resolving to live this day in a good and joyful manner, you will come to see the day as glorious and precious. Your lips will train your heart and your mind. Your affirmation of the beautiful will make your heart and your mind feel the glory and the majesty of the world.

Accustom yourself to see the beauty in other humans, the glory in every soul, the tenderness in every heart. Penetrate to the Divine depths of others' nature. Be attracted to the overwhelming beauty of each soul and heart. Form the habit of seeing others as the children of a loving God.

Smile in the face of seeming calamity. Your smile will carry you through the day, filling you with renewed energy and bringing you hope. Force your lips to smile for a short time period each day even if your heart is heavy, making it difficult to awaken your heart to smile. Force a put-on, pretend smile to appear on your lips. Repeat this process for two weeks. Smile mechanically in the beginning, and gradually your smile will become genuine, emanating from the depths of your heart.

Through your efforts to make your lips smile, you remove the layer of darkness that surrounds you, allowing light to filter through. You stimulate your inner power of cheerfulness. Soon your heart, your mind, and your spirit will smile.

Find an occasion, a recreation, or a person who can elicit from you joyous, hearty laughter. Laughter will cause the clouds of despair to disappear. Laugh and your fears will lose their hold, your worries their grasp. Your sorrows will not crush you; pessimism will not approach you.

Take yourself away from your situation. Distract yourself from your troubles. Do something pleasurable, something you enjoy. Refill your mind with cheerful thoughts and recharge your heart with hopeful feelings. Do not listen to or identify with pessimistic thoughts or people or read about or watch tragic events on TV. Rather, read cheerful books and magazines; listen to upbeat music and radio programs; watch hopeful videos, movies, and TV shows; be in the company of optimistic people.

Be selective in the people with whom you associate. Avoid any situation or anyone who interferes with your hopeful and optimistic outlook on life. Do not identify with gloomy people or environs. Seek out aspects of life as well as people who will charge you with joyful influences. Always seek the company of cheerful individuals.

During the day, do not permit shadows to spread over your joy. Think in terms of success, achieving positive goals, and continuing to plan and build. Let your creative powers assert themselves. If your mind is optimistic, permanent failure is impossible.

If you suffer reverses at work, in your business, in your relationships, or in your aspirations, water your heart, mind, and spirit with fresh hopes. New dreams will bloom bearing the fruits of success.

Do not let setbacks, which slow your momentum, foil your pursuit of your goals. Regroup quickly and be flexible in finding new ways to move forward. Continue to persevere; do not despair. You may need to alter the means of how you go about achieving your goals. Find alternative paths to reach your goals. Always put your setbacks into proper perspective. Step back. Do not let the temporary obstacles you face mushroom into major disasters. Avoid blaming yourself if things go slowly.

Remind yourself of your inner strengths and good points and put them to work for you. Remember that you have valuable qualities. Reread Rabbi Nachman's admonition on page 114 in chapter 8, and begin by first searching out and finding one of your positive qualities.

Remember the power of your mind. Replace your negative, self-limiting thoughts with positive, empowering ones:

- Learning how to be hopeful is a means to joyfulness.
- Expect good things to happen.
- Do not dwell on disappointment or sadness.
- Strive to create a positive environment.
- Do not associate with negative people.
- Develop a self-talk that is life affirming.
- Be a love finder, not a fault finder.
- Look for goodness in yourself and in others.
- Act as if you are happy; eventually you will dispel the gloom and feel better.

The Jewish tradition emphasizes joyfulness and the continual need to bring it into our life through action. As Rabbi Nachman of

Breslov put it: "Never despair! Never! It is forbidden to give up hope."[10]

LEARNING THE SKILLS OF OPTIMISM

For some, the power of positive thinking is sufficient. They can force themselves to be cheerful, thereby overcoming hardship or disappointment. Others, however, need to learn the skills of optimism, particularly the technique of reframing a situation, which involves changing thought patterns and mental habits.

Martin E. P. Seligman,[11] a psychology professor, advocates learning the coping skills of optimism to change your personality; help fight depression, anxiety, and pain; and raise your self-esteem. You need to change the way you think about misfortune. Your thoughts create your feelings, good or bad. Learning optimism helps those who are discouraged, especially chronically negative persons.

Seligman's clinical experiments indicate that if we feel empowered, assume credit for our triumphs, expect good things to happen, learn to challenge negative beliefs, and perceive events as susceptible to our influence, then we grow with hope and optimism. An optimist sees misfortune as temporary, controllable, and rooted in circumstances.

Conversely, if we understand good events as temporary and fortuitous, believe that others control our destiny, and attribute our successes to others' doing or to luck, then we grow pessimistic and helpless. A pessimist sees a defeat as permanent, catastrophic evidence of personal failing or ineptitude.

Optimists persist in the face of setbacks. Pessimists crumple and quit.

Learned optimism focuses on the power of non-negative thinking—specifically, controlling your attitude to people or events. Optimism can be learned as a coping skill; you can unlearn a negative outlook on life. How?

As you daily experience frustration, rejection, failure, or setbacks, you need to differentiate situations that are changeable from those you simply cannot alter. Do not waste your time and energy worrying over something beyond your control. Rabbi Yechiel Michel of Zlotchov—the Zlotchover Maggid, who lived from 1721 to 1786—related this wisdom that he learned from his ancestors. There are two things you should not worry about: that which is impossible to fix and that which is possible to fix. What is impossible to fix, how will worrying help? What is possible to fix, fix it, and why worry?[12]

In situations that are changeable, focus on what you can do to effect change. Where change is possible, try to change things. When facing a difficult situation, one that is within your power to change, commit yourself to finding a solution, not to hiding your head in denial. Do not become hopeless or helpless.

Where you cannot change a situation, learn to cope with your emotions and reactions. By altering how you interpret a situation, you can learn to turn a negative event into something positive. Make the best of a challenging situation by viewing it in a positive light or growing from it.

Let us take a specific situation. Suppose a colleague at work does not say "Hello" and avoids making eye contact with you. You could interpret this behavior as "unfriendliness," a negative thought. However, your colleague might have been preoccupied with other thoughts and meant nothing unfriendly to you.

As Seligman points out, you need to dispute your interpretation of "adversity."[13] Ask yourself whether your negative thoughts are in fact accurate, whether your beliefs are in fact correct. If your negative thoughts and beliefs are distortions, challenge them. Argue with yourself about thoughts and beliefs flowing from what you perceive as an adversity. Are your conclusions logical? Is an alternative conclusion more logical? Change how you interpret a situation or another person and shift your feelings and your conduct. Do not misinterpret data or lose your perspective.

A childhood story of the Kobriner Rabbi well illustrates reframing:

> When the Kobriner Rabbi was a child, his region suffered a terrible drought. Beggars wandered from city to city, seeking food. A number of them came to his mother's house and she prepared a fire to cook food for them. Some of the beggars, growing impatient, began to abuse her with aggressive words. She became so upset she started to weep.
>
> Her small son, the future rebbe, said to his mother: "Why should you let their abuse bother you? You help them with a pure heart and carry out a good deed with a perfect spirit. If, on the contrary, the beggars had praised and blessed you, your gesture of love would be less worthy, because doubt would exist that you performed it to gain recognition."[14]

In situations that are not changeable, that are beyond your power or control, learn to cope with your own emotions. Try to make the best of it. Do not obsess about the negative. Remember, "This too will pass." Interpret every facet of your existence with optimism. See life's traumas as challenges, not threats. Shift how you assess the meaning of day-to-day events. Seek to foster a joy that puts a positive interpretation on everything in your life. Remind yourself of your past triumphs. Make and implement a plan to achieve a more favorable outcome. Set modest, immediate, and achievable goals.

Each day, take one negative thought and look at its bright side. Focus on one event you responded to with distress and reframe it so that the good you now see nullifies the distress you experienced.

People can learn to be hopeful and optimistic or helpless and pessimistic. Learn to reframe events and situations in order to find the good, rather than the negative. As Rabbi Barukh of Mezbizh once said, "What a good and bright world this is if we do not lose our hearts to it, but what a dark world if we do!"[15]

OTHER PRACTICAL STRATEGIES TO ENHANCE YOUR JOYFULNESS AND OPTIMISM

In addition to forcing an optimistic attitude and reframing events, four other practical techniques can enhance your joyfulness.

First, visualize your primary goal (or goals) in life and what it or they mean to you. Ask yourself why you initially established the objective (or objectives) and to what extent it or they still matter to you. This will help you overcome short-term crises.

Second, if life becomes overwhelming because a task or an obligation seems too burdensome, take constructive action. Break it into smaller, more manageable parts.

Third, each evening before you go to sleep, write down what has been bothering you during the day. Keep paper and pen near your bed and during the night write down your fears, your worries, and your sorrows if you cannot do so before going to sleep. In the morning, you will be ready to deal with what you have written down. Make and implement a plan to solve the problem. Take specific action and defined steps to remedy a defined problem. By making concrete plans, you take the problem out of the zone of apprehension and bring it into the area of remediation.

Fourth, let go of the past. Uproot the past from your heart; banish it from your mind. Free yourself from your past. Forget the failures or the emotional hurts of the past, which may have brought humiliation or fear, a tendency to unhappiness, a disposition toward doubt, or a susceptibility to despair. Yes, these failures and hurts, as well as your attendant suffering, were obstacles you encountered. These failures and hurts represent stepping-stones that you were able to overcome on your way to higher reaches.

If you erred in the past, revisit the situation and determine how to set it right. Demonstrate sincere repentance by taking appropriate action, particularly during the period between Rosh Hashanah and Yom Kippur. Offer an apology, express your sincere forgiveness, using the techniques discussed in chapter 6, then drop the matter and do not give it further thought. Let go of the past and move on. Do not wallow in the past.

Each day before you go to sleep, evaluate your day's activities. If there is anything you regret, especially in an interaction with another human, do not let it fester. Determine to offer an apology. Visualize how you will act differently in a similar situation or with that person in the future. Then, let go of the day.

THE IMPORTANCE OF SPIRITUAL OPTIMISM

The cosmos is a friendly place with sufficient spiritual, emotional, and physical nourishment for everyone. As good is dominant in God's creation, everything that exists is good. The purpose of things is for the good.

If existence is good, if everything is for good, human life—your life—is designed for good. You must see the bright side of things. Know that good must come ultimately. Do not let your mind or your heart tolerate negativity or pessimism.

Train your mind to interpret life in happy terms. Train your disposition to escape the grasp of misery. Train your heart to harbor hope, shutting out discouragement.

When you see obstacles in the way of your goals, do not be discouraged. When your plans are overthrown, you lose your job or do not get the job you avidly wanted, a relationship ends, or you are disappointed or rejected or people let you down, do not be dispirited. Try to learn the lessons from these difficulties.

Everything is for your good. If you fail in one direction, suffer a loss in one avenue, another channel, even more useful and beneficial, will open for you.

See life's trauma as challenges, not threats. In the face of difficult circumstances, if at all possible commit yourself to a solution and do not go into denial. Reframe a situation, find the good, not the negative. Encourage positive expectations and avoid destructive beliefs. Address positively the challenges you face. Remember that whatever happens to you helps you grow in wisdom and love.

As Rabbi Moshe of Kobryn (1784–1858), the Kobriner Rebbe, taught: "When a person suffers, she should not say: 'That's bad!' Nothing God imposes on us is bad. But it is all right to say: 'That's bitter!' It is like a bitter medicine a physician prescribes to cure the patient."[16]

Do not surrender to helplessness; rather turn to God, in whatever way you feel comfortable. Learn to look to the Eternal for help and guidance. Face life with faith and trust in God. Your faith and trust will sustain your efforts, encouraging and animating you in difficult times. Do not be overwhelmed by apparent difficulties that are only temporary. These obstacles will spur you to even greater efforts and self-assertion.

Hope even in the midst of misfortune and suffering. Rabbi Yechiel Michel of Zlotchov, the Zlotchover Maggid, lived in great poverty early in his life. However, not for one hour did happiness desert him. When asked how he could offer a prayer of thanksgiving, "Blessed be Thou . . . Who has supplied my every want," day after day, he replied: "My want is, most likely, poverty, and that is what I have been supplied with." He also once said to his son: "My life was blessed because I never needed anything until I had it."[17]

Because we never know how things will turn out, never give up hope. Rather maintain your faith and optimistic outlook no matter what happens. To make these points, Rabbi Nachman of Breslov told this story:

> There was once a poor man, named Moshe, who earned a living by digging clay and selling it. Once, while digging clay, he discovered a precious stone that was obviously worth a great deal. Since he had no idea of its worth, he took it to an expert to tell him its value.
>
> The expert answered, "No one here will be able to afford such a stone. Go to London, and there you will be able to sell it."
>
> The man was so poor that he could not afford to make the journey. He sold everything he had and went from house to house, collecting funds for the trip. Finally, he had enough to take him as far as the sea.

He then wanted to board a ship, but he did not have any money. He went to a ship's captain and showed him the jewel. The captain immediately welcomed him aboard the ship with great honor, assuming that he was a very trustworthy person. He gave Moshe a special first-class cabin, and treated him like a wealthy person.

Moshe's cabin had a view of the sea, and he sat there, constantly looking at the diamond and rejoicing. He especially did this during his meals, since eating in such good spirits is highly beneficial for the digestion.

Then one day, he sat down to eat, with the diamond lying in front of him on the table where he could enjoy it. Sitting there, he dozed off. Meanwhile, the steward came and cleared the table, shaking the tablecloth with its crumbs and the diamond into the sea. When he woke up and realized what had happened, he almost went mad with grief. Besides, the captain was a ruthless man who would not hesitate to kill him for his fare.

Having no other choice, he continued to act happy, as if nothing had happened. The captain would usually speak to him a few hours every day, and on this day, he put himself in good spirits, so that the captain was not aware that anything was wrong.

The captain said to him, "I want to buy a large quantity of wheat and I will be able to sell it in London for a huge profit. But, I am afraid that I will be accused of stealing from the king's treasury. Therefore, I will arrange for the wheat to be bought in your name. I will pay you well for your trouble."

Having nothing to lose, Moshe agreed. But as soon as they arrived in London, the captain died. The entire shipload of wheat was in Moshe's name, and it was worth many times as much as the diamond.

Rabbi Nachman concluded, "The diamond did not belong to Moshe, and the proof is that he did not keep it. The wheat, however, did belong to him, and the proof is that he kept it. But he got what he deserved only because he remained happy."[18]

When Moshe returned home, his neighbors saw that he was as joyful as ever. His joy became infectious.

A sense of spiritual optimism is important as we face evil in the world, pain and suffering in our life, and ultimately death. We need to overcome our sense of despair and to believe that the world we inhabit is not a chance configuration of material particles that accidentally gave rise to life and the mind, a place of fear and death, but rather that it is an arena for the evolution of the human spirit, a place where our individual and collective efforts can make a difference as we strive to perfect the world. Encourage the spark of goodness, the spark of the Divine, in everyone by helping each person realize his or her highest self.

In addition to promoting a positive belief in each of us; in our families, neighbors, and communities; and in the fulfillment of the spiritual possibilities of humankind, the notion of cause and effect underpins spiritual optimism. No one ever really gets away with anything. While righteous humans may suffer in this world, Jewish sages indicate that they will be rewarded by God, a just judge, on another plane—the World to Come, as we shall see in chapter 13— or when they are reincarnated through multiple lifetimes.

Believers in spiritual optimism, from my perspective, are life affirming and generally set for themselves high standards of personal conduct and aspiration, enabling them to meet life's trials and temptations with more patience, courage, and strength.

If you are joyful you not only benefit yourself, but also contribute to the well-being of others. As our lives are interwoven with each other, your mind and your spirit, consciously or unconsciously, influence others. We often make others gloomy from our gloom, sad from our sorrow. You can, however, transmit to others your hope, your inspiration, and your joy.

Your mind can send forth messages of joy to others, enhancing their lives. By keeping your mind and your heart cheerful, you help not only yourself but others as well.

A great expression of lovingkindness and compassion consists in giving your positive spirit and attitudes to others. Among your highest duties include imparting enthusiasm, confidence, and optimism to others; inspiring others with hope; and creating an atmosphere of joy.

Your laughing eyes and smiling lips emanate rays of cheer and joy that permeate the atmosphere. A joyous person has the power to impart joy to others.

Joyful, optimistic people inspire others with their exuberance and their enthusiasm. The Talmud teaches: Two jesters were declared "dwellers in the afterlife World to Come" because they made others happy (Ta'anit 22a).

Wherever you go, whatever you do or say, whomever you meet, look for ways to establish yourself as a positive presence in others' lives. Your overflowing joyfulness will enable you to connect with and be open to others. Furthermore, only with joy can you attain tranquility.

NOTES

1. I have drawn on Rabbi Morris Lichtenstein, *Judaism: A Presentation of Its Essence and a Suggestion for Its Preservation* (New York: Society of Jewish Science, 1934), pp. 98–101; Rabbi Morris Lichtenstein, *Jewish Science and Health: The Textbook of Jewish Health* (New York: Society of Jewish Science, 1986), pp. 142–148 and 183–213; Rabbi Morris Lichtenstein, *Peace of Mind: Jewish Science Essays* (New York: Society of Jewish Science, 1970), pp. 75–90, 147–154, 162–169, and 182–188; Rabbi Morris Lichtenstein, *How to Live: Jewish Science Essays* (New York: Society of Jewish Science, 1957), pp. 149–155, 163–171, and 218–224; Rabbi Morris Lichtenstein, *Joy of Life: Jewish Science Essays* (New York: Society of Jewish Science, 1938), pp. 16–29; Menachem Mendel Schneerson, *Toward A Meaningful Life: The Wisdom of The Rebbe*, adapted by Simon Jacobson (New York: William Morrow, 1995), pp. 134–142 and 153–160.

2. Chaim Kramer, *Crossing the Narrow Bridge: A Practical Guide to Rebbe Nachman's Teachings*, ed. Moshe Mykoff (New York: Breslov Research Institute, 1989), p. 33.

3. Martin E. P. Seligman, Ph.D., *Learned Optimism* (New York: Knopf, 1991).

4. Howard S. Friedman, Ph.D., *The Self-Healing Personality: Why Some People Achieve Health and Others Succumb to Illness* (New York: Henry Holt, 1991), pp. 93–97.

5. Adapted from *The Hasidic Anthology: Tales and Teachings of the Hasidim*, trans. Louis I. Newman (Northvale, NJ: Jason Aronson, 1987), p. 213.

6. Norman F. Cantor, *The Sacred Chain: The History of the Jews* (New York: HarperCollins, 1994), p. 11.

7. Sherwin T. Wine, *Judaism Beyond God* (Hoboken, NJ: Ktav, 1995), pp. 190–192.

8. Cantor, *Sacred Chain*, p. 3.

9. Noah benShea, *Jacob the Baker: Gentle Wisdom for a Complicated World* (New York: Ballantine, 1989), p. 19.

10. *The Empty Chair: Finding Hope and Joy: Timeless Wisdom from a Hasidic Master*, adapted by Moshe Mykoff and The Breslov Research Institute (Woodstock, VT: Jewish Lights, 1994), p. 110.

11. Seligman, *Learned Optimism*. David Mahoney and Richard Restak, *The Longevity Strategy: How to Live to 100 Using the Brain-Body Connections*

(New York: John Wiley, 1998), pp. 72–86, also develop the concept of learned optimism.

12. Simcha Raz, *Hasidic Wisdom: Sayings from the Jewish Sages*, trans. Dov Peretz Elkins and Jonathan Elkins (Northvale, NJ: Jason Aronson, 1997), p. 101.

13. Seligman, *Learned Optimism*, pp. 233–234.

14. Adapted from *The Hasidic Anthology*, p. 9.

15. Martin Buber, *Tales of the Hasidim: The Early Masters*, trans. Olga Marx (New York: Schocken, 1947), p. 97.

16. Adapted from Martin Buber, *Tales of the Hasidim: The Later Masters*, trans. Olga Marx (New York: Schocken, 1948), p. 163; *The Hasidic Anthology*, p. 483.

17. Adapted from Buber, *The Early Masters*, pp. 138 and 156.

18. Adapted from *Rabbi Nachman's Stories*, trans. Rabbi Aryeh Kaplan (Brooklyn: Breslov Research Institute, 1983), pp. 467–468.

CHAPTER TEN

Strive for Equanimity and Inner Peace of Mind to Overcome Stress, Anger, and Envy

Peace of mind is essential to achievement and accomplishment. Great works are not achieved in a time of agitation or excitement; they are the offspring of a serene vision and calm judgment. Lasting achievements that really count are produced when your inner life is peaceful and harmonious.

We also need peace of mind to achieve personal happiness and fulfillment. If the mind is in a chaotic, disturbed condition, happiness cannot penetrate it. If you live calmly, your sleep at night is normal and tranquil. Your self-esteem, your joyfulness and optimism, and your love for and forgiveness of others flourish on a serene background, a mentally peaceful atmosphere.

In contrast, restless people render those with whom they come in contact restless as well. If your thoughts, words, and deeds are agitated, you transmit streams of unease and disturbance to others.

This chapter discusses the Jewish tradition's emphasis on equanimity and techniques for achieving inner peace of mind every day, throughout your life.[1] Spiritual and practical suggestions are offered for living calmly, in contentment with yourself and in harmony with others, avoiding stress, anger, and envy.

STRESS IN OUR DAILY LIVES

As you reflect back over the past week, you probably realize that you have experienced stress at some point. The subject of stress in our daily lives almost needs no introduction. Reflect on the following: You are running late for an important meeting and are tied up in gridlock traffic. Your teenager is three hours late in coming home from a Saturday night date. After last month's shopping binge, the credit card bills arrive and you must face paying them. You are about to undergo a painful medical procedure. The supermarket checkout line you pick turns out to be the slowest. Stress bears down on us relentlessly and intensely.

We live in an age of discontent that makes us restless and uneasy as we go through each day. In addition to our anxieties over our relationships and our money worries, many of us are overworked and overstressed. Our work atmosphere is ever more pressured and stressful. We feel we must work harder just to stay in place. We are on a treadmill, never quite able to catch up with all of life's demands.

The workaholic culture spills over into our personal lives. We experience difficulty in balancing our work and the demands for a successful career with our home life and our desire for a more fulfilling personal and inner life. We feel we work too much and neglect our families, yet we are ready to work longer hours for career advancement and more money. We also need the extra money to pay for the goods and services we consume.

We want to do and have it all: success at work, material achievement for our families, and participation for our children in the best possible activities. New interests and new entertainments constantly crowd our lives.

We drive our bodies and our minds recklessly; we are in constant, breathless motion. We become restless, rushing beings. We feel pressured in order to achieve. Our hectic actions; impatient gestures; tense, straining faces; and rapid speech waste our energy and power. We hurry throughout the day.

However, most of us cannot bear too much strain; we cannot carry too many burdens and responsibilities. Creative individuals become passive, the young suddenly age, and the strong become weak. We are irritable and impatient during the day and sleepless at night. Life lacks fulfillment; it becomes meaningless. Every phase of our existence turns dark and unhappy; we simply cannot cope. We can do so much and no more. We look to alcohol, narcotics, stimulants, or prescription drugs to correct our ailments. However, nothing seems to solve our plight. We are not quite sure how to handle it all.

Stress exacts its toll on our health in physical and mental illness, and even on human life. Stress prepares the body to respond to danger. A stress-triggering incident sets in motion a physiological survival mechanism called the "fight or flight" response. We accelerate the production of stimulating or exciting hormones, such as adrenalin, which are sent throughout the body. These stress-generated hormones result in the body becoming all charged up, which, of course, is useful in emergencies. The heart races, blood pressure increases, muscles in arms and legs tighten. When we feel stressed, our breathing accelerates, becoming very short and shallow.

In the modern world, we are unable to fight off the stress-inducing crises, physically and emotionally. Our tension never gets released, leading to a type of emotional suicide. We cannot downshift. Our revved-up mind and body lead to the familiar complaints: headaches, backaches, muscle tension, sleeplessness, and stomach problems. High blood pressure, heart disease, ulcers, asthma, and eczema are exacerbated. In women, stress upsets the hormonal balance and interferes with the reproductive system. We are more vulnerable to dementia, anxiety, and depression.[2]

Because stress depresses the immune system, there is a correlation between stress levels and susceptibility to colds and the flu.[3] In one study, researchers found that individuals who experienced severe, chronic (lasting one month or more), stressful life events—with underemployment, unemployment, or enduring interpersonal difficulties with family or friends having the greatest influence on risk—were between two and nearly four times more likely to develop colds than those without such experiences.[4]

Experts have concluded that stress-related health problems manifested in physical complaints, such as backaches, headaches, undue fatigue, high blood pressure, eating disorders, and gastrointestinal disturbances, account for sixty to ninety percent of all visits to physicians.[5]

In addition to the emotional and physical consequences of stress, our work suffers. We achieve less when in an excitable state, failures of judgment mount, we often lack a clear mental vision, and our energies become exhausted. Being stressed-out brings fatigue and irritability, a lack of accuracy, deficiencies in concentration, gaps in attention, diminished powers of judgment, and a tendency to err and make mistakes. In short, when stressed we are unable to cope.

As ambitious as we are, we need to face the finiteness of time: 24 hours in a day, 168 hours in a week. We suffer from what Rabbi David A. Cooper describes as TDS: Time Deficiency Syndrome.[6] So much to do, so little time. We must, however, face the limits of our energy. We are only capable of working so many hours in a day or a week.

Many of us find that we lack the energy to enjoy life. As our body becomes impaired, we become frazzled and our reserve of energy and strength becomes depleted. We see nothing but unhappiness in life. Every phase of our existence, every circumstance turns dull and unhappy. We see less and less hope. We become easily discouraged. We lack fortification against the vicissitudes and hardships we all encounter. We are helpless when confronted with a dilemma or when we are in the midst of crisis. We are simply overwhelmed by trying to do it all.

By over-straining our energies, the body and the mind become enfeebled. Our peace of mind ebbs. As our stress increases, we dread each new day with its new burdens, anxieties, and ever more pressing tasks. We are on a treadmill, never quite able to catch up with everything we rush after.

HOW JUDAISM CAN HELP US DEAL WITH STRESS

How can we bring Judaism into our daily lives to deal with stress? Let us consider two alternatives: first, the traditional observance of the Sabbath as a time of peace, which is difficult for most of us; second, equanimity as a key virtue of spiritually oriented Judaism.

JEWISH SPIRITUALITY AND SABBATH OBSERVANCE

For Jewish traditionalists, the answer to the question of how Judaism can help deal with a stressful lifestyle is easy: Observe the Sabbath— once a week commit to twenty-four hours of rest and peace. Orient your overly hectic life around the Sabbath, a day for rest and relaxation.

Sabbath observers work six days a week to make a living. For them, the high point of their week is the Sabbath, around which the other six days revolve. They withdraw from the demands of the workaday world and try to fill the day with spiritual significance. It is a day to recharge the body, the mind, and the soul; a refreshing pause, a sense of peace and tranquility, derived from not working, physically or emotionally. In short, traditionalists view the Sabbath as a "glorious release from weekday concerns, routine pressures. . . . It is what is needed most in the competitive, tension-packed, hurried, frenzied life of this society."[7]

In striving to help the ritually observant withdraw from the demands of the workaday world, Jewish law provides an elaborate set of rules distinguishing between two types of activities: those that are prohibited and those that are permitted. Prohibited are work-like activities such as writing or typing; driving a car; switching on or off electric lights or any electric apparatus, such as a computer or a television; and engaging in exercise or athletic activities, gardening, or lawn maintenance.[8]

These prohibitions emanate from the Hebrew Bible. The authors of the Torah tell us not to perform any task—really work—prohibited on the Sabbath. (Exodus 20:10; Deuteronomy 5:12–14)

The Talmud goes on to list thirty-nine categories of prohibited activities, including cooking, washing clothes (today, by machine or hand), sewing, gluing, constructing or repairing (such as household repair tasks), shaving or cutting hair, lighting (or extinguishing) a fire, smoking, cutting or tearing (but not the cutting of food), fishing, gardening, carrying, and pushing or moving an object more than six feet within a public domain or from a public domain into a private domain (or vice versa). (*Shabbat* 73a)

Rabbinic law also forbids activities resembling a prohibited task, which in practice may lead to them, including buying or selling, riding an animal, boating, playing a musical instrument, and switching on or off electric lights or any electrical device. Avoided are other tasks that detract from the sanctity of the Sabbath, including watching television, engaging in exercise, reading business correspondence, or performing heavy tasks such as rearranging household furniture.

In contrast, permitted activities include reading and studying (particularly Torah study), resting, walking, eating, praying, thinking, talking, and socializing with neighbors and family.

Sabbath observance, from the perspective of Jewish Spirituality, represents a matter of individual preference. For most of us, the complicated and repressive prohibitions probably have little to do with rest and tranquility for the body, mind, and soul. They are burdensome and inconvenient; they are spiritually choking. The theme of commands, abstinence, and the long list of prohibited activities—as human constructs, not Divine ordinances—override the theme of prayer and study.

Most of us do not work on Saturday; it is part of the weekend. Unless you were brought up on all the rules and have regularly observed them (or are a "born again" Jewish traditionalist), most of us do not view the Sabbath as the high point of our week, an eagerly awaited day of joy and delight, around which the other six days revolve. We want to indulge in rest and recreation on our two days of leisure as we choose to do, without the intrusion of the anxiety- and guilt-producing prohibitions.

In the twenty-first century, we may increasingly come to view the Sabbath not as a rest day, but as a time to reaffirm our Jewish identity. There are many possibilities: participating in a Friday evening service, holding a family dinner on Friday night, reading a Jewish book, or participating in a discussion session with Jewish friends.

Thus, for most of us, Shabbat is not a day of release, rest, and serenity, designed to bring sanity to our lives. Rather, as spiritual Jews, we are free to make Shabbat "as Jewish as we want, in whatever way we want, and for however long we want."[9]

How then can we deal with a stress on a daily basis? Let us begin by looking at the Jewish tradition, apart from Sabbath observance, focusing on the character trait of equanimity.

EQUANIMITY, ANGER, AND ENVY
IN THE JEWISH TRADITION

A key Jewish virtue is equanimity, genuine inner peace of mind—not chutzpah, nerve, brashness, or passionate intensity, as many might assume.

We crave calmness and serenity. It reflects our desire to be godlike. Our natural state is contentment, which brings forth a calm mind and a warm and sympathetic heart. Thus, the Jewish sages admonish us to strive for tranquility—not anger or envy, which destroy our spiritual potential.

ANGER AND ITS COSTS

Anger, a strong feeling of displeasure and antagonism rather than a calm, controlled expression of assertiveness in confronting evil people or solving problems (as discussed in chapter 9), represents a very bad quality into which we can quickly fall. Manifesting anger becomes a habit. Many of us get angry ten to fourteen times a day.[10] Yet anger, whether experienced in the home, community, or place of employment, works great mental, emotional, physical, and spiritual harm.

In the Jewish tradition, anger does not bring us joyfulness. It is equated with foolishness. (Ecclesiastes 7:9) Jewish sages observe in the Talmud: Whoever becomes angry is considered as one who serves idols. (*Shabbat* 105b) The Talmud also notes: "He who loses his temper, even the Divine Presence is unimportant in his eyes." (*Nedarim* 22b)

When a person is angry, whether it takes the form of explosive anger or chronic anger, she is not herself, her inner peace is impaired, and her finer judgment is silenced. She becomes, as the author of the Book of Proverbs so aptly puts it, "like an open city without a wall." (Proverbs 25:28) The Talmud warns us: "As to every person who becomes angry, if he be wise, his wisdom departs from him; if she is a prophet, the spirit of prophecy forsakes her. . . . if heaven allots a high rank to him, it will be taken away." (*Pesachim* 66b)

Anger, which can manifest itself in quick, dangerous outbursts or as a long period of stewing, debilitates our minds and our spirits. When a person becomes angry, he or she loses control over normal reason. Anger saps good judgment and clear understanding. Losing oneself in anger leads to lashing out recklessly.

Anger burns out a person's finer feelings, the nobleness of one's soul. As Rabbi Raphael of Bershad has observed, "Anger poisons both the inside and the outside: It destroys the soul."[11] An angry person becomes oblivious to others and their needs and desires.

Anger has its interpersonal and physical health costs. Anger makes us irritable and impatient. It burns out the heart; it poisons the mind. It often leads to hostility, manifested by resentment and aggression and marked by overly antagonistic behavior toward others. Anger may culminate in the hatred of others.

Anger often creates an atmosphere of bitterness and resentment. It arouses the hostility and contempt of others. Angry words cannot be taken back, the damage often cannot be undone.

An excessive expression of anger further separates quarreling spouses or lovers by making them even angrier and more aggressive with each other. Displays of parental anger adversely impact children. Anger can ruin friendships by turning friends into enemies. An angry person has few friends; not many want to associate with one in whose presence they must refrain from expressing their natural selves or any contrary opinion or else risk exposing themselves to uncontrolled wrath.

Reflect on an antagonistic, angry person you know, someone who is aggressive and quick to explode at the most minor excuse for provocation. How do you deal with him or her? Think of how he or she seeks out opportunities for manifesting irascibility, the object of which is to throw off bitterness. You try to stay out of his or her way, don't you? An angry person's antagonism keeps you at a distance. It creates a barrier between people, leading to the angry person's social isolation.

Anger causes suffering and can even result in premature death. (Job 5:2) One prone or habituated to anger, the Talmud tells us, will be exposed during life to all sorts of bodily afflictions, and in the afterlife, as we shall see in chapter 13, to all the torments of Purgatory. (*Nedarim* 22a) Anger reduces our vitality and lessens our resistance to disease.

The kindling of anger quickens the pulse, heightens blood pressure, contracts heart muscles, and increases stomach secretions. Anger makes one's face flush, enlarges eyes, tenses muscles, and throws the entire body into a disturbance. With anger a blazing headache may appear, or ailments may develop in the stomach or heart. Energy pours out from the body, leaving every organ in a deteriorated condition. Physical problems, especially the risk of suffering a heart attack or a stroke, mount with every rage, every expression of aggressive, inflammatory, hostile anger.

Modern research findings bear out these anecdotal observations.[12] In a classic study over a twenty-five year period of 255 physicians, those with high hostility scores were nearly five times more likely to develop coronary heart disease than were those with low scores.[13]

Even short of aggressive hostility, anger plays a significant, negative role in our physical health. One study of 1,623 heart attack victims found that an angry episode within the previous two hours raised an individual's risk of suffering a heart attack more than twofold.[14] In another study of 1,305 men, those reporting higher levels of anger had a two- or threefold increased risk of coronary heart disease.[15] In short, anger, especially in its chronic, intense, sustained variety, is not conducive to longevity.

ENVY AND CONTENTMENT

Along with anger and hostility, avoid envy, which results in a loss of the finer powers of the mind, spirit, and body. Many of us are haunted when we see others who possess more than we do. We are jealous of those who possess more, those who have more wealth. We lose our ease at others' abundance. We are unable to enjoy our possessions because others possess even more.

We are also jealous of others' happiness, real or imagined. We often grow miserable at others' joy. We cannot bear to see a neighbor or a friend rise, personally or professionally. We are unable to hear of a neighbor or a friend's achievement.

As a result of our envy and the accompanying jealousy, we often live in an extravagant fashion, as we put forth all kinds of pretensions. Our mind does not center itself on life's vital values, goals, and issues; it ceases to identify itself with deeper human interests. We become consumed by envy and jealousy.

Turn away from envy and jealousy. Rather, strive for contentment, especially with your material possessions. Contentment softens disappointment; it brings forth your finer elements. It keeps you serene; your mind calm, your heart warm, and your spirit sympathetic.

With what you have cultivate contentment. You have what you need. Be happy with your life, your health, and your friends. Take delight in a friend's or neighbor's comfort and achievement as you do in your own.

But do not mistake contentment with the passive acceptance of your attainments—with what you are. Contentment with what you are leads to stagnation. Reach out to achieve higher ideals. Expand the depths of your soul and your mind. Do more, know more, think more, achieve more, and always strive to be more loving, forgiving, and truthful in your interactions with others.

THE IMPORTANCE OF EQUANIMITY

Equanimity is counted as a high virtue in the Jewish tradition. In the Wisdom Literature, we read that calmness gives us superiority and power. Proverbs 16:32 states: "Better to be forbearing than mighty, to have self-control than to conquer a city." The Talmud counsels us to train ourselves to acquire a calm disposition by removing vexation from our hearts (*Ta'anit* 4a).

When we are serene, each of us is ruled by his or her wiser self. When we are calm, our mental balance enables us to receive and accept whatever happens to us. By living a serene life, our human and spiritual powers function at their best. We receive unpleasant news calmly and take all that life has to offer tranquilly.

When we are serene, we express the best aspects of our noble spirits. We feel the wonder of life. Our best qualities, our better selves, and our best ethical tendencies and virtues assert themselves when we are calm. The wellsprings of love, compassion, and forgiveness open up. Hearts feel closer when tranquility rules our lives.

When we are serene, we can best express our mental powers. Our thoughts come more readily. Our concentration is at its best. Our powers of memory are heightened. Sound ideas come to us more quickly and more abundantly. Errors of judgment diminish. We produce our best thoughts and form our clearest plans. We are able to see and solve the most difficult problems when our inner life is possessed of harmony and a sense of inner peace.

Achievement and accomplishment burst forth from a calm mind. We do our best work when our inner life is peaceful and our reason and judgment are free to act.

A serene mental state enables us to better face and solve the problems life holds for us. A tranquil nature better preserves our physical and emotional well-being. When the mind is serene, ease and calmness mark our bodily expression. Our physical and mental energy does not dissipate so rapidly. Our mind does not feel lost in the face of a crisis; it does not become hopeless when confronted with a dilemma.

When we are tranquil, rays of inner peace spread out from our soul, bringing even more serenity to the world. We transmit our equanimity to others.

Tranquility averts strife and mends fraying relationships. Calmness preserves peace. It prevents misunderstanding and misjudgment. As Proverbs 15:18 reminds us, "A hot tempered person provokes a quarrel; a patient individual calms strife."

Try to be tranquil not only externally but also internally. Avoid a double nature, that is, one nature that we show to the world—a calm appearance—and another nature by which we live in our private lives.

If your inner being is split into two parts, with each part hostile to the other and the two sides fighting each other, this inner conflict takes away the joy of life.

Always strive for equanimity even in the midst of life's storms. Do not become angry, even when you encounter events or people that justifiably provoke anger. Take a breather and wait out the commotion. Do not interrupt a tirade; let another wear himself or herself out, then try to mollify him or her. Look for the chance to prod an explosive person to focus on the solution rather than dwelling on the problem. Do not be envious of others' wealth or happiness. Strive to be the calm person God created you to be.

To deal with your stress, your anger, or your envy, you need to develop a rich inner life. This can be accomplished by various spiritual techniques and practical approaches.

HOW SPIRITUAL SEEKERS CAN ATTAIN AND MAINTAIN THEIR EQUANIMITY

Stress, anger, and envy, the opposites of equanimity, generally result from our reaction to external factors—they are our own creation. We are fundamentally calm and serene, but we need to see to it that tranquility expresses itself in all of life's dealings and activities.

To surmount the stress- or anger-inducing events in your life—whether it is rush hour traffic, waiting in line at the post office or the supermarket, attending family gatherings for the holidays, or facing an unreasonable boss or an unreliable colleague—begin by reestablishing your spiritual connection with God, the Ultimate Good in the universe, Who is within each of us.

Restore your faith and trust in the Holy One's help and beneficence. Remember that you can turn to God for hope and help, for guidance and sustenance. Turn to a life filled with the realization of God's presence in your daily life. The Supreme Sovereign watches over each of us throughout the day, every day of our lives.

Realize that a Divine Presence fills the cosmos and from Whose goodness comes your life, your health, and your sustenance. A living, loving God exists to Whom you may turn in times of difficulty. The Eternal will help, guide, protect, and sustain you in every aspect of your life.

You can attain a more tranquil heart and a more peaceful mind knowing that you can put your burdens on God's shoulders and in the Eternal's hands. You can rely on God, the Source of Good, to give you everything you need.

Feel the power of God within you, realizing this Power with your mind, your heart, and your spirit. Living with faith, confidence, and joy, open your heart to God; surrender your being to Divine care and protection, always trusting and hoping in the Eternal. You can always find God's love—at any moment, in any adversity. Beyond your faith and trust in God, cultivate patience and moderation in your daily living.

CULTIVATE PATIENCE

Through patience you can endure the difficulties and unpleasantness that beset you in life with a greater measure of serenity. Patience teaches us to wait for a better future. Having confidence in God's goodness and believing that everything that the Eternal does is for the good, remember that the best will come even if it is delayed a bit.

Patience is extremely essential if you are not to fall under the burden of the obstacles you face daily. Realize that stumbling blocks exist in any undertaking. Face these impediments, however, with patience.

You need to know when to be patient. Be patient in all the difficulties that life brings. In particular, be patient with others. Others do not think as you think; others do not feel as you feel; others do not do things as you would wish them; others do not have the same strivings as you have. Your impatience with others indicates that you do not really understand others. Be patient with people as long as they are not doing anything illegal, unloving, untruthful, or otherwise "evil." When you feel agitated, do not unleash your fury by shouting at or interrupting others. Slow down and listen. Put yourself in the other person's shoes.

PRACTICE MODERATION IN YOUR DAILY LIVING

The practice of moderation provides you with a clearer sense of what gives meaning and purpose to your life and what you really need to survive and flourish as a human being. Learn to follow a middle way, the golden mean, pursuing moderation and balance—another virtue in Jewish tradition—in all of your actions, including eating and drinking, sleeping, working, and pursuing pleasures. Be the ruler of your desires, not their subject.

Focus on the big picture: You possess an immortal soul. As we shall see in chapter 13, the Jewish sages view earthly life, death, and the soul's afterlife as a continuum. As Rabbi Pinchas Shapiro of Koretz, the Koretzer Rebbe, stated, "All pleasures come to you from your afterlife share in Paradise. The more you enjoy in this world, the less will be left over to you in the World to Come. Be wise, therefore, and restrain yourself in the pursuit of pleasures. Leave a portion for your enjoyment in the afterlife, which is everlasting."[16]

Moderation represents a key to self-mastery. However, approach moderation slowly, in gentle, gradual increments. As developed later in this chapter, set your priorities by slowing down, reflecting, and simplifying. Each of us has more of a voice over our destiny than we think. You can respond differently to events and people. You can exercise discipline in your thoughts, words, and deeds.

Whatever spiritual practice you use—whether you pray, meditate, or visualize—remember that you possess free will. Someone once asked Rabbi Nachman of Breslov, "What is the nature of free will?" "Simple," the Rebbe answered: "If you want, you do. If you don't want, you don't do."

Reb Noson, Rabbi Nachman's closest follower, adds, "I recorded this because it makes a very important point. Many people are confused. They see themselves caught up in their habits and helpless to change their ways. They feel that they no longer have the power of free choice. It is just not so! Everyone has free will to do or not do as he or she chooses."[17]

It is up to you to make choices daily enhancing your equanimity. Your brain, your intellect can (and should) rule over your heart, your emotions. As the author of the Book of Deuteronomy reminds us, "Choose life so that you and your offspring may live. . . . " (Deuteronomy 30:19) Remember your health—physical, mental, and emotional—is given to you for use, not waste; for achievement, not dissipation. Train yourself in moderation. Order and regularity should be an unalterable part of your life.

Remember also that your middle way and mine are probably not the same. You must find out for yourself. No one can tell you how to pursue the path of moderation. Let me, however, offer some suggestions.

MODERATION IN FOOD AND DRINK

Do not indulge in an excess of food or drink to satisfy your impulses. In addition to practicing healthy eating habits, eat moderately and regularly both at definite mealtimes and at leisure. Eat only when you are hungry. At every meal satisfy your bodily requirements, but do not eat more than your system requires. In the Talmud, Jewish sages admonish us to eat slowly and chew our food well. (*Shabbat* 152a) Eating slowly helps you refrain from overindulgence, by giving your natural feedback system time to provide an adequate internal signal that you are satisfied.

MODERATION IN SLEEP

Practice moderation and regularity in sleep, creating order in your life. Avoid too much or too little sleep. Excessive sleep is harmful; a person becomes dull and sluggish, destroying keenness of thought, stupefying the mind, and weakening one's desires.

For most of us, however, the problem is too little sleep. Insufficient sleep is not wholesome. It makes the mind restless, edgy, and irritable. It leads to attention lapses, reduced short-term memory capacity, and impaired judgment.[18]

Each day, your body needs a period of complete rest to replenish its reservoir of strength; your mind needs time to be recharged with fresh energy. Hardships dissipate, discouragements vanish, and stresses are eased with sleep.

Retire and get up at a specific, regular time. Do not stay up late pursuing amusements, thereby robbing yourself of the essential hours of rest your body and mind require. Do not exchange rest for restlessness. Pursue diverse entertainments, but not at the expense of your needed hours of rest.

MODERATION AT WORK

Learn moderation in the time and energy you devote to your work. Do not invest all of your energy, strength, and time in your workaday concerns. Do not give your work your whole life. A life spent only in toil is unnatural, weakening and ultimately destroying the mind and the body.

Even if you thrive on a fast work pace and a heavy workload and the challenge of your work provides you with much-needed stimulation, excessive toil and working more than what is normally required represents an evil; it banishes happiness and causes stress, weakening and destroying the mind and body. You cannot continually overload your body or overcrowd your mind; otherwise your work will overwhelm you, breaking down your essence rather than bringing you joy and delight. Your body and mind will be driven to states of fatigue and exhaustion.

With your store of energy, you are capable only of working so much in a day or a week. If you insist on overworking or are forced to do so, you will strain your energy and overtake your capacities. Your mind and body will rebel. You will find yourself ill and feeble before your time.

Some of us work with too much haste or too much intensity. We place too strenuous, too exacting a drive on our human powers and faculties. Do not let your work drive you breathlessly day after day, week after week until you collapse, exhausted. Do not rush furiously in performing your tasks. You can only bear so much stress.

Reexamine the amount of time and energy you devote to your work. Change your attitude toward your job. Make work a pleasure, more creative and challenging, not a burden, in which the day is tiresome and your life miserable. Other options include scaling down (or redefining) your ambitions; switching to a lower paying, less stressful and time-consuming job; taking a position in a different, perhaps smaller, organization where you can use your talents more fully; or opting out of corporate life.

Work with effort proportionate to your strength. Do not try to do more than you are able to do. Labor with a controlled energy that knows its time and its limits. Work with ease, with smooth evenness throughout the day. Your mind will be clear and work with great efficiency. By avoiding fatigue, you will be more accurate and your powers of judgment and concentration will be enhanced.

Do not overwork your body and your mind. Conserve your physical and mental energies. When you reach the point of fatigue, take a break, if possible, from your work. Give your physical and mental systems the opportunity to restore and replenish themselves.

Try not to carry your work troubles and anxieties into your nonwork hours. Carrying your work with you all the time ruins your rest and sleep. Separate your office and home and keep them apart. Technology and 24-hour commerce lets us work continuously. Avoid the tendency to turn the anywhere, anytime office into the everywhere, every time office.

MODERATION IN PLEASURE

Judaism does not teach asceticism or self-denial. There is no need to suppress human needs and desires. Do not renounce the world: God is in the world. Do not regard human joy as incompatible with Divine attributes. The flesh and its desires are not evil. Self-abnegation is not a virtue.

Do not absent yourself from pleasurable, wholesome experiences. However, control your pleasures. Pleasure with control is salutary; pleasure without control is harmful, destroying your finer qualities. As with most things in life, take pleasures that recreate the body, refresh the mind, and rejuvenate the spirit with a strong dose of moderation. Pursue wholesome pleasures that do not destroy the foundation of future pleasures and do not conflict with your better judgment.

Mental and spiritual pleasures are lasting, while those of the body are fleeting. The body grows accustomed to physically pleasurable things and the desire for them grows less potent. Mental and spiritual pleasures are endless. The aftereffects of a stimulating book or concert or a reflection on the beauty of nature are just as pleasurable as the experience itself. The pleasures of the mind and especially those of the spirit are vast and timeless. Spiritual strivings develop your eternal soul.

SPIRITUAL PRACTICES DESIGNED TO
HELP YOU ACHIEVE EQUANIMITY

During the day, even before you feel stress, anger, envy, or impatience getting the best of you, you can attain and maintain a sense of calm through prayer, meditation, and visualization. You can transform yourself and create a healthy, serene atmosphere about you. You can reset your mind to its naturally joyful, tranquil state of radiant calm.

Petitionary and affirmative prayers can help reduce your stress, anger, envy, and impatience, thereby enhancing your equanimity.

Petitionary Prayers for Equanimity

To purify your heart and your mind of stress, anger, envy, or impatience, offer the following petitionary prayers twice daily, in the morning and the evening, for ten to fifteen minutes. Close your eyes and relax your body. Slowly repeat one of the following:

O God, drive away my [stress, anger, envy, ———] and grant me a tranquil nature.

or

Purify my heart and mind, O God, so that I may serve You in truth, humility, and joyfulness.

Affirmative Prayers for Tranquility

You may want to offer an affirmative prayer for your peace of mind, twice daily for ten to fifteen minutes each morning and evening or whenever you face a situation likely to trigger stress, anger, envy, or impatience. Close your eyes and relax completely, while sitting in an easy, relaxed posture or while walking with measured steps. Slowly repeat one of the following:

I affirm that the presence of God expresses itself in my calmness and inner peace of mind.

or

I accept things or people as they are.

or

I am untroubled by events or people.

To loosen your attachment to your various desires, the negative particles attached to your heart, mind, and soul, offer the following affirmative prayer twice daily, in the morning and the evening, for ten to fifteen minutes. Sit quietly, close your eyes, breathe in and out normally, and slowly repeat:

I affirm that God is at my side, helping me overcome my unhealthy urge to [eat or drink too much, sleep too little or too much, work too much, or ——— too much]. Strengthen my resolve to reject this harmful habit. Guide me to triumph over this unhealthy inclination.

If your stress, anger, envy, or impatience interferes with your sleep, try an affirmative prayer for a restful, pleasant sleep. Before you go to sleep, sit or lie down quietly for ten to fifteen minutes, close your eyes, and relax completely. Repeat the next affirmation in a trusting frame of mind, expecting a restful sleep, without any skepticism. Concentrate on hope, joy, and calmness, banishing surging thoughts and anxious desires. If you expect a restful sleep, it will come. Your faith will be justified; your expectations will not suffer disappointment.

> I affirm that God will give me complete rest and that I will rest in God's love.

In offering any of these affirmative prayers, remember that if you have faith and expect the best, then God will send you the best.

MEDITATE TO CALM YOUR MIND AND BODY

You can meditate to restore tranquility in your mind and spirit by inducing a relaxed state of being. Through meditation, you can develop an attitude of detached introspection about yourself and your relationship to the world.

In his best-selling book *The Relaxation Response*,[19] Dr. Herbert Benson presents the Relaxation Response, a demystified form of meditation, a turning inward, designed to induce short-term calming and long-term health benefits including lowering blood pressure, strengthening the immune system, generating energy, and decreasing the heart rate. According to Dr. Benson, the point is " . . . when the mind quiets down, the body follows suit."[20]

What is going on? The relaxation response breaks the pattern of our everyday thoughts. Giving the brain and the body a respite results in a physiological relaxation. A significant drop in the body's oxygen consumption accompanies a downshifting in metabolism. Blood pressure drops, heart rate decreases, breathing slows and becomes deeper, and muscles relax and require less blood.[21] The more dramatic effects of using the Relaxation Response are cumulative over time.

Six basic steps must be followed[22]: (1) Sit in a comfortable position, with your eyes closed. (2) Let your muscles relax, starting with your face and working down to your feet. (3) Become aware of your breath as you breathe in and out through your nose. Each time you exhale, repeat a word, a prayer, or a phrase—for example, *Shalom, Sh'ma*

Yisroel or "The Eternal is My Shepherd." (4) Disregard everyday thoughts that come to mind. Do not fight these distracting thoughts. Return to your repetition and your breathing. (5) Continue the repetition for ten to fifteen minutes. Once you finish, do not stand immediately but continue to sit quietly, allowing your thoughts to return. Then open your eyes and sit another minute or so before standing up. (6) Practice this technique once or twice daily; morning and evening are best.

Using the Relaxation Response, you will start and end your day in a more tranquil state. After several months of meditation, your body will be less affected by everyday stress. A tense meeting will still trigger the speed-up of hormones, but your heart, back, stomach, and other systems will not react as strongly. The practice of meditation enhances your control over your life and the daily situations you face. It also promotes your self-esteem and your sense of equanimity.

According to Dr. Benson, religious conviction, such as Jewish Spirituality, enhances the beneficial effects of the Relaxation Response. Using a focus that is drawn from a religious tradition reinforces the Relaxation Response. You are more apt to adhere to the routine, to look forward to and enjoy it. Dr. Benson concludes: "When present, faith in an eternal or life-transcending force seemed to make the fullest use of remembered wellness because it is a supremely soothing belief, disconnecting unhealthy logic and worries. . . . It appeared that beliefs added to the response transported the mind/body even more dramatically, quieting worries and fears significantly better than the relaxation response alone."[23]

As an alternative to the Relaxation Response, you may also want to try one of the next meditations, for ten to fifteen minutes daily, twice a day for at least three weeks. Be patient.

Meditations for Tranquility.   Introduction: Find a quiet place. Create a warm, welcoming atmosphere, an environment of serenity and spaciousness for the journey within. Lower the lights in the room, close your eyes, sit quietly, and calm and relax your body. Breathe in and out normally, feeling where your breath flows in and out of your body. Adjust your breaths so that the in and out breaths are the same length.

Mindfulness Meditation: Focus your awareness on your breathing. Observe your breath as you inhale and exhale. Continue to remain aware of and observe your breathing. If your attention drifts and you are not observing your breath, refocus your attention and return your awareness to your breath.

Meditation to Facilitate Equanimity: Reflect on a current, recent, or past event involving you that you found quite emotional, particularly in a negative way—a stress-, anger-, or envy-inducing event. Reflect on this event and the emotions it generated in you from the viewpoint of your immortal soul.

Why were (and are) you distressed? Ask yourself how this event will impact you and the entire universe now, in the near future, and in the distant future. Is it really important? Contemplate the magnitude of this event from the perspective of more than one billion Chinese. Ask yourself whether this event and the emotions generated is of the magnitude of the death of a parent. Does your stress, anger, or envy arise from trivial matters?

To help you place this event and your emotions in perspective, reflect on what the psalmist wrote: "For in Your sight a thousand years are like yesterday when it has passed. . . . " (Psalm 90:4)

Strive to build a reservoir of understanding that will help you deal with various turbulent events as mere ripples in your life. Remember that a disturbance in a deep lake triggers only minor ripples, not major waves.

Concluding Instructions: Come back to the here and now. Take your time to ease yourself back. Slowly bring awareness into your body. Feel yourself back in the room and open your eyes.

You need to live "mindfully," giving each moment, each situation, and each human interaction your full and immediate attention. By focusing your attention on your breath, a meditation such as the Mindfulness Meditation helps you learn to be present in the moment. Your breath can be an extraordinary ally as you shift your focus from your habitual reactions to the moment. You slow down to listen and feel—to really listen and feel. Focus on the joy of the present moment. Through this process, you will find peace and openness. Step back and give yourself some room.

The Relaxation Response and the Mindfulness Meditation are breathing exercises emphasizing slow, deep breathing which helps us relax. The increased blood flow, supplying oxygen to the brain and removing biochemical wastes from our system, energizes us.

You may want to link the Relaxation Response or a meditation with some form of focused exercise. The sustained, repetitive quality of walking or swimming, for example, helps engender the benefits of Relaxation Response or other meditation, reducing anxiety and diminishing your negative thoughts.

In view of everything we think we should be doing, for some of us "quiet time," when our minds and feelings are at ease, may make us feel especially anxious. It is hard for many of us to sit still and do nothing. If may be difficult for you just to be with yourself. There is often something in the present moment we are trying to escape. We may be afraid to confront who we are when we are stripped of our busy, active nature. We keep busy to avoid facing our real feelings.

Perhaps the most important—and often the most difficult—thing for many of us centers on finding the time to practice the Relaxation Response or engage in any form of meditation. Being obligated to meditate may only add to your stress. What if your schedule is so crowded that you do not have time for the Relaxation Response or another meditation?

Try some type of mini-meditation: Learn to become conscious of your breath. Stop, close your eyes, and take a deep breath in. Let your breath out slowly. Draw the inhaled air deep into your lungs and exhale as your diaphragm contracts and expands. Allow your belly to rise and then fall about one inch. Breathe evenly. Repeat this for just two minutes. Open your eyes.

You will find this type of deep breathing exercise, done even for a short time period, takes your mind off a stressful situation. It enhances your perception of control and inner peace, even when things seem out of control.

If you are really pressed for time, use the "Freeze Frame"[24] technique, developed by the Institute of HeartMath, which can help you reduce tension in one minute. The Freeze Frame technique is as follows: Stop and recognize your stress, anger, envy, or impatience; take time out. Focus your attention on your big toe, then shift your focus to your right index finger. Place this finger on your left chest, over your heart. Focus your attention on this area. Imagine breathing through your heart. Recall a person, a place, or an experience that creates genuine feelings of pleasure for you, or a time in your life when you felt really good. For about one minute, reexperience these feelings. Ask your heart what would be a better response to your current situation—and listen to your heart's answer.

Once you have mastered the Freeze Frame technique, you can do it with your eyes open, even while talking to others or continuing to work. Basically, you use positive thoughts to alter and calm your heart's rhythm in stressful situations.

VISUALIZATIONS FOR SERENITY

Visualizations are helpful when you feel overcome (or about to be overcome) by stress, anger, or envy. Use one of these visualizations twice a day, for ten to fifteen minutes. Remember that change in our lives is gradual and cumulative.

Visualizations for Calmness and Tranquility. Introduction: Create a warm, caring atmosphere, an environment of serenity and spaciousness. Lower the lights in your room. Close your eyes, sit quietly, calm and relax your body, and breathe in and out normally, feeling where the breath flows into and out of your body.

Visualize serenity and calmness coming from God, filling your heart, your mind, and your spirit, spreading over your entire body and remaining with you. Recognizing that your serene self is your natural, healthy self, ask God to grant you a tranquil, balanced nature. Visualize that you are in a serene state, enabling you to perform your tasks in a calm manner, confronting challenging problems and facing difficult obstacles with equanimity.

Or, visualize these words or form a mental picture: Your serene self is your natural self, your healthy self.

Or, visualize an internal ball of light moving through your body and spreading peace and tranquility. If you feel tension in your mind, your neck, your back, or anywhere, visualize something that makes you feel calm and relaxed, such as a garden or flowing water.

Or, visualize your day, your current situation, your future, or whatever is appropriate in bright, harmonious, pleasing colors.

Concluding Instructions: Come back to the here and now. Take time to ease yourself back. Slowly bring your awareness back into your body. Feel yourself back in the room and open your eyes.

At the beginning of the day, you may find it helpful to visualize your goals for the day and the steps you will take toward meeting them. In previewing your day, visualize what may go wrong, what may lead you to stress or other unhealthy, negative behavior, such as anger or envy. Visualize how you will handle these obstacles, events, or people; visualize the positive choices you will make.

A Hasidic tale involving Rabbi Itzchak Kalish of Vorki—the Vorker Rabbi, who lived from 1779 to 1848 and was known for his gentleness and rectitude—wonderfully illustrates the benefits of previewing your day. Once, the Vorker Rabbi was traveling with a friend in a carriage. His friend complained that the driver was going too fast. To this complaint, the driver reacted in a violent manner, insulting both passengers. "How can you be so calm and accept this abuse?" asked the rabbi's friend. The rabbi answered, "Because I was prepared for even more insolence and abuse than we are receiving."[25]

Take a more modern situation. Suppose you dislike commuting; you really dislike it. Imagine a major traffic jam on the only route to your office. Imagine the most negative consequences. Will your delay in getting to your office be the end of the world? Once you imagine the worst scenario, the hassles of your daily commute may not be so bad after all.

In addition to the spiritual practices set forth in this chapter, you can train yourself to act serenely. You can use practical techniques to cultivate tranquility and thereby weaken the ascendancy of stress, anger, envy, or impatience.

SOME PRACTICAL TECHNIQUES FOR ATTAINING AND MAINTAINING YOUR EQUANIMITY

Let us consider some practical techniques to attain and maintain your equanimity. In addition to following the path of moderation previously discussed in this chapter, to feel more in control of your life it helps to prioritize your time, avoid the excessive consumption of goods and services, and manage your finances wisely.

You can also enhance your tranquility by modifying your thoughts. As discussed in chapter 9, you can change how you think about the challenges you face. Reframe events and personal interactions. Do not let your emotions jump into the midst of every problem, whether large or small. Do not let every dilemma, great or tiny, overwhelm your mind. Also, once you have calmed down, try to express your anger directly to the person who caused it, not to others.

PRIORITIZE YOUR TIME

To reduce your stress and anxiety, learn to prioritize your time, rebalance your life, and refocus your energies. You cannot do everything. You cannot encompass all activities. You cannot identify with everything the world offers. You cannot be present everywhere or keep up with everyone.

Your stress may arise from being unable to balance all of the competing demands you face. You may be forced to determine which commitments you need to give up.

Poor time management, an important source of stress, leads to a number of negative consequences, including unfulfilled expectations, a continual feeling of being overwhelmed, an inability to achieve objectives, worry about how to get projects done, insecurity about the future, missed commitments and deadlines, inadequate time for rest and relaxation, frequent lateness, and procrastination.

Remember: You have more choice over your destiny than you realize. Fundamentally, it is a matter of reflecting, setting priorities, rebalancing and refocusing your energies, simplifying, slowing down, having a more purposeful life, and reconnecting with your long-term values.

Selectivity starts with your thoughts. Bring the power of your mind to focus on what is useful and beneficial. Use your mental energies to count for something in your life and in the lives of others, not on irrelevancies and frivolities such as mindless TV watching or endless Internet surfing.

Center your mind on the most important elements of your life. What is the essential object of your thoughts? Keep that object in your field of mental vision.

Focus your heart, your mind, and your thoughts. Starve out unwholesome, negative desires and impulses: hatred, deception, pride, fear, worry, sorrow, anger, envy, bitterness, and destruction. Rather, encourage what is wholesome in you: humility, self-esteem, joy, optimism, equanimity; and in your relationships with others: love, compassion, forgiveness, and truthfulness.

Be selective in your actions. Focus your energies on certain aspects of your life, which may vary over time. Focus on making contributions and achievements. As discussed later in this chapter, find purpose and meaning in your life. Discover an outlet for constructive action where you can give expression to your talents, energies, and finer emotions. Identify with the needs of others, lift up those who have stumbled, cheer those who are unfortunate, and encourage the disheartened. Do not dissipate your will on small things so that little is left for big endeavors.

Give yourself a better sense of direction by prioritizing your tasks and allocating your time accordingly. Plan properly so that you accomplish a few key desires. As part of your plan, focus on your long-term goals—personal, professional, social, and spiritual—and short- and intermediate-term objectives to accomplish these goals. Ask yourself whether your goals are consistent with your values.

Be selective and focus on certain aspects of your life. Ask yourself: What do I need to devote more (or less) time to?

Think and decide what you want to achieve and make a focused effort to optimize your time. Implement a written plan of priorities to manage your time more efficiently, encompassing both a long-term perspective and the present accomplishment of daily activities.

As part of your plan, containing a step-by-step description of how you are going to meet your goals and objectives, evaluate how you spend each day. Then organize your time.

Each day map out and write down your tasks so that you are not in doubt as to what you should do today, this week, this month, and this year; what you can postpone; what you can delegate to someone else; or what you should just not do. In focusing on your daily activities, you may want to draw up lists and priorities each evening (or morning, whatever works for you). Then when you wake up (or before you start the day), you will feel ready to tackle that day's challenges. Try to designate a specific time period to take care of each item on your list.

Give priority to a few critical activities. Focus on one thing—the most difficult thing or the one that counts the most—that must be attended to first. Begin this task without procrastination or delay. Do it sooner, so achievement becomes easier and benefits are received sooner. Focus on the limiting step—the one thing that must get done— that stands between you and what you want to achieve.

Postpone small, trivial, nonessential, low priority tasks. Do not let distractions consume you.

When you face a problem, solve it. Do not put off a decision. When you feel down and things are not going your way, force yourself to focus on your work. Gradually you will learn the value of sheer discipline rather than procrastination.

As part of your time management plan, remember to give yourself adequate time for rest and relaxation. Balance and alternate work and toil with rest and relaxation, not sacrificing your health and your strength for material possessions. Allow sufficient time—if not daily, then several times a week—for rest and recreation to replenish your spent energy, recharge your strength, and revitalize your spirit. Spend time on something outside of your work from which you draw encouragement, inspiration, and joy. For some, family; for others, a hobby, vacations, volunteer endeavors, or a physical activity.

In addition to various forms of passive recreation to restore our energy and replenish our strength, such as relaxation, rest, and sufficient sleep, most of us need to pursue some sort of active recreation. Do something different with your leisure time than what you do during your workaday hours. For instance, if your daily tasks are mental, emphasizing left-brain skills such as analysis, pursue some right-brain activity; a little artistry or an active, physical form of recreation consisting of bodily effort, such as exercise. By calling your physical aspects into action, you give a respite to your mental faculties, which have labored during the day. By alternating labor with rest and active relaxation, you will toil more efficiently and enjoy your work more. You will be able to give the best that is in you, and attain the best results.

As part of the prioritization process, set boundaries, particularly time boundaries. Set aside a part of each day or each week when you can be on your own. Beyond your work and your personal priorities, such as your family, your children, and your volunteer endeavors, find a quiet time for yourself, for your own health and inner peace of mind. During this quiet time, take a break from stress-creating activities and individuals. Reflect and assess where you are and where you want to be, and how you can get there.

Each of us needs time to be with ourselves and the Divine Presence within us. We need unplanned, spontaneous time where we may seek guidance and find it.[26] Make time, at least fifteen minutes, for yourself every day, a daily time period without obligations to catch up on or goals to achieve. Set boundaries so that others honor your time to be yourself. To maintain your time boundaries, develop the ability to say "No." You cannot please everyone all the time.

AVOID THE EXCESSIVE CONSUMPTION
OF GOODS AND SERVICES

Our mad desire to keep up with others and our consumption-oriented lifestyle make our existence ever more costly and frenetic. "Excessive" consumption of luxurious goods and services pressures us to earn more and more to indulge our ever increasing extravagance. Many of us have taken long strides away from a plain and simple lifestyle that brings peace of mind, health, and happiness.

We work breathlessly to obtain luxuries that the global economy produces: trophy homes, designer clothes and shoes, fancy watches, and expensive cars. We race and tear ourselves apart to obtain the superfluous, luxurious standards of modern living. These pleasures are not among life's fundamental requirements.

As we labor to meet our heightened financial demands, our stress and our envy increase. We dread each new day, each new week, each new month with its ever mounting burdens and ever more pressing tasks. In short, part of our stress and our envy comes from our pursuit of a material nirvana and the accompanying struggle most of us face in paying our monthly bills and in managing our ever mounting financial obligations. We are so stressed out that among our avenues of escape, we spend even more.

Strive to simplify your lifestyle by cutting back (or eliminating) expenditures on luxuries that burden your financial resources. Rather than mindless consumption that fails to satisfy the heart and the spirit, focus on meeting your family's basic needs. Simplicity in living will bring you more contentment. With simplicity you are free to achieve far more than you ever imagined.

Pursuit of a simple lifestyle does not mean deprivation, returning to an agrarian past or the wilderness, or separating ourselves from humanity. As urban and suburban dwellers, we have the power to select items fundamental to our physical, mental, emotional, and spiritual well-being and growth.

Strive to reduce (or eliminate) your quest for luxuries that breed discontent in your heart and trigger stress by taxing your strength and your resources to the breaking point. Meet your essential needs for food, clothing, education, shelter, and medical care without requiring anything in "excess" or things having no enduring value. Simplicity brings peace of mind.

Eliminate nonessential luxuries that bring no lasting return. Avoid mindless consumption in an effort to fill your emptiness, for it fails to satisfy your heart and your mind. Avoid competitive consumption. Do not crave goods and services that have no ultimate value, even though they may exert a stimulating impact on your system for a short time period. Do not sacrifice your health for any material acquisition.

Focus on your values and goals. What is really important to you? Establish your own values and goals; do not borrow others' values and goals.

Cultivate spiritual practices, such as those discussed throughout this book, to help clear your vision. Work to attain your sustenance and basic comforts. Creating a simpler lifestyle requiring less money often will give you more time for the things and the people in your life that really matter.

Select interests and things fundamental to your physical, mental, emotional, and spiritual growth and development, eliminating nonessential luxuries that tax your strength and your resources. Learn to say "Enough"—specifically, "I have enough" for my (or my family's) dignity and security.

Some of us can simplify our lives by taking a less demanding, less stressful, less time-consuming job. This is, of course, difficult if the measure of your self-worth consists of money, power, authority, and status. However, you are far more than what you own. Most of us can live with less money and still be quite happy.

MANAGE YOUR FINANCES WISELY

Frugality pays big dividends.[27] Financial success, most basically, involves setting realistic goals and priorities backed by self-discipline. Do not live on a scale higher than your means, without regard to your income or assets. To cut costs, learn to share goods and services with others. Hunt for the lowest prices especially when purchasing big ticket items, such as a car. Look for expenses you can reduce or eliminate, thereby creating funds for investment. Restaurant meals and vacations are two key areas where spending typically spins out of control. In sum, be much more careful about how you spend and invest your money. Thriftiness is critical.

Our basic needs are small; our fundamental wants are few. Try to live well below your means and invest soundly, avoiding conspicuous consumption that depletes funds otherwise available for building your assets. Cut back on high-status purchases even if you must lower your current lifestyle or seem more downscale than your neighbors.

Before you buy something, ask yourself: Is my spending wasteful or unnecessary? Do I really need it? Can I do without it? How many do I already have? How long will it last? Do I own anything that could substitute for it? Remember: Never shop for entertainment, to alleviate loneliness, to dispel boredom, as an escape or fantasy fulfillment, or to relieve your depression.

Part of your income should be yours to keep. Your paycheck must, of course, be used for many necessary items, including shelter, food, transportation, health care, and clothing. Too often, however, you forget that a part of your earnings should be yours to keep.

On your list of monthly expenses put yourself first. Every month, put aside some of the money you earn now for the future. Make saving money an obligation. Launch a disciplined saving and investing plan. Try to save at least ten percent of your gross income between your employer's savings plan, your IRAs, and your investments. Sign up for an automatic savings plan, in which money is taken directly from your checking account and deposited into, for example, one or more mutual funds. Establish the habit of regular saving and investing.

Do not enslave yourself through debt to support a lifestyle that has little to do with your self-esteem, joy, or equanimity. Do not hock your life for mindless luxuries. Debt can be a double-edged sword. Debt gives you the ability to purchase whatever you want, whenever you want. It gives you an initial, temporary feeling of freedom and power. The other side of the sword is that debt can put you into financial bondage. If you do not control the amount of debt you incur, then, as you become debt-laden, your debt will control you.

Purchases made with credit cards can pile up so fast that the amount of money you owe, plus the interest, can take too much of your monthly income. You may reach the point where you no longer have enough money left over after the monthly credit card payments to meet the balance of your living expenses.

Debt must be used wisely. Here are some suggestions on how to handle debt:

- Do not use debt for "consumer purchases," such as food, clothing, and entertainment.
- Do not borrow money for items that will not outlast the amount of time you will make payments on the loan.
- If you have accumulated large amounts of debt, you should consider locking up or canceling credit cards to avoid the further mounting of your indebtedness.
- Consolidate your debts: Shift from high-interest debt accounts

to a single low-interest account. Consider a home equity loan or borrowing against cash value life insurance. If these options are not possible, consider using a single low-interest credit card. Many credit card companies have one-year promotional deals. After the first year, switch cards, taking advantage of another promotion. Then, reduce the number of cards and begin to pay off your indebtedness without incurring any new debt. Try to pay off your credit card balance each month.

- In the future, pay cash. Create a wish list and save regularly until you have sufficient funds to purchase what you want without using plastic. Use debt only for major items, such as the purchase of a home or a car. When you do borrow, attempt to keep the debt as small as possible and keep the payments well within your budget. It is even better pay to off your debt and live within your means. Except for a home, do not buy it if you cannot afford it. Do not go into debt for a car or for a lavish wedding or a bar/bat mitzvah. Limit gift buying on birthdays or holidays.

Implementing these practical techniques—prioritizing your time, avoiding the excessive consumption of goods and services, and managing your finances wisely—hopefully will lead you to a better balance in life. Strive to combine a sound material base with the achievement of emotional and intellectual growth and development as well as spiritual fulfillment. The search for a more balanced approach, integrating both the material and the spiritual aspects of life, involves an ongoing personal reexamination of the "right" use of your time, your energies, your money, and your possessions. If you want, you can find time for the people, activities, and values you really cherish.

Seeking to live a life of greater balance and moderation will, hopefully, lead you to consider the material base you really require to meet your needs and permit your growth and development while enabling you to give more fully of yourself to others. You need to ask: How much money and how many material possessions do I need to help fulfill my path, my destiny, my bliss in my earthly life? In answering this question, you may lessen your urge for materialistic consumption and your desire to try to impress others by spending and consuming. You may be led to bring your expenditures in line with your values and your life purpose, thereby diminishing your stress, your anger, and your envy.

FINDING AND LIVING THE MEANING
AND PURPOSE OF YOUR LIFE

The quest for equanimity and inner peace of mind begins, most basically, by reflecting on what your life is all about. There is much more than our everyday physical world; there is transcendent meaning beyond our materialistic culture and our earthly bodies.

As we search for our deeper needs, increased knowledge and awareness—from the Jewish tradition and other belief systems—provide a means to rethink our values and our goals. As we become more aware of our potential and our essence, we become cognizant of the tradeoffs we make in our daily quest for our material existence.

Many of us search for a calling, a passion, so that our daily existence becomes an expression of our beliefs and our dreams. In our workaday world, we want to do something meaningful and significant. We seek to find our bliss—here and now—which will enable us, fully using our capabilities, to make a genuine contribution not only to our personal growth and development but also to the well-being of humanity. Striving to be of genuine service to others, we want to make the world a better place than when we found it.

Many of us want to find the meaning and purpose of what life is about: some work that has to be done, some outlet for our talents and energies. We need to strive and struggle for a worthwhile goal. We want to leave a positive mark on the world. But how?

Each of us needs to discover his or her bliss, his or her destiny, here and now. The more clearly you can follow your life's purpose— what you understand to be your unique function here on earth, in being, relating, working, and creating—the more meaning your life will have to you.

Our talents and gifts are very varied. Some have musical or artistic abilities. Others can express themselves in words. Some have a talent for making people laugh. Some love to cook and entertain. Others have a knack for gardening. Some work well with their hands; they enjoy building or repairing things. Some have a special way with kids. Others are great with animals.

Each of us has a unique and special place in God's creation; a place that can be filled only by that person.

Your purpose need not be on a grand scale, such as a national political leader or a world famous entertainer or athlete. Rather, your destiny may be as a good parent or spouse, an effective teacher, a contributor to community betterment, or in using a skill in some form of artistic endeavor or creative expression.

How can each of us discover our destinies, our bliss here and now? Beyond the rather mechanical inventories of skills, likes, and dislikes, ask and try to answer some basic questions. What really matters to me? What is truly important and meaningful in my life? What do I value most deeply? How do I really want to live my life? What activities and relationships enhance and nourish me and which do not? Remember: You are the only one on this quest.

The following Hasidic tale tells of Rabbi Hanokh's quest to be himself:

> For a whole year I felt a longing to go to my master Rabbi Bunam and talk with him. But every time I entered his house I felt I wasn't man enough. Once though, when I was working across a field and weeping, I knew that I must run to him without delay.
>
> Rabbi Bunam asked: "Why are you weeping?"
>
> I answered: "I am, after all, alive in this world, a being created with all the senses and all the limbs, but I do not know what it is I was created for and what I am good for in this world."
>
> "Little fool," Rabbi Bunam replied, "that's the same question I have carried around with me all my life. You will come and eat the evening meal with me today."[28]

As you face the perplexing question of who you are and what you should do and be, take time from your life regularly to ask: Who am I? What is my purpose in life? What am I doing with my life? What are my goals? What problems and obstacles hold me back? How can I overcome them? Take time daily to connect with your inner thoughts and feelings and sort out your priorities. What does your soul yearn for? What is it your heart really wants?

Pay attention to the "call" of your destiny. In an era when nearly everyone wants to speak and few of us really want to listen, be quiet long enough to hear and abide God's clear call. The Divine will reveal to you your special purpose in life, which you should embody in a written, personal mission statement. Finding your destiny not only will assist you in charting your life but also hopefully enable you to serve others, for instance through work and community activities or raising children who will make the world a better place. You have the capacity to be God's partner in perfecting the world and you also need to focus on projects having lifelong importance that are not especially urgent: self care, your family, rest and recreation.

Learn to control your inner world. Self-mastery represents the key to life mastery. When you see a weakness in your character, whether pride, negativity, anger, envy, or impatience, energetically strive to correct it. By achieving your goal, whether humility, joy, optimism, or equanimity, you have made the supreme conquest. One who succeeds in conquering himself and attaining self-control is greater than the warrior who captures a city. (Proverbs 16:32) Remember: You can develop the finer feelings in your heart, mind, and spirit and in your dealings with every person.

Each evening, review the day's events and the people you have encountered to identify the sources of your stress, anger, envy, or impatience: deadlines at work, unreliable colleagues, an unreasonable boss, unsettling economic events, interpersonal relationships, etc. Map out for the next day equanimity-inducing practices.

You may find it helpful to keep a journal detailing your stress, envy, or anger. Write down the day, time, place, triggering person or event, the circumstances, and your mood and fatigue levels. Try to understand what was the real emotion—such as shame, guilt, fear, loss, heartbreak, or hurt—behind your stress, anger, or envy.

Your friends and colleagues make a difference. Spend time with people who demonstrate the character traits and the lifestyle you wish to make your own. Avoid those who will disrupt the personal virtues you wish to cultivate.

Pain, suffering, and tragedy mark nearly everyone's life. Let us turn and see how Jewish Spirituality can help you deal with your own or a loved one's serious illness, the process of dying, and ultimately your death or the demise of a beloved. Remember: You do not always get what you want because God may have other plans for you.

NOTES

1. I have drawn on Rabbi Morris Lichtenstein, *Judaism: A Presentation of Its Essence and a Suggestion for Its Preservation* (New York: Society of Jewish

Science, 1934), pp. 89–91 and 98–100; Rabbi Morris Lichtenstein, *Jewish Science and Health: The Textbook of Jewish Science* (New York: Society of Jewish Science, 1986), pp. 87–94, 161–166, 214–226; Rabbi Morris Lichtenstein, *Peace of Mind: Jewish Science Essays* (New York: Society of Jewish Science, 1970), pp. 54–68, 131–137, 147–154, 162–169, 182–188, 251–258; Rabbi Morris Lichtenstein, *How to Live: Jewish Science Essays* (New York: Society of Jewish Science, 1957), pp. 85–92, 141–148, 156–171, 218–224, 234–243; Rabbi Morris Lichtenstein, *Joy of Life: Jewish Science Essays* (New York: Society of Jewish Science, 1938), pp. 16–19, 37–44, 136–144, 167–182, 206–212, 244–251.

2. Robert M. Saplosky, *Why Zebras Don't Get Ulcers: A Guide to Stress, Stress-Related Diseases, and Coping* (New York: W. H. Freeman, 1994), pp. 196–215.

3. Jane E. Brody, "Personal Health: A Cold Fact: High Stress Can Make You Sick," *New York Times*, 12 May 1998, C7.

4. Sheldon Cohen, Ellen Frank, William J. Doyle, David P. Skoner, Bruce S. Rabin, and Jack M. Gwaltney Jr., "Types of Stressors that Increase Susceptibility to the Common Cold in Healthy Adults," *Health Psychology* 17:3 (1998): 214–223.

5. Herbert Benson, M.D., with Marg Stark, *Timeless Healing: The Power and Biology of Belief* (New York: Scribner, 1996), pp. 49 and 226.

6. Rabbi David A. Cooper, *God Is a Verb: Kabbalah and the Practice of Mystical Judaism* (New York: Riverhead, 1997), p. 166.

7. Rabbi Hayim Halevy Donin, *To Be a Jew: A Guide to Jewish Observance in Contemporary Life* (New York: Basic Books, 1972), pp. 62 and 64.

8. Further explanations are provided by Rabbi Shlomo Ganzfried, *Kitzur Shulchon Oruch: The Classic Guide to the Everyday Observance of Jewish Law*, trans. Rabbi Eliyahu Touger (New York: Moznaim, 1991), pp. 339–393, and Donin, *To Be a Jew*, pp. 89–96.

9. Sherwin T. Wine, *Judaism Beyond God* (Hoboken, NJ: Ktav, 1995), p. 159.

10. Bruce Felton, "When Rage Is All the Rage: The Art of Anger Management," *New York Times*, 15 March 1998, Business Section, 12 (quoting Dr. Hendrie Weisinger).

11. Simcha Raz, *Hasidic Wisdom: Sayings from the Jewish Sages*, trans. Dov Peretz Elkins and Jonathan Elkins (Northvale, NJ: Jason Aronson, 1997), p. 180.

12. Jane E. Brody, "Personal Health: Controlling Anger is Good Medicine for the Heart," *New York Times*, 20 November 1996, C15; Redford Williams, M.D., and Virginia Williams, Ph.D., *Anger Kills: Seventeen Strategies for Controlling the Hostility that Can Harm Your Health* (New York: Times Books, 1993), pp. 25–60; Matthew McKay, Ph.D., Peter Rogers, Ph.D., and Judith McKay, R.N., *When Anger Hurts: How to Change Painful Feelings into Positive Action* (New York: MJF Books, 1989), pp. 23–31.

13. John C. Barefoot, W. Grant Dahlstrom, and Redford B. Williams Jr., "Hostility, CHD Incidence, and Total Mortality: A 25-Year Follow-Up Study of 255 Physicians," *Psychosomatic Medicine* 45:1 (March 1983): 59–63.

14. Murray A. Mittleman, Malcolm Maclure, Jane B. Sherwood, Richard P. Mulry, Geoffrey H. Tofler, Sue C. Jacobs, Richard Friedman, Herbert Benson, and James E. Muller, "Triggering of Acute Myocardial Infarction Onset by Episodes of Anger," *Circulation* 92:7 (1 October 1995): 1720–1725.

15. Ichirco Kawachi, David Sparrow, Avron Spiro III, Pantel Vokonas, and Scott T. Weiss, "A Prospective Study of Anger and Coronary Health Disease," *Circulation* 94:9 (1 November 1996): 2090–2095.

16. *The Hasidic Anthology: Tales and Teachings of the Hasidim*, trans. Louis I. Newman (Northvale, NJ: Jason Aronson, 1987), p. 2.

17. Chaim Kramer, *Crossing the Narrow Bridge: A Practical Guide to Rebbe Nachman's Teachings*, ed. Moshe Mykoff (New York: Breslov Research Institute, 1989), pp. 12–13.

18. Jane E. Brody, "Personal Health: Facing Up to the Realities of Sleep Deprivation," *New York Times*, 31 March 1998, C7 (quoting Dr. Stanley Coren).

19. Herbert Benson, M.D., *The Relaxation Response* (New York: William Morrow, 1975).

20. Benson, *Timeless Healing*, p. 127.

21. Ibid., pp. 131–133 and 145–148.

22. Ibid., pp. 134–137.

23. Ibid., p. 155.

24. Bill Thomson, "Change of Heart," *Natural Health* (September/October 1997): 98–101, 155–158. The Freeze Frame technique works by stabilizing the heart's electromagnetic field and producing a regular pattern of electromagnetic waves generated by the heart. The Institute of HeartMath is located in Boulder Creek, California (1-800-616-8846, http://www.heartmath.org).

25. Adapted from *The Hasidic Anthology*, pp. 366–367.

26. Stephan Rechtschaffen, "Learning to Timeshift," *New Age Journal* 13:3 (May/June 1996): 70–71; Stephan Rechtschaffen, M.D., *Time Shifting: Creating More Time to Enjoy Your Life* (New York: Doubleday, 1996), pp. 86–88.

27. Thomas J. Stanley, Ph.D., and William D. Danko, Ph.D., *The Millionaire Next Door: The Surprising Secrets of America's Wealthy* (Atlanta: Longstreet Press, 1996) present case studies of who is really rich in the United States and how they got that way through hard work, frugality, and planning for the future.

28. Martin Buber, *Tales of the Hasidim: The Later Masters*, trans. Olga Marx (New York: Schocken, 1948), p. 251.

PART FIVE

DEALING with PAIN, SUFFERING, and TRAGEDY

In nearly everyone's life, terrible things happen. Most of us will encounter pain, suffering, and tragedy during our lifetime. They are an unavoidable, inexorable part of life.

This part of the book discusses three of life's crises: illness (chapter 11); terminal illness, dying, and the death moment (chapter 12); and death, grieving, and the afterlife (chapter 13). Let us see how Jewish Spirituality can help us better cope and deal with the way life is, full of pain and suffering, as we face seemingly tragic events.

As we consider pain, a physical signal, and suffering, our response to the signal provided by pain, let us remember that life's adversities may help us actualize our spiritual potential. Every experience can serve as a teacher and an opportunity for growth and learning.

None of us can comprehend the nature, design, and purpose of God's plans. There are no accidents in the Divine plan for each of us. We do not know what is involved in our life plan, which includes both joys and sorrows. Handled correctly, the challenges we all face make us stronger, at least from a spiritual perspective. Every event can nourish the soul. Also keep in mind that God offers us assistance, support, and love, particularly through the other people we encounter.

We face the challenge to continue to maintain a positive approach when we encounter hardships including physical and emotional pain and suffering, the death of loved ones and our accompanying grief, and ultimately our own demise. Find meaning in your pain and suffering. Recommit to your spiritual growth and development. As developed in this part of the book, reframe life's trials and difficulties into positive experiences.

CHAPTER ELEVEN

Facing Serious Illness, Curing Symptoms, and Promoting Healing

Perhaps our greatest treasure is our health—physical, mental, emotional. If we were to lose our health, most of us would give away our worldly possessions to regain it.

Although we have come to rely on modern medicine to deal with sickness, we are in the midst of an era characterized by widespread dissatisfaction with the prevailing, physician-controlled, disease-treatment model for illness. We are not happy with the overuse of pharmacological and procedural/interventionist therapies and modern medicine's focus on technology and technique. We are witnessing a marked antipathy to health care professional expertise, authority, and elitism. Many view modern medicine, and even alternative practices such as acupuncture and homeopathy, as inadequate and insufficient because they only address the superficial physical symptoms and causes of illness. Emphasizing materialism and the impact of things on the body, they do not treat the whole person.

In this chapter, I want to put aside the need for preventative self-help, marked by the healthy lifestyle considered in chapter 10, including proper nutrition and exercise, cessation of smoking, and stress and time management—all of which will lessen our suffering from lifestyle illnesses, particularly stress-related, degenerative diseases, as well as anxiety and depression. I want to focus on sickness, particularly physical ailments, and healing.[1] We cannot, however, detach sickness from its emotional consequences. As we are all aware, serious, life-threatening physical illness may bring with it apprehension about visits to physicians and medical tests, nervousness about medical treatments and the accompanying side effects, the threat of pain and disfigurement, the prospect of death—as well as anxiety, despair, and stress marked by interruption of our social and work routines, financial drain, and forced dependency.

Note that I do not use the term "cure," the relief from symptoms or the recovery from the purely physical or emotional dimensions of health conceptually linked with a discrete pathology. Physical illness may be a manifestation, at least in part, of much deeper emotional, social, and spiritual problems.

Based upon a holistic approach positing a person as an interconnection of physical, mental, emotional, and spiritual elements, for me healing—more specifically, spiritual healing—connotes a process: the attaining of wholeness (or at least the striving to become whole again) by reuniting the body, mind, and spirit. By reintegrating the parts that are split off you can achieve a completeness, even if some parts are missing or do not quite fit together, as well as a greater measure of comfort and inner peace of mind.

All of us seek the restoration of a healthy relationship within ourselves, with those around us, and with God. An inner healing connotes increased self-acceptance and higher self-esteem. We heal our relationships with others through our unconditional love, forgiveness, and truthfulness. We also strive to come closer to God. In other words, the healing of the total person and a return to our unity—to be made whole again.

In many instances, when you are on the road to recovery your physical condition will clear up and improve enormously. If you are healed—even if you are not cured—you will be able to live with your illness, the intensity of your symptoms may ease, and your ability to function will improve. You learn to cope, to accept what you cannot change or avoid. You will be healthier.

In this chapter we shall first consider healing and curing in the Jewish tradition and today, in the twenty-first century. Then, we shall take up specific spiritual techniques—prayer, meditation, and visualization—designed to facilitate healing and recovery. Suggestions are also offered on enhancing the efficacy of these spiritual practices. Although focusing on healing, because of our interest in the restoration of health, the spiritual practices and practical suggestions also encompass recovery.

HEALING AND CURING IN THE JEWISH TRADITION

In the Jewish tradition, sickness is recognized as a fact of life. Pain and suffering—whether a broken bone in your arm or cancer in your body—is a real and unpleasant experience.

The Jewish tradition recognizes the limitations of medicine, or what we now call scientific, Western medicine. In the Hebrew Bible, physical ailments were sometimes cured by prayer and concentration. Healing and even the curing of symptoms is not the exclusive province of the New Testament.

In Genesis 20:17 we read that the legendary patriarch of the Jewish people, Abraham, prayed to God for Abimelech, the king of Gerar. We are told that God "healed" Abimelech.

When Miriam, the sister of the legendary Moses, became ill with leprosy, a skin disease, Moses cried out to God, saying, "O God, heal her." Miriam was healed. (Numbers 12:10-15)

The Hebrew prophets Elijah and Elisha, who lived in ninth century B.C.E., stand out for their use of curative spiritual practices. In I Kings 17, the son of the woman in whose home Elijah had often taken refuge suddenly became dangerously ill. The boy's vital signs sunk very low, almost to the point of death. Elijah prayed to God for the life and health of the child, who regained consciousness and was revived. (I Kings 17:17-24)

Elisha cured the leprosy of Naaman, the general of the Syrian forces. (II Kings 5:1-19) Elisha advised him, "Go and wash seven times in the Jordan and your flesh will be restored and you will be clean." (II Kings 5:10) Naaman ultimately complied with Elisha's prescription and "his flesh became like a little boy's, and he was clean." (II Kings 5:14)

Elisha also raised a child from the dead using prayer and what we would today call cardiopulmonary resuscitation, popularly known as CPR. (II Kings 4:18-37)

The psalmist is often steeped in pain and suffering. He feels the tortures of his body and agony in his heart, but the healing spirit of God dissolves his wounds. He finds release from his physical pain and his mental hurt through prayer. For instance, the psalmist offers the following prayer:

> Bless the Eternal, O my soul, all my being, bless God's holy name
> . . .
>
> Bless the Eternal . . . Who forgives all your sins and heals all your diseases. (Psalm 103:1-3)

In the Psalms, an individual in distress, in a time of weakness, or ill appeals for Divine help. The psalmist lays bare his emotions, hopes, doubts, fears, and longing—all of which we experience—in the presence of the Eternal. The prayers offered in the Psalms are those of a soul in need, pouring itself out before God, Who is viewed as a loving and ever present Helper. Each psalm ends with the metamorphosis of sorrow into joy or inner peace.

When the psalmist appeals to the Supreme Sovereign with his whole heart, the Eternal in the Divine goodness answers his prayers. As the psalmist recounts: "O my God, I cried out loudly to You and You healed me." (Psalm 30:3) The psalmist declares, "You turned my lament into dancing; you loosened my sackcloth and girded me with gladness that my whole being might sing hymns to You endlessly. . . . " (Psalm 30:12-13)

Healing in the Jewish tradition recognizes that we are more than material beings and physical creatures. We are essentially spiritual beings. We have a spark of the Divine encased in each of us.

God is present with you in your pain and suffering. Realizing that the Eternal is close to you helps you reconnect not only with yourself and with others but also with the Source of Life.

A modernized story from the old country puts in perspective God's role in healing and even curing physical symptoms. Yankel suffered from cancer. His primary care physician told him he would be dead in one day. Yankel ran to the window, looked up at the sky, and said, "God, please save me." Out of the blue, a wonderful, melodious voice said, "Don't worry. I'll save you." Yankel climbed back into bed, feeling reassured.

Yankel's physician called a surgeon, who walked into Yankel's room saying, "If I operate today, I can save you." "No, thanks," said Yankel, "God will save me." Then an oncologist and a radiation therapist each told Yankel, "I can save you." Yankel replied, "I don't need you. God will save me."

The next day, Yankel died and found himself in the world beyond. Facing his Maker, Yankel asked, "What happened? You said you'd save me and here I am, dead." "Help came your way," was the response.

"I sent you a surgeon, an oncologist, and a radiation therapist. You didn't do your part."

This story makes the point that in addition to participating in our own healing and recovery through prayer and other spiritual practices, we must remain open to the many perspectives on healing and curing symptoms. Yes, God is the ultimate Source of Healing. As we read in Exodus 15:26: "I am God Who heals you."

However, spiritually oriented Jews do not rely only on God. Healing and the restoration of health comes from many sources. The medical and spiritual approaches to illness are complementary, not mutually exclusive. Medication, procedures, and other services provided by health care professionals represent gifts from God. You need to integrate Divine and human action by making therapeutic use of all the resources the Eternal has placed in this world.

HEALING AND CURING IN THE
TWENTY-FIRST CENTURY

For us in the twenty-first century, health care consists of a four-legged stool: first, medication; second, procedures, such as surgery and radiation; third, alternative practices, such as acupuncture; fourth, a spiritual component—prayer and devotion, meditation, inspiration (positive thinking), and imagery, as well as communal support and love. When we'are sick, we need to achieve a greater balance among these four legs.

Medication and procedures, the centerpieces of modern Western medicine, can do great things for you if your particular health problem falls within that realm. Recognize the clear efficacy of medication or procedures, including immunization against polio and other diseases, anesthesia for surgery, dentistry for cavities, antibiotics for bacterial infections, joint replacement procedures, and organ transplants.

In other situations, a spiritual component can play a major role in healing (and even curing) asthma; ulcers; various forms of pain, fatigue, or drowsiness; congestive heart failure; rheumatoid arthritis; dizziness; hypertension; and insomnia.[2] For many illnesses, there is a place for both spiritual practices and the techniques of scientific, Western medicine or alternative procedures. A need exists for cooperation between health care professionals, alternative practitioners, and those whose expertise lies in the spiritual realm.

I am urging then, from the perspective of Jewish Spirituality, a broad, a holistic vision of health and healing, a re-creation of the unity of mind-body-spirit. To achieve this wholeness, so that the mind, body, and spirit constitute fully integrated aspects of one's self, recognize that when illness strikes your recovery depends upon a partnership with God. Look to the infinitely Loving Mind and Presence. God invites you to be partners with the Eternal in the healing and regenerative process. God's—and your—partners also include health care professionals and alternative practitioners.

A desire for healing and restoration on your part represents an important component of the equation. In II Kings 20 and Isaiah 38, we read that King Hezekiah, the ruler of Judah from about 715 to 687 B.C.E., became ill and was told by the prophet Isaiah he would die. Hezekiah prayed for his recovery, reminding God of his sincere and wholehearted faith. Isaiah returned with the word of God that not only would Hezekiah be cured but also that fifteen years would be added to his life. Faith and medicine worked together for King Hezekiah. In addition to Hezekiah's prayers, the prophet Isaiah prepared a salve made of figs that he and Hezekiah successfully applied to the king's rash (II Kings 20:7; Isaiah 38:21).

SPIRITUAL PRACTICES TO PROMOTE HEALING AND CURING

You need to consider what types of spiritual practices work best to promote healing. Spiritual healing focuses on practices based in your faith in God as the Supreme Healer, the Fountain of Health and Well-Being. Drawing on a number of research studies dealing with the spiritual aspects of health and healing, let us discuss the benefits of faith in God; attendance at religious worship services and participation in religious activities; and prayer, meditation, and visualization.

FAITH AND TRUST IN GOD

No matter how bleak the present may seem—or in reality be—have faith and confidence in a loving God Who created you, Who sustains you, and Who will heal you. Invite God into your healing. Invoke the Divine to help with your pain and suffering. The Eternal will care for you. Face the future with hope. You can acquire and sustain your hope through faith and trust in God Who preserves and shelters you. Remember that the Supreme Sovereign watches over the destiny of all whom the Eternal created. Faith in and a connection with God is beneficial for your health.

Studies indicate that a belief in God promotes health. According to Dr. Herbert Benson, this belief is triggered by faith because humans are "wired for God." We "have the wiring that predisposes us to find faith enormously healing."[3] Benson concludes, "Across the board, in groups of different ages, ethnicities, and religions, among patients with very different diseases and conditions, religious commitment brings with it a lifetime of benefits,"[4] including better general health, lower blood pressure, and longer survival. Conversely, a lack of religious involvement represents a risk factor contributing to poorer physical health.[5]

A number of research studies detail the curative health benefits, specifically more rapid recoveries, derived from a belief in God. Let us focus on four noteworthy studies. In one study of heart disease, of 232 patients over age 55 who had open-heart surgery for coronary artery or aortic valve disease, those who received strength, solace, and comfort from their religious beliefs were three times more likely to survive than those who did not.[6] Patients in this study with a strong religious faith and active social lives were far less likely to die in the six months following heart surgery than similar patients who were not as religious and did not get out as much. Those who were both religious and socially involved had a fourteen-fold advantage over those who lacked faith and were isolated.

Forty heart transplant patients were interviewed in a second study three times: two months, seven months, and twelve months after their transplants. Those who expressed strong religious beliefs in their initial interview (and also participated in religious activities) experienced better physical and emotional well-being, fewer health worries, and less difficulty in following their demanding medical regime than those who were less religious.[7]

In another study of thirty elderly women recovering from surgical corrections of broken hips, researchers concluded that those with strong religious beliefs were able to walk significantly farther on discharge and were less likely to be depressed.[8]

Finally, among severe burn patients who faced long, painful recoveries, researchers found anecdotal evidence that religious commitment was associated with an enhanced ability to cope.[9]

ATTENDANCE AT RELIGIOUS WORSHIP SERVICES AND PARTICIPATION IN RELIGIOUS GROUP ACTIVITIES

Attendance at worship services may correlate positively with health. Though at present this is unproven, epidemiological data from observational studies in which an association is gauged between a particular measure of religious involvement and the subsequent incidence of disease "suggest that religious involvement is a protective factor in healthy populations and thus apparently acts in a primary preventive fashion,"[10] including lessening hypertension, degenerative heart disease, and cervical cancer; and contributing to improved longevity. Another article reviewing twenty-seven epidemiological studies indicates that twenty-two of these studies show a positive correlation between frequent attendance at worship services and better health.[11]

Worship services and religious group activities provide a number of potentially therapeutic elements and health affirming and calming activities: music (including active participation in worship music), familiar rituals, prayer and contemplation, a sense of community as well as group support, distraction and respite from everyday tensions and the busyness of our hectic schedules, and increased social ties including opportunities for friendship and socializing.[12]

These benefits may be conferred due to an enhanced relationship with God or because of other factors including the commitment and effort required to participate in religious services, the lifestyle associated with regular participation, the social contact involved in worship services and other religious group activities, and the feelings of trust and interconnectedness accompanying a religious activity. At this point, experts do not know for certain.

What seems clear, however, is that we seem to feel better when we are with others who share our beliefs, values, and traditions. Group worship often elevates our mood, easing our anxieties and fears, increasing our energies, enhancing our sense of being loved, and helping overcome our social isolation.[13]

Co-worshipers can offer sufferers practical help, emotional support, and spiritual encouragement during times of crisis, such as illness. Coming together in worship provides a solid foundation on which we can build a supportive social network. Researchers have noted the existence of a strong relationship between worship attendance, larger social networks, and additional types of social support.[14] A heightened degree of social support is associated with fewer emotional problems and improved coping by those who are ill. One notable study of more than fifty-two hundred persons over twenty-eight years concludes that frequent attendance at religious services correlates with lower mortality rates, particularly among women, partly explained by improved health practices, increased social contacts, and more stable marriages.[15]

When we pray in a community we also gain the benefit of the company of others and may find comfort in knowing that the psalms, prayers, and blessings were and continue to be spoken by millions of Jews past and present who also yearn for healing. We relax in a feeling of safety. Being part of a meaningful community encourages a greater degree of self-expression, which can affect the course of an illness and promote our healing and our recovery.

Group worship also enables many of us also to reflect on the quieter, more peaceful time of our childhood. We are transported back to another time and place. According to Dr. Herbert Benson, "[T]he words you read, the songs you sing, and the prayers you invoke will soothe you in the same way they did in what was perhaps a simpler time in your life. . . . [T]he brain [retains] from childhood a visceral, active memory of the songs, symbols, words, and gestures so the body is invigorated and nourished when they are remembered."[16]

The interest of sufferers and the contemporary cry for a greater degree of community and social support has led to the emergence of free-standing Jewish worship services for healing. A service of healing combines traditional and contemporary prayers and blessings, as well as psalms, meditations, singing, and other Jewish elements. Some services incorporate relaxation exercises or guided imagery visualizations in which each participant imagines being transported to a comforting place. The services focus on helping people open up to God. The mood is warm and intimate. A healing service not only provides a liturgy designed to help people cope with the physical, emotional, and spiritual pain and suffering in their lives but also creates a community of comfort where individuals who suffer can gather. It is a structured time and place for prayer, personal sharing, reflection, meditation, and community connection for those coping with sickness as well as with all types of grief and loss. Thus the participants in this type of worship service include those who are ill (including the recently diagnosed as well as the chronically ailing), caregivers and friends of the ill, the bereaved, the spiritually needy, people with inner conflicts and interpersonal problems (including those going through divorce), and individuals who want to give thanks for being healed (or cured).

A stand-alone service provides a context of community with and for people who collectively acknowledge their pain and suffering and share the complex emotions emanating from their personal difficulties. The time for personal sharing and reflection provides comfort to the attendees and inspires a sense of lessened isolation.

The National Center for Jewish Healing (c/o Jewish Board of Family and Children's Services, 120 West 57th Street, New York, NY 10019, telephone 212-632-4705) can provide you with information on Jewish healing services in your community.

THE EFFICACY OF PRAYER AND MEDITATION

We pray and meditate when we are stricken with illness, whether physical or emotional, and experience the accompanying pain and suffering, especially when we are convinced that human assistance has exhausted its possibility of helping us. When hope in a human agency of curing is dimmed, we turn to God.

Prayer represents a universal way to achieve a union with God, the Master Healer. By keeping our attention anchored in the present moment, meditation enables us to go deeply within our own experience, our own uniqueness. Prayer and meditation represent powerful healing techniques. Through prayer and meditation we attain wholeness, integration, and harmony. Prayer and meditation can even facilitate physical and emotional recovery.

Prayer and meditation work. Studies indicate that spiritual practices are beneficial for illnesses with psychological components or those that can be aided by a more relaxed heart rate, lower blood pressure, or reduced muscle tension.[17] Researchers have concluded that a form of meditation, called the Relaxation Response, discussed in chapter 10, helps with chronic pain (including headaches and back pain), hypertension, heart disease, diabetes, ulcers, asthma, arthritis, and cancer. Specifically, cancer patients experienced decreased symptoms and better control of nausea and vomiting associated with chemotherapy. Individuals who had undergone open-heart surgery encountered less anxiety and fewer postoperative heart irregularities. Patients with cardiac irregularities experienced fewer of them. There was less anxiety and less need for medication for those undergoing painful X-ray procedures.[18]

At present, however, we do not exactly know how and why prayer and meditation work. Does God step in and heal? Or does prayer and meditation trigger a psychological or biochemical palliative in a patient?

Although entering into the realm of speculation, it is not unreasonable to conclude that prayer and meditation can invoke the Divine Presence. In the Talmud, Jewish sages indicate that God's presence hovers over the bed of a sick person, staying close to him or her. (*Nedarim* 40a) We are not alone because the Eternal is with us. We are also reminded that we are images of the Divine and that each of us is a special being with a spark of Divinity. Prayer and meditation connect us to the Jewish tradition, linking us to countless Jews over the centuries who have yearned for healing.

These spiritual practices, in the context of sickness, help us take a greater degree of control over a situation that may seem wildly out of our hands. We demonstrate that our illness has not rendered us powerless. Prayer and meditation permit us to change how we look at our plight. They allow us access and a connection to the deeper regions of our inner selves, helping us get in touch with our essential wholeness and strength and setting free our spirit's full resources.

Prayer and meditation also enhance our will and engage our capacity for hope and expectancy, the concerns and feelings of our heart for healing. They often provide a release and relief from our fears and anxieties that otherwise heighten physical and psychic pain. Prayer and meditation provide a refuge, a sense of calm and reflection, a sanctuary from often painful procedures and treatments, a distraction, some place to go. These practices are calming, quieting, grounding, and relaxing.

The mental relaxation accompanying prayer and meditation brings us comfort. Dr. Benson characterizes this as "remembered wellness," messages of healing that mobilize the body's resources. Through "remembered wellness," our bodies tap their design "to remember and revive health and well-being."[19] We remember our vigor from the time we felt our healthiest.

Ultimately, by invoking God's Presence, we realize that our well-being is not only in our hands, but, rather, in God's hands, and that the Eternal is the Source of all healing. Prayer and meditation help magnify our sense of gratitude, even for a small improvement in condition.

Prayer and meditation work in promoting healing, but as Dr. Larry Dossey concludes, "[T]here is no formula, no 'one best way' to pray that everyone should follow."[20] The one size, one approach does not fit all. There are many types of prayer and many ways of praying.

Dr. Dossey recommends choosing "a method that intuitively feels best," and fits your personality.[21] It depends on your temperament and your personality. For some, solitary, quiet, contemplative prayer and meditation, not traditional group worship, work best.

TYPES OF PRAYER

In focusing on prayer, let us examine two aspects: first, who is praying, the person who is suffering or others on his or her behalf; and second, the types of prayers offered, directed or nondirected.

Prayers Offered by a Sufferer

Many of us pray for our own healing and recovery when we are sick. Prayer serves as a powerful healing and curative technique and it's available to everyone. You do not need an intermediary to speak with God. Each of us has the opportunity to seek healing wherever and whenever we need it—in our residence, in a hospital room, or in our car. You can seek and discover God's Healing Presence on your own at any time.

Prayers Offered By Others

What about intercessory prayer, that is, prayer on behalf of another who is ill? As the Talmud tells us, if a person is sick for more than one day, he or she should let others know so that they can pray for him or her (*Berakhot* 55b).

If you are ailing, ask others to pray for you. Add your name to a synagogue or temple's prayer list, used by members to pray for those in need of healing. Jewish organizations should sponsor these prayer groups. By offering members' prayerful voices, these groups give God a channel through which to act and help provide sufferers with the strength to go on. To meet the needs of those who request prayers, take call-in requests through phone lines, voice mail, e-mail, and fax.

Prayers by others—relatives, friends, neighbors, and even strangers—contribute to the well-being of those who are sick and ailing. These are ways we let those who are ill know that they are important, they matter, and they are not alone. They foster a sense of belonging and being supported. Through the act of prayer, those who suffer feel the love of the Jewish community embracing them in their time of need.

Our prayers operate at a distance and are nonlocal. Distant, nonlocal prayer works, at least some of the time. In perhaps the most famous empirical study of distant, nonlocal prayer,[22] patients did not know anyone was praying for their recovery. Three hundred ninety-three patients, who had been hospitalized in the San Francisco General Hospital coronary care unit with actual heart attacks or severe chest pain, were studied for ten months. Half of the patients were assigned someone to pray on their behalf; the other half were not. Roman Catholic and Protestant home-based prayer groups from across the United States were invited to pray for 192 patients, at a distance, without their awareness. The prayer groups were given patients' names but little information about their conditions. They were asked to pray for the patients daily with no instructions on how to carry it out. Thus, each pray-er prayed for many different patients.

The results of the controlled, double-blind study in which neither the patients nor the physicians and nurses knew who was or who was not being prayed for are quite striking. In contrast to the unprayed-for control group, the prayed-for group was five times less likely to require newly prescribed antibiotics and three times less likely to develop fluid in the lungs as a result of a faulty heart. No one who was prayed for needed a breathing machine; twelve in the unprayed-for control group did. Fewer prayed-for patients died during the study, although the divergence is not statistically significant.

This study of distant, nonlocal prayer is not without its methodological questions. The patients may have suffered from too wide a range of heart problems to comprise a meaningful sample. No data was collected as to a patient's psychological state on entering the study, so that patients with psychological characteristics predisposing them to a better physical recovery might have been randomly allocated in greater numbers to the prayed-for group. The habits and techniques of physicians treating the patients were not controlled for. We lack information on amount, duration, and style of prayer practices among pray-ers. Did members of prayer group pray; if so how earnestly? Also, with respect to the unprayed-for control group: did their family or friends pray for them? What about prayer by the patients themselves and the degree of their religious convictions? The study leaves open all of these questions.

Intercessory prayer remains a "hot" research topic. More recently, researchers recruited forty advanced AIDS patients, half of whom received prayers and "distant healing" from spiritual healers throughout the United States chosen by reputation and experience; the other half received no such prayers. The forty subjects did not know to which group they were assigned. The twenty in the prayed-for group received ten weeks of daily prayers and healing from the spiritual healers, who were given a photograph of the patient, a first name, and basic medical information. Healers were assigned to patients on a rotating schedule that changed every week, thereby distributing the healers across the prayed-for group. This study indicates that the prayed-for group acquired fewer AIDS-defining illnesses, required fewer hospitalizations and physician visits, and showed more significant psychological improvement than the group that received no prayers from the healers.[23]

Stepping back from these specific studies of distant, nonlocal prayer, in summarizing a number of empirical studies, physician Larry Dossey states: "More than 130 controlled laboratory studies show, in general, that prayer or a prayerlike state of compassion, empathy, and love can bring about healthful changes in many types of living things, from humans to bacteria. This does not mean prayer *always* works, any more than drugs and surgery always work but that, statistically speaking, prayer is effective."[24] Over half of the studies cited by Dr. Dossey show statistical evidence that prayer has a significant, positive effect even if the recipient did not know that he or she was being prayed for.[25] People can exert healing influences on distant organisms at statistically significant levels. As Dr. Dossey concludes, "The evidence is simply overwhelming that prayer functions at a distance to change physical processes in a variety of organisms, from bacteria to humans."[26]

Thus prayer, which involves information being sent, not energy sent or received, is effective both at close range and at vast distances.[27] The degree of spatial separation does not matter. When you pray for another, your consciousness affects that person. You can help a sufferer recover. The pray-er and the patient are in some sense one. Connected and blended, they are united.

Why does distant prayer work? Once again we enter into the realm of speculation. However, from the perspective of Jewish Spirituality, God is omnipresent. The Eternal, Who transcends time and space, exists everywhere and in everyone. Whenever prayer is offered, it is always in God's presence.

Directed and Nondirected Prayer

Prayer can be either directed or nondirected. In a directed prayer—what I call petitionary prayer—the pray-er asks for a specific definite outcome—for instance, positive changes in his or her body, mind, or spirit. A directed prayer represents an intentional—if you will, an aggressive—prayer form.

Surprisingly enough, nondirected, open-ended prayer—what I call a prayer of surrender, such as "Thy will be done" or "Let it be,"—works. A nondirected prayer is not a petition for anything, such as an improved physical condition. It is free of any specific goals. It just asks for what is best. You let go of your preferred outcome and your demands, asking only that the greatest or highest good will prevail.

Through nondirected prayer, we accept without being passive, we are grateful without giving up, we honor the rightness of whatever happens. In a nondirected prayer, we experience feelings and emotions, but not as specific goals or preferred outcomes. In offering a nondirected prayer, we have faith and trust in God that the best outcome will prevail.

A nondirected prayer allows for pain and suffering, even death. Like Job, we need to realize that our knowledge is in fact limited. Thus, we can pray for the best potential in any situation because we do not know exactly what that is. The best outcome may be death in this earthly life, not a physical cure or even a holistic healing.

Nondirected prayers may be more effective than directed prayers, according to Dr. Dossey, at least for certain types of personalities who prefer a quiet, still type of prayerfulness. In reaching this conclusion, Dossey cites studies that nondirected prayer techniques "appeared quantitatively more effective, frequently yielding results that were twice as great, or more, when compared to the directed approach."[28]

Let us next focus on spiritually oriented prayers, meditations, and visualizations for healing and recovery. You can use these spiritual practices before taking medication or undergoing a conventional or alternative medical treatment or procedure. By connecting a particular medication, treatment, or procedure with God's healing power, these spiritual practices may not only facilitate your healing but also raise your hopes and expectations for a beneficial outcome.

HOW SPIRITUAL SEEKERS CAN PROMOTE
HEALING AND CURING

Whatever spiritual technique you use, you need first to admit you are sick. As the psalmist writes: "Have mercy on me, O God, for I languish; heal me, O God, for my bones are in agony." (Psalm 6:3) By acknowledging your illness, you can proceed with the healing process, requesting a reuniting of your mind, body, and spirit; and attain help from God, health care professionals, alternative medical practitioners, and loved ones.

Prayer

Through prayer, whether for your own healing or someone else's healing, you seek to connect to and communicate with God. Before considering prayers for another, let us first discuss prayers for your own healing and recovery.

You can offer various types of prayers—petitionary, affirmative, or surrender—for your own healing and restoration of health. Experiment with different forms of prayer. There are many ways of praying: verbally, silently, or with music. Prayer can be playful or serious. Realizing that words are not the only acceptable form of prayer, you need to discover what is appropriate for you. Prayer need not be a conscious, waking activity. You can pray in your dreams, unconsciously.

To engage in prayer for your own healing or recovery, select a quiet location. Get away from or turn off your answering machine, your computer, and your fax. Close your eyes to eliminate distractions. Relax and calm your body and mind with deep breathing. Sit or recline comfortably. Repeat whatever prayer you select once or twice a day, for ten to fifteen minutes, for several weeks. Be patient.

Petitionary Prayers

You can offer one of these petitionary prayers to invoke God's aid:

> Bring healing (or a cure) to my suffering, [specify the problem] O
> God, the most powerful and compassionate Healer.

Blessed are You, O God, Who brings healing (or curing). Please heal me. (Please cure my ———.)

God, please increase in me Your lifegiving and healing (or curing) power.

Affirmative Prayers

You can offer affirmative prayers for either your general health or a specific malady.

For your general health:

God fills me with perfect health and strength, strengthening the parts in me that can do the regeneration.

God expresses the Divine Presence in me through my perfect health and well-being.

God, Who gave me life, repairs me, restores my strength in accordance with the Divine goodness and lovingkindness.

God, the Source of all health, works wonders.

For a specific physical malady or an organ or limb:

The stream of Divine health and goodness flows into my ——— [specify organ or limb], filling it with abundant wellness, restoring me to perfect health and strength.

Health and wellness saturates my ——— [specify organ or limb], obliterating all my pain and suffering.

God removes the pain from my ———; the Eternal is restoring me to perfect health.

For mental or emotional illness, especially depression:

God fills me with joy.

Prayers of Surrender

You can give the situation over to God, after health care professionals and alternative practitioners have done the best they can for you. In praying for what is best for you, because you do not know what that is, offer one of the following prayers of surrender. Remember that God has many ways of helping you.

Thy will be done.

Whatever You think is good for me, what You think I should go through, please do it.

I trust in You, O Loving God, Who created and sustains me. I realize I am in Your control, an infinitely loving Presence. I am loved by the Eternal One.

Into God's hands I entrust my spirit, when I sleep and when I wake, and with my spirit and my body also, God is with me, I will not fear. (The last line of the *Adon Olom* [God Eternal] prayer, probably composed by Solomon ibn Gabriel [1021-1058 C.E.], Spanish-Jewish poet, hymn writer, and philosopher.)

If you are in such pain and suffering that you are unable to concentrate on any form of prayer, whether petitionary, affirmative, or surrender, then try to pray whenever you are as calm as you can be. With your eyes closed, repeat very slowly for as long as you can (or up to fifteen minutes): God removes all pain from my ———— [part of body or mind] and restores me to perfect health.

Crying Out To God

Express your anguish by crying out to God. Repeat your cries daily, for ten to fifteen minutes at a time. Pour out your heart to God—your hopes and your fears.

The Baal Shem Tov, in commenting on the psalmist's declaration, "O my God, I cried out loudly unto You and You did heal me" (Psalm 30:3) states, "This signifies that the act of crying unto God is itself a source of healing for spiritual ailments."[29]

Offer your own cries from your heart to God, the Supreme Healer. Express your feelings openly and honestly to God. Share your pain. Appeal to the Eternal for strength and guidance, for healing and comfort. Ask God to provide a helping hand to lift you up. Strive to reach out to God as never before.

Prayer for Lovingkindness

As you reflect on an appropriate mode of prayer, you might try to send a prayer of lovingkindness to your worst enemy or your most despised relative. Consider the following.

Dr. Melvin Morse, in his book *Transformed by the Light*,[30] recounts the story of a thirty-nine-year-old woman who had a non-life-threatening form of skin cancer, basal cell carcinoma, but who was convinced it was serious. The night before her surgery she was visited by a ball of light. She realized she was in the presence of something holy. As she started to pray for her cancer to be cured, the light told her that what we generally think of as prayer is more like complaining. If she wanted to pray, the light advised her to send love and light to her worst enemy. As she did so she felt that love reflected back, as though coming off a mirror to her. She also felt a physical shift in her body. It was as if her cells were coming alive with the life force. When she finished, the light told her that she had prayed for the first time in her life. In the morning, when she went to her doctor, the cancer was gone.

Recitation of Psalms

The late-eighteenth-century Hasidic master Rabbi Nachman of Breslov endured personal illness and suffering, including the deaths of two children and his wife. Viewing physical illness as the outward manifestation of an inner spiritual disturbance, he designated ten of 150 psalms as healing psalms, powerful spiritual remedies, capable of bringing about a wholeness of the body, mind, and spirit and a reintegration of the self. Rabbi Nachman called those ten psalms *Tikkun Haklai*, the Complete Remedy.[31] For Rabbi Nachman the therapeutic powers of these ten psalms could remove some of the underlying causes of illness, negativity, frustration, and especially depression (in other words, a lack of joy), the bane of our health and well-being.

As you recite the ten psalms designated by Rabbi Nachman, try to identify with first, the psalmist and the expressions of pain and longing; and second, the contents of the psalms in a deep and meaningful way, seeking to apply the words to yourself. A summary of the ten psalms is as follows:

Psalm 16. The psalmist, who is ill, asks for God's protection and rejoices that the Holy One will not abandon his soul. The psalmist feels the nearness of God and expresses confidence in the Divine protection.

Psalm 32. The psalm expresses the serious physical and mental consequences flowing from disharmony within one's soul. The psalmist concludes that God will save those who trust in the Eternal. Return to God as the Source of joy.

Psalm 41. In this psalm, a sufferer's prayer, the psalmist expresses thanks to God for the possibility of healing.

Psalm 42. The psalmist, in the depths of depression, realizes that God directs the flood of troubles but will be certain that the psalmist does not drown in them.

Psalm 59. This psalm, written as a prayer in a period of danger, manifests the psalmist's faith and trust in God to deliver us from the forces that oppress and cast us down.

Psalm 77. In this psalm of anguish and distress, the psalmist imagines that God may cast off the Jewish people. However, the psalmist is reminded of the wonders the Eternal has performed for the people of Israel. Despite appearances to the contrary, God is ever present and compassionate.

Psalm 90. Although each person's existence is transitory, the psalmist asks for God's help in understanding the consequences of a life wasted on unworthy and ineffectual pursuits. The psalm concludes with a desire for God to endow human striving with some of the Eternal's own enduring power and significance.

Psalm 105. The psalmist offers us ways to heal, including not sinking into victimhood. By singing songs to God, each of us can raise our soul, aiding the healing process.

Psalm 137. The psalmist points to the importance of continuing to sing and how the thought of Jerusalem brings the promise of hope and some degree of spiritual healing.

Psalm 150. Again, the psalmist, in mentioning some of the instruments played more than two thousand years ago and used to praise God, reminds those who are ill to continue to sing to the Eternal.

MEDITATION

Meditation helps you clear your mind of its ongoing, crazy chatter. By calming and focusing your mind, freeing it from negative thoughts and helping you relax, meditation enables you to enter into a state of awareness, stillness, and inner silence for a period of time. You begin to experience an inner peace and a transcendent vision. As you forget yourself, you feel the presence of God. You reconnect to the Eternal, the Source of comfort and healing. Thus, meditation helps provide the psychic space for you to identify and connect with the Holy One.

In addition to Relaxation Response, set forth in chapter 10, sufferers find the Guardian Angel Meditation of considerable help.

Although most Jews in modern times are uncomfortable with the idea of angels, the Hebrew Bible contains numerous references to various angels—not the Hollywood variety with halos and wings.[32] The term "angel" generally denotes a messenger. Angels are spiritual forces given human form: the angel who stops Abraham from sacrificing Isaac (Genesis 22:11-12); the angels who appear on Jacob's ladder (Genesis 28:12); the angel who tells Manoach and his wife of the impending miraculous birth of Samson. (Judges 13:9-20) These are some of the Bible's many nonhuman messengers.

Biblical literature also refers to other, rather strange kinds of angels. For example, the prophet Isaiah describes the seraphim, winged, burning angels. (Isaiah 6:6) The prophet Ezekiel has a vision of the Divine chariot-throne moved by four strange, four-faced winged creatures. (Ezekiel 1:4-20)

In short, angels fill the Jewish tradition. Although portrayed as having a wide range of power they usually, but not always, represent spiritual forces for goodness. Angels are sent to help us, and individuals who are ill often receive a sense of comfort and healing from the Guardian Angel Meditation.

Guardian Angel Meditation. Introduction: Try to create a warm, welcoming atmosphere, an environment of serenity and spaciousness for the journey within. Lower the lights, if possible. Candles can set a mood that enhances meditation. Close your eyes; sit quietly; calm and relax your body by sitting, reclining or lying down; breathe in and out normally, feeling where the breath flows into and out of the body. Adjust the breaths so that the in and out breaths are the same length, thereby bringing about both a relaxation of the body and an alertness of the mind. (Obviously, vary these instructions depending on your physical condition.)

Invoke the angel Michael, the angel of love and kindness, on your right side. Shift your attention and focus it there. Ask Michael to be with you because sometimes your own love fails, when you are unkind or judgmental. Tell Michael that you wish to receive an experience of caring and generosity, which will warm you more than you could have ever imagined. Stay with this experience.

Then, invoke the angel Gabriel, the angel representing the strength and courage of God who helps us overcome fear and worry, on your left side. Again, shift your attention there and focus on it. Ask Gabriel to help you overcome your fears and worries related to your illness. Tell Gabriel that you wish to draw strength and courage from God to overcome the challenges that you face. Stay with this experience.

Invite Raphael, the angel who represents the healing power of God, who is behind you, to come into your body, specifically into the painful areas. If it is God's will, tell Raphael that you want to experience a healing in the physical, mental, and spiritual realms and even a cure.

Imagine the angel Uriel, the light of God, in front of you. Allow this light to be as bright as you wish. Ask Uriel, who provides insight and understanding that come from outside our own minds, to help you know and understand what is happening.

Feel the presence of these four angels. Call on each of them. They are there for you.

Finally, imagine the Divine Light above your body flowing into your heart and through your body. That light is the Shekhinah, the feminine aspect of God. Allow the light to surround you with love and encompass you with a protective inner peace. Help is all around you.

Concluding Instructions: Come back to the here and now. Take time to ease yourself back. Slowly bring your awareness back into your body. Feel yourself back in the room and open your eyes.

VISUALIZATION

Visualization—imagery—is an effective tool for helping you see the changes you need to make and how you can go about making them. A mental picture serves as one of the most powerful commands you can send your mind.

Visualization helps you develop healthy ways to meet the needs represented by an illness. Your symptoms, your pain, and your suffering indicate that something within you is out of balance, that something needs adjustment, adaptation, or change. Imaging lets you see the big picture and experience the way an illness is related to events and feelings you may have considered unimportant. You see how a single piece is connected to the whole.

Visualization can be either receptive-passive or active.[33] A receptive, more passive visualization helps you become aware of your unconscious patterns and needs as well as your potential for change. It is a form of diagnostic imagery. Relaxing and emptying your mind, you pose a question and await a response. You make contact with your inner, subjective reality. You pay attention to images arising in response to questions you ask in a relaxed state of mind.

This type of visualization aids you by pointing to one or more physical, emotional, or spiritual problems needing resolution before a more profound and enduring healing (or even the curing of symptoms) can proceed.

An active visualization communicates your conscious intentions to your mind. You imagine your desired goal, a specific, favorable experience—for instance, your healing, a wholeness of your body-mind-spirit, or your immune system's cells carrying away your cancer cells away—as if already achieved, while maintaining a relaxed state of mind. Identifying with what you want to achieve, you sow the seeds of healing information into the unconscious levels of your mind.

An active visualization is therapeutic, promoting healing, helping alleviate symptoms and facilitating your recovery. In triggering physical, mental, and emotional reactions, the images possess the power to affect your mind and body. Whatever you think and imagine deeply impacts on your mind and body. The visualization process enhances your innate capacity to attain and maintain your health. An active visualization will help you relax, relieve your anxiety and pain, provide a greater degree of tolerance for medical procedures, heighten your ability to cope with your illness, and in general assist you in gaining a greater sense of control over your situation.

A spiritually oriented, active visualization, focusing on God's healing and restorative powers and asking them to work for you, helps you. By visualizing the Eternal giving and you receiving healing (or the desired cure), you place yourself more directly in tune with the Infinite and make yourself more susceptible to the influx of God's blessing.

Engage in a visualization exercise once or twice a day for ten to fifteen minutes, for three weeks. Remember to select a quiet location. Turn off your answering machine, your computer, and your fax. Take the phone off the hook. Relax your body, calm your mind, and go to your still inner place. Be patient.

The more fully you visualize something, the more real it seems to your brain. Use as many of your senses as possible during your visualizations.

Active Visualizations for Healing and Recovery.   Introduction: Relax your body by getting into a comfortable position; lie or sit down. Close your eyes, thereby eliminating external distractions from the range of vision. Take several deep, full breaths, then let go of these breaths. Allow your breath to enter your nostrils and follow it through your throat to your chest, heart, and lungs. Exhale gently through your nostrils, allowing the release of all that is stale and hurting your body-mind-spirit, to go back to the Source of Life. As you continue to breathe comfortably and easily, relax your body and let go of unnecessary tensions.

For a physical illness: Bring your attention to each part of the body, thinking of how it is made up. As part of this tour of your body, invite each part to relax. Begin with your scalp, then the muscles of your face and eyes, arms, hands, torso, legs, and feet. Relax your muscles as much as you can.

For a mental illness: Place your mind in a state of calmness and ease.

Visualize the affected part of your body or mind receiving the stream of Divine well-being, penetrating the place from which the pain comes, and washing away the affliction. Visualize yourself, the whole of yourself, your body, mind, and spirit, as healthy.

Or, visualize the state of physical or mental health you want to attain. Then visualize God giving you the desired health and your receiving this desired health. Visualize waves of health-promoting energy coming from God. Feel the bliss and joy.

Or, visualize yourself surrounded by a white, healing light, a warm glowing energy of God. Visualize that you are healed and restored to wholeness. Visualize that your specific ailment—physical or mental— is cured.

Or, visualize waves of curative energy of warmth and bliss, a cleansing stream of light, coming from God, passing through the painful part of your body or your mind, and washing away the pain in your ———.

Or, visualize the breath of life, coming to you from the Eternal and penetrating your ———.

Or, visualize your illness, for example, cancer cells growing in your body. Visualize a health-promoting solution coming from God, for example, disease-fighting white blood cells carrying away your cancer cells.

Concluding Instructions: Come back to the here and now. Take time to ease yourself back. Slowly bring your awareness back into your body and mind. Feel yourself back in the room and open your eyes.

Another Visualization Combining Passive and Active Imagery. Introduction: Follow the introductory instructions for the active visualizations above.

Visualize your special inner place of peacefulness and healing. Look around and notice the shapes and colors. Listen to the sounds and smell the fragrances. Make certain that the image is detailed and evocative.

Imagine being at the top of an imaginary staircase. Descend one step at a time, going deeper ever more comfortably, relaxing with each descending stair—ten, nine, eight, seven, six, five, four, three, two, one steps. You are more relaxed, comfortable, and pleasant. Your body is relaxed yet your mind is aware.

Go into your special inner place of deep relaxation and healing, a place of total peacefulness and complete safety for you. See the shapes and colors. Hear the sounds. Smell the smells.

Focus your attention on your physical or mental symptoms. Allow an image to emerge for each symptom. Accept the image, familiar or strange, whether it makes sense or not, whether you like it or not. Take time to observe the image. Ask yourself: What is it that represents the symptom?

Let another image appear that represents the curing of each symptom coming from God. Allow it to arise spontaneously. Allow it to become clearer and more vivid. Ask yourself: What is it about this image that represents curing of this symptom and the healing and restoration of wholeness of your mind-body-spirit?

Consider the images of your symptom and your healing together. How do they relate to each other? Which is larger? More powerful? Visualize the image of the healing (and curing) becoming stronger and more powerful than the image of your symptom. Visualize the image of the symptom turning into the image of healing (and curing). How does transformation happen: suddenly or gradually? Is what is happening related to anything in your life?

Focus clearly and powerfully on the healing (and curing) image. Visualize the healing (and curing) taking place now in your body or mind just at the right place. Do you feel or imagine any changing sensations as you visualize the healing (and curing) taking place? Affirm to yourself that the healing (and curing) is happening now— and the healing (and curing) continues whether you are sleeping, waking, or going about your daily activities.

Concluding Instructions: Slowly open your eyes. Prepare to return to your waking consciousness. Visualize yourself at the bottom of your imaginary staircase. Begin to ascend one, two, three . . . ten steps. Become more aware of your surroundings. When you reach the tenth step become awake and alert, feeling refreshed, relaxed, and more whole than before.[34]

As you work with any type of visualization, keep a journal or a notebook to record your experience with healing; your feelings, thoughts, and questions; and your progress. Record your symptoms and your levels of stress and activity. Regularly review your journal to see what you have learned and spot recurring patterns needing more attention and exploration.

PRAYER, MEDITATION, AND VISUALIZATION FOR OTHERS

Techniques for praying, meditating, or visualizing for others depend on whether or not you are in the presence of the sufferer. When you invoke spiritual practices on behalf of another, remember to place yourself in the other's situation.

In the Presence of a Sufferer

You can offer a prayer or a guided meditation for a sufferer. A guided meditation represents another way of going within—but in this instance, the journey is led by someone outside who guides the sufferer, with a focused message, to a place where he or she can have the opportunity to meet with God. A guided meditation thus provides the sufferer with an opening beyond his or her ordinary state of being, affording the opportunity to experience a deeper and more profound state of being.

In a guided meditation (or visualization), the guide serves as the facilitator. For a successful guided meditation (or visualization), the guide-facilitator needs not only to direct the process but also to enter into the spirit of the meditation (or visualization).

The Guardian Angel Meditation in this chapter serves as an especially powerful guided meditation. The guide can also offer the following guided visualization for ten to fifteen minutes, once a day, for three weeks. Again, the guide and the sufferer should be patient.

Guided Visualization for Recovery. Introduction: Both the guide and the sufferer should relax their bodies, eliminating all tensions from mind and body, and close their eyes. The guide should remain active and awake.

The guide should visualize the sufferer as the recipient of God's curative powers.

For a physical ailment, the guide should visualize a stream of curative powers coming from God and flowing into the body of the sick person, penetrating and saturating the ailing body part, purifying and carrying away the pain. Visualize the sick person becoming completely well and in perfect health and well-being.

For a mental illness, the guide should visualize the sufferer as receiving Divine rays of serenity and inner peace. Visualize the sufferer as filled with joy, calmness, and equanimity. Visualize the sufferer as radiant, happy, full of optimism, with his/her mental agony receding, the storm in his or her mind cleared away, with tranquility and peace of mind restored.

Concluding Instructions: The guide should invite the sufferer to come back to the here and now. Tell the sufferer to take time to ease himself or herself back. Slowly bring awareness back into his or her body and mind.

Outside the Presence of a Sufferer:
Distant Prayers and Visualizations

A pray-er can offer prayers and visualizations outside the presence of the sufferer. Jews have traditionally offered the *Mi-Shebeirakh* prayer, "May God Who blessed our ancestors, bless and heal ———, a sick person," on behalf of others outside their presence.

The *Mi-Shebeirakh*, a holistic prayer for a full healing (*refuah shlayma* in Hebrew)—a spiritual healing, a healing of body and soul, the attaining of wholeness—asks God's blessing and compassion and for a sufferer's restoration and strength as follows:

> May the One Who blessed our ancestors Abraham, Isaac, Jacob, Sarah, Rebecca, Rachel, and Leah, bless and heal ———, who is ill. May the Holy One of Blessing shower abundant miracles on him/her, fulfilling his/her dreams of healing, strengthening him/her with the power of life.
> Merciful One:
> restore him/her,
> heal him/her,
> strengthen him/her,
> enliven him/her,
> Send him/her a complete healing from the heavenly realms, a healing of body and a healing of soul, together with all who are ill, soon, speedily, without delay; and let us say: Amen!

The *Mi-Shebeirakh* is recited in the synagogue after the reading of the Torah. If the sufferer cannot be present at the worship service, a close relative or friend is called up to the Torah for an honor (*aliya* in Hebrew). The prayer is offered after the completion of the *aliya* to the Torah reading, filling in the name of the person who is ill. The prayer can also be said before and after surgery, during treatments, or on admission or discharge from a hospital.

At the end of the *Mi-Shebeirakh* prayer, we pray for the individual person, who is called by name together with all who are ill. If you are ill, being included in a collective prayer can be a source of comfort. You are not alone; there are many who suffer. Pain and suffering is a part of life. When we are ill there is a natural tendency to isolate. Realizing that you are not the only one singled out for hardship furthers your spiritual healing. The prayer provides comfort, letting sufferers know that they are still part of the community.

In addition to the *Mi-Shebeirakh* prayer, as part of the *Shemoneh Esreh*—the most important part of the traditional Jewish weekday worship services next to the *Shema*—we recite the *Refaeinu* prayer, a petitionary prayer for healing those who are sick and relieving all who suffer pain.

Heal us, God, and we will be healed; save us and we will be saved, because You are our praise. Bring a full healing for all our pains and sufferings, because You are God, the most powerful, faithful, and compassionate Healer. God please heal ——[designate specific individuals]. Blessed are You, God, Who heals the sick.[35]

A communal worship service can also include other prayers for sufferers. For example:

May the Source of strength Who helped the ones before us help us
find the courage to make our lives a blessing.
Let us say: Amen
Bless those in need of healing with *refuah shlayma*
The renewal of body, the renewal of spirit
Let us say: Amen.

A pray-er can also use one of the following visualizations for a sufferer outside the pray-er's presence. Again, this can be offered once or twice a day, for ten to fifteen minutes, for at least three weeks.

Distant Visualizations for Healing and Recovery. Introduction: The pray-er should place himself or herself in prayerful state of mind, eliminating extraneous thoughts. The pray-er should relax his or her body and mind, and close his or her eyes.

Visualize the sufferer as present, seated opposite in a relaxed position, eyes closed, body at ease. Visualize the sufferer surrounded by a bright, healing light. Imagine that he or she is healed, restored to wholeness.

If the affliction is physical, visualize restoration as coming from God in the form of a stream of light, penetrating into the affected part of the sufferer's body and purifying the sufferer's body from all pain and suffering. If the affliction is mental, visualize rays of joy and tranquility radiating from God, saturating the sufferer's mind and restoring his or her inner peace and wholeness.

Concluding Instructions: The pray-er should come back to the here and now. Slowly bring awareness back to your body and mind. Feel yourself back in the room and open your eyes. On completing this visualization, the prayer may want to recite the *Refaeinu* prayer, indicating the name of the sufferer.

How you pray, meditate, or visualize—the quality of your spiritual practices—is more important than how often you pray, meditate, or visualize—their quantity. Remember to be patient.

ENHANCING THE EFFICACY OF SPIRITUAL PRACTICES FOR HEALING

The efficacy of your spiritual practices for healing and recovery depends upon a number of factors, including: not blaming yourself, developing your faith and trust in God, taking on more responsibility, cultivating a positive outlook, reframing your situation, engaging in selfless service and altruism, participating in social support networks, and recognizing the need for patience.

DON'T BLAME YOURSELF

Guilt often enters into the equation when you are ill. Do not blame yourself for getting sick. Do not ask: Why me? Rather, thank your limbs, organs, cells, and molecules for faithfully sustaining you for as long as they have. Adopt a forgiving, rather light-hearted attitude to your body and your mind.

Even if you have done the "right" preventative things and you get sick (or a chronic condition fails to improve), your illness is not a spiritual failure. A multitude of causal factors—such as genes, family and personal history, environment, lifestyle, nutrition, general health habits, and accidents—all enter into the picture. Modern Western medical science, as well as alternative medicine, simply does not know what causes some diseases or their cures.

Do not worry that you brought your condition, physical or mental, on yourself as a result of some type of behavior or personality characteristic. God is not punishing you. Illness is not sent to purify your character. Your illness is not deserved.

DEVELOP YOUR FAITH AND TRUST IN GOD

Spiritual practices for healing and recovery depend on a clear realization of the Divine Presence, an unfaltering faith in God's infinite goodness, and an unbounded trust in God's love. The future remains open, no matter how bleak the present may be or seem. You are not alone. You can draw on the Holy Presence as a source of guidance, support, and benefit. God is with you in your time of need. Remember that somehow the Eternal suffers when you do.

Bear in mind that you are inherently a Divine being and an integral part of God's plan for the cosmos. Reaffirm daily that you are a child of God, Who will not desert you. Thus, a positive belief in spiritual practices, a realization that your prayers are acceptable, and the beneficent spiritual influences God constantly sends each of us are of vital importance in helping you remain alive.

Develop and deepen your faith and trust that everything is in God's hands and everything the Eternal does is for the best: your joy and sadness, your health and sickness, your hope and loss. Realize your life as ultimately being one with God, our Creator and Sustainer. See God as a partner working with you in your healing.

Effective spiritual practices must be sincere; they must come from your own heart. God wants your wholeheartedness, your genuine devotion. Reach out to, communicate with, and connect with the Supreme Sovereign. Pray, meditate, or visualize with concentration and a total effort of your entire being. Sincerely yearn for a wholeness and a healing of your body, mind, and spirit.

When you pray, meditate, or offer a visualization for yourself or for another, whether in his or her presence or not, offer your spiritual practices with faith and trust in the Eternal. Rely on Divine help. Offer your spiritual practices when you are steeped in serenity; with a cheerful heart (not a heart submerged in sorrow); when your mind is not excited, irritated, or impatient. Be free from worry, fear, anxiety, stress, anger, hatred, envy, or bitterness.

TAKE ON MORE RESPONSIBILITY

Each of us has a responsibility to pull himself or herself along. Play an active, responsible role not only in preventative health care but also in your healing and recovery when facing a life-threatening illness.

You must take responsibility for your own health and well-being. You are the central factor. Bernie Siegel, the noted oncologist and best-selling author of *Love, Medicine, and Miracles*,[36] concludes that an unshakable relationship with one's own internal will and its encounter with God characterizes "exceptional cancer patients," not their faith in a physician's medical skills and powers.

These exceptional patients feel more in control of their fate. They perceive that they are the masters of their destinies. They are willing to take on responsibility for and participate in decisions related to their health. They want to enter into more equal relationships with their health care professionals. Being empowered can speed their recovery and minimize their discomfort.

They are not submissive, passive sufferers. Rather they are responsible, assertive participants, who express their personal rights and feelings. They argue with their health care professionals. Seeking solutions, they are open to exploring new avenues for healing and curing.

These exceptional patients also manifest a fighting spirit, an attribute of optimism: hoping for the best—associated with a realistic appraisal of their illness—yet preparing for the worst. They communicate clearly and openly with health care professionals, and express appropriate emotions.[37] They are also willing to look at their lives beyond their physical illness to what they have contributed in the past and what they will accomplish with the time they still have.

As part of this new healing paradigm, health care professionals and alternative practitioners will serve as valuable resources for these confident, resilient, more self-reliant, high self-esteem individuals, each of whom will define his or her own personal visions of health and learn from and respond to life's adversities. These empowered individuals will, to a significant degree, pursue their own healing and recovery. Armed with new skills, resources, and capacities; a more expansive understanding of health and disease; and their faith and trust in God Who is able to contribute to human emotional and spiritual empowerment, they will assert their primary role in healing and, if possible, recovery from illness. They will make more conscious and self-directed choices. Increasingly, they will not look to health care professionals as the final authority on issues of health and healing.

Whether through your spiritual practices, your social support network, or your assertiveness, as a patient you must desire to be helped. Cherish hope and foster encouragement. Always remember that you can appeal to God for the things requisite to your healing and regeneration that cannot be obtained through Western (or alternative) medicine.

CULTIVATE A POSITIVE OUTLOOK

Hope and optimism help in healing, leading to a wholeness of mind-body-spirit and to better medical outcomes. Drugs and procedures are more effective when you are in a hopeful state of mind. Our thoughts have a magical power. You have probably heard stories of critically ill people whose cheerful attitudes helped them recover.

When you are ailing, try not to be fearful or to worry. Do not sink into a morass of negativity. Of course, this is not easy; however, strive to face life with optimism and courage. Sometimes illness may appear to crush us, mentally and emotionally. Do not brood over your ailment; otherwise you will encourage it. You can help drive out or destroy illness by minimizing your physical or mental problems, making light of its dangers, and striving for cheerful thoughts and talk. The more joy you hold in your thought, speech, and deeds, the faster you will drive illness away.

In *Anatomy of an Illness*,[38] Norman Cousins championed the ideal that humor can help restore one's health. Cousins provides anecdotal evidence of the benefits derived from his own use of old episodes of the television show "Candid Camera," Marx Brothers movies, and humor books to overcome a rare and painful illness. As the saying goes, "laughter is good medicine."

Cousins notes that laughter has rejuvenating effects on the body and the mind. It relaxes muscles and reduces blood pressure and heart rate. Laughter, what Cousins terms "internal jogging," gets your attention off of yourself and your situation. It provides the distance needed for a new and better perspective on your situation.

For many of us, music provides useful opportunities for opening our hearts and getting in touch with inner feelings of joy and optimism. When recovering, to lift your spirits and keep in a positive mental framework, listen to your favorite joyful music.

If you worry and become fearful and dejected when you are sick, you prevent the stream of Divine healing from asserting itself. A gloomy mental state often has a pernicious impact on your health. Hopelessness and despair kill. You can die as a result of negative beliefs and a sense of overwhelming futility. If your mind and your heart believe that your body is beyond hope, if they are convinced that recovery will not come, your progress will be greatly prolonged or will prove impossible. The natural killer cells of your immune system, which protect you against invading viruses, are weakened by a number of emotional factors, including loneliness and depression.

Studies indicate that people who suffer a heart attack while depressed (or who become depressed subsequent to a heart attack) are significantly more likely to die in the following six to twenty-four months than nondepressed heart attack victims.[39] Patients with a low level of blood flow to the heart (ischemic heart disease) who had depressive disorders and severely negative thinking, had, on average, 1.6 times as many episodes of the disease. They were 1.5 times as likely to die from it.[40] Physical symptoms mirror emotional issues.

Place yourself in a state conducive to and compatible with healing and the restoration of health, which flows when your inner state is relaxed and serene. Be a receptive channel through which Divine healing may flow. Your peace of mind and self-love send a "live" message to your body.

A degree of realism is in order. When facing a situation beyond cure, those who are able to find the means to deny cope best. Such denial is not only permissible, it may be the only means of sanity. Also, as one expert on coping with stress and stress-related diseases concludes, "Hope for the best and let that dominate most of your emotions, but at the same time let one small piece of you prepare for the worst."[41]

REFRAME YOUR PAIN AND SUFFERING

Listen to your body and try to put your pain, which may be a blessing in disguise, in perspective. Physical distress, such as headaches or back pain, or emotional discomfort, such as depression or anger, are messengers drawing attention to unhealthy conditions developing within you. They are messages from your body and mind. If you are in physical pain, you know that some destructive process is at work—some irregularity in your conduct, some excess in your habits—requiring immediate attention. As a physical signal, pain enables you to seek help for the restoration of your health.

In particular, physical pain provides a warning and may protect us from even greater woe. Without the warning provided by pain, an even more severe illness might develop without your knowledge, to the point where you could die prematurely. Without the warning of physical distress, your body might be abused to the point where it could suffer irreparable damage. Thus, physical pain serves a warning light. It urges you to seek the needed measures for healing and to bring your body, spirit, and mind back to their complete and healthy state.

How you interpret and respond to your pain, a physical signal, and suffering, your response to the signal provided by pain, may make you stronger, at least from a spiritual perspective. Try to reframe your situation, searching out positive ways of viewing your difficulties.

In one of Rabbi Nachman's tales, "The Seven Beggars,"[42] all of the seven heroes are beggars, at the lowest of most people's scale of success. Each of them is terribly disabled: One is blind, another deaf, a third dumb, one has a crooked neck, another is hunchback, one has no hands, and the last no legs. Yet each turns his or her seeming disability into an advantage. They all owe their success to their special disadvantage. As beggars, each knows he or she has nothing in this material world and must depend on God for everything. The moral of the story: You must ask God to show you how to take advantage of even the worst of situations. Focus on the deeper meaning of your pain.

See a life crisis, such as a severe, life-threatening illness, as a wake-up call, a challenge sent by God. As the author of Proverbs reminds us: "For whom God loves, does God reprove, as a parent its child." (Proverbs 3:12) The Holy One, in the Eternal's Wisdom, may be choosing you for an extra-difficult assignment.

Perceive a life crisis as something enabling you to grow in wisdom and love and to learn from. It is an opportunity for positive change, not a threat. Sickness may serve as a teacher, a source of spiritual insight and renewal of strength. The worst can yield some benefit. Pain and suffering represent an opportunity to turn your life around. Illness may serve, paradoxically, as an agent of your healing.

An ailment may represent a wake-up call to shock you out of complacency, or spiritual sleep. The noted author C. S. Lewis, a widely known defender of Christianity, writes, "God whispers to us in our pleasures, speaks in our conscience, but shouts in our pains: it is [the Divine] megaphone to rouse a deaf world."[43]

Your pain and suffering contain a meaning and an opportunity for growth. Ask yourself: What is it that God is trying to get me to learn about myself? What can I learn from my illness? How can my affliction help me heal my life and find out who I am?

Your illness opens the pathways to self-examination. What is your purpose in life? What are your values, needs, and priorities? What are your strategies for attaining your goals and priorities? Where do you want to put your time and your energies?

Through your illness, you may begin to see what you truly believe in life. You may find new meaning in life and new reasons for living. As developed in chapter 10, we all need a sense of meaning and direction in our lives, a sense of purpose. What is your unique life purpose?

A sense of meaning and purpose gives you the strength to endure life's upsets. Ask yourself what it is that you are here for. From the perspective of Jewish Spirituality, it is to contribute love to the world, to express and experience unconditional love, and to be drawn out of yourself into a larger whole.

Find your fulfillment in spiritual values and interactions with others. You may need to learn to open your heart in love to others— your family, friends, neighbors, colleagues, even God; to forgive; and to be more truthful. Ask yourself what is preventing you from living your life with as much lovingkindness, forgiveness, and truthfulness as you can?

Fever, exhaustion, and pain, of course, may make sustained introspection difficult, or almost impossible. Yet physical and emotional suffering can be conducive to deeper insight and self-understanding.

As you recover, you may need to alter the bad habits that brought about the affliction from which you suffered. You may also need to heal your deeper, spiritual maladies. You may need to pursue a life of calm, not excitement; a life of inner peace, not anger, envy, or impatience; a life of humility, self-esteem, self-reliance, self-confidence, and courage, not pride, fear, worry, or sorrow. Hopefully, you will experience a more joyful and meaningful life—how good it feels to be at peace with yourself, with others, and with God.

The poet and environmental activist Gale Warner was thirty years old in November 1990, when she went into the hospital for an investigation of a light but persistent cold. A chest X ray revealed a mass in her lung the size of an avocado. A biopsy the next day confirmed the diagnosis: an aggressive form of non-Hodgkins lymphoma.

Warner recorded her experiences in a journal until her death nearly thirteen months later. *Dancing at the Edge of Life*,[44] her posthumous memoir of her fight against cancer, records Warner's determination to carve meaning out of her life. "I tell my friends that my first six months of cancer was my master's degree in love and life," she writes. "Now I'm in the doctoral program." Even on her worst nights, when Warner starkly faced the fear of failure and her own despair, she continued to seek out the lessons from her suffering. She continued to recount: "This is another teaching." News of a relapse was followed by even greater dedication to her living with meaning.

Like Gale Warner, your pain and suffering can be turned into a source of profound insight and strength. Endure and maintain a happy face. Proceed on your life despite your affliction. In so doing, you inspire others to continue their lifelong journeys, and to say "yes" to life.

Ultimately, you may be thankful for your pain and suffering. Your ailment may help you achieve self-improvement and a measure of enlightenment. Make the most of the situation. Even if you are not cured, you can be healed by linking your outer self to your inner self, your spirit within to others and to God. Remember: Healing represents a movement to the wholeness of your body, mind, and spirit.

BENEFITS OF ALTRUISM

Love, compassion, and selfless service may enter into healing and even into curing physical symptoms. Love and compassion influence the effectiveness of our spiritual practices. Conversely, if love and compassion are not present, prayers, meditations, and visualizations are less effective. Thus, as you turn to others, pray-ers on your behalf, you need to enlist people whom you love and who love you.

To overcome physical or mental infirmities, develop a sense of altruism—a fuller life shared with the rest of humanity—through your unconditional love, your selfless service, and your participation in the life of the community. There is a healing power in "doing good."

You can begin by performing small acts of kindness toward others in daily life, out of your unconditional love for them. Look at each person you meet during the day and love him or her without expecting anything in return. You will experience the fact that you are not alone. As you extend your love, your very essence, you will gradually forget about your pain and suffering, whether physical or mental. You will gradually detach yourself from your mental image of weakness, isolation, or hopelessness.

Those who are suffering from serious illness can strive to help repair the world through selfless service. Even with a disability, you should do what you can for others. This will bring new meaning to your existence. Experiencing the joyfulness of living, through a useful, other-directed activity, will help you begin to transcend your pain and suffering.

In his book *The Healing Power of Doing Good*,[45] Allan Luks summarizes surveys he conducted involving the relationship between altruism and well-being. Luks discovered that people who help others report better health than their peers in their respective age groups. Luks calls this phenomenon the "helper's high."

Luks concludes that people who regularly engaged in helping activities involving personal contact, particularly with strangers who needed the help, without regard to the outcome, experienced "feel-good" sensations directly associated with better self-perceived physical health. Volunteers surveyed indicated they experienced relief from pain symptoms, including chronic headache, back pain, and stomach ache. Biochemical changes, particularly increased production of endorphins, muffle the pain message and distract the sufferer from his or her discomfort. Also reported were relief from symptoms of chronic diseases, including arthritis, lupus, and asthma, as well as a hastening of recovery from surgery.[46] Volunteers also claimed emotional benefits, both short-term—a sense of euphoria, a greater sense of calmness and relaxation, increased energy, and a general sense of emotional well-being—and long-term—a feeling of tranquility, improved self-esteem, greater optimism, and decreased depression.[47]

The benefits of helping strongly correlated to the consistency of their helping behavior. For instance, the long-term emotional benefits occurred only when people engaged in a regular regime of helping activities over sustained time periods. The frequency of helping is also critical: Weekly (about two hours a week of one-to-one helping) is much better than monthly or one-time volunteer endeavors. It is also important to let go of the results, Luks maintains, and just feel close to and empathize with the person you are trying to help.[48] Exert yourself to reach out; extend yourself, either physically or emotionally.

Volunteer endeavors help the volunteer. Helping others improves the health of the helper. By focusing on others, we forget our own problems. We are distracted from the source of our pain.

The act of helping others may be an especially effective means of developing a network for healing social support. Why? Volunteering enables helpers to develop close relationships and provides purpose and meaning to their lives. A sense of social connection paves the way for the sensation of the "helper's high." By enriching the lives of others you enrich and heal yourself.

PARTICIPATE IN SOCIAL SUPPORT NETWORKS

Sufferers should also participate in social networks. Social support helps us. We realize that we are not alone in facing life's difficulties. Friends and family can offer practical help and information, emotional support, and spiritual encouragement. All this is beneficial for your recovery. Empirical studies show that social contact helps extend the length and quality of life. Close social relationships correlate with a lower risk of dying at any age. They are also associated with the increased likelihood of recovery from serious illness and triumph over the dark shadow of depression.

Researchers have concluded that diversified social networks—being married; interacting with friends, family, colleagues, and neighbors; and belonging to social and religious groups—lead to better health. Two studies at opposite ends of the illness spectrum, the common cold and breast cancer, illustrate this point. One study of 276 subjects reported that individuals with a greater variety of social relationships were more able to resist cold viruses.[49]

Even more significantly from the perspective of those suffering from catastrophic illnesses, in a widely cited study researchers found that women suffering from advanced breast cancer who participated in support groups lived an average of eighteen months longer than those patients who did not—a significant difference.[50] This study demonstrates the power of interpersonal connectedness to improve physical health.

Groups composed of people linked only by a common chronic condition offer particularly effective emotional support. Sufferers experience the benefits of being linked to and in a growing relationship even with strangers. They let down their walls, begin to communicate openly, and get in touch with and honestly share their feelings through close, self-revealing discussions with others. They talk about who and what they really are without judgment, criticism, or rejection. Support groups create safe spaces where people are able to talk about what is going on in their lives and enable them to create a sense of intimacy they might not have experienced for a long time. Members offer nurturance, reassurance of each person's worth, and a general sense that they can always turn to other participants. Hearing others' stories, one's own story falls into perspective.

The breast cancer support group participants, for instance, discussed how to cope with cancer. They expressed their feelings about the illness, their grief, their anger, and its impact on their lives, thereby enabling them to carry on with their daily existences. The support group also helped them overcome the alienation that often divides cancer patients from well meaning but anxious family members and friends, improve their communication with family members and physicians, better control pain, and face and master their fears about death and dying.

PATIENCE: AN IMPORTANT PREREQUISITE

As you utilize various spiritual practices for your healing and the restoration of your health, you must exercise patience. Healing as a wholeness of mind-body-spirit comes gradually. Recovery, whether physical or mental, generally does not come all at once. When you invoke God's help, you typically regain your wholeness or health day by day, step by step.

Do not lose patience if your healing or your recovery is slow and the restoration of your health requires a long process. Encourage the process with your hope, strengthen it with your faith, and cooperate with your patience. Avoid despondency and impatience, which are the most potent assistants to the forces of sickness.

VISITING THE SICK IN THE JEWISH TRADITION

Traditionally, Eastern European towns maintained Jewish visitation groups (*bikur holim* in Hebrew) to visit the sick. Synagogues and temples now sponsor these groups so that individuals do not suffer or recuperate alone.[51]

These visits respond to the isolation, the lack of community, and the sense of abandonment experienced by those who are seriously ill. Those who visit offer sufferers comfort, encouragement, and the caring reflecting of human interdependence—in other words, the sense of community nearly all of us need.

The visitor provides the patient with a link to the Jewish community, reaffirming a sense of connection and purpose. The visitor often cheers the sufferer, inspiring a sense of hope: infusing the ailing with a sense of meaning and a resolve to continue to fight his or her illness, and freeing the sick person from his or her prison of fear, worry, hopelessness, and isolation. Perhaps bringing a smile, the visitor also shows the sufferer the bright side of life, lessening despondency and darkness.

The visitor need only be present to listen to the patient and be there for the moment, to provide "company" and share the burden, without any preconceived agenda. In addition to having someone listening to what he or she wishes to share, a sufferer generally wants the comfort, understanding, and friendship of others. The visitor, even in offering a smile or a touch of the hand, hopefully conveys a sense of God's loving presence and reaffirms the sufferer's wholeness.

The practice of *bikur holim* illustrates the healing power of relationships. The Talmud recounts many stories about Rabbi Yohanan ben Zakkai, a great leader who when he heard about another rabbi being sick would visit and speak with him about his illness. After their conversation, Yohanan ben Zakkai would hold out his hand and the other rabbi would rise.

One day Yohanan ben Zakkai himself became ill. He was visited by Rabbi Hanina, who, after speaking to the stricken sage, held out his hand and Yohanan ben Zakkai stood up.

The question is posed: "Why couldn't Yohanan ben Zakkai raise himself?" Jewish sages gave this answer: "Because the prisoner cannot free himself from prison." (*Berakot* 5b) Even the greatest of Jewish healers needed another to help him be free of the burden of fear, isolation, and hopelessness. When we fall ill, we realize how much we need each other.

These visits also change the visitor. We are softened. We become more compassionate and caring, more grateful and aware of life's blessings.

Beyond visitation groups, synagogues, temples, and other Jewish organizations should create three other types of social networks. First, they should establish healing centers and healing networks to aid the health and well-being of people who seek help. These centers would surround people who are ill with optimistic and joyful people who share a belief in spiritual growth and personal transformation, thereby helping those who suffer.

Second, Jewish institutions should create a list of volunteer buddies to befriend those challenged by a particular illness (or other crisis). These volunteers should have experienced (or be facing) the same circumstance encountered by those seeking their advice. Particularly with stress-related illnesses, patients want to speak one-on-one with someone having the wisdom to bring them through this difficult time, to help them transform their pain and suffering. Individuals who fought an illness vigorously and who mastered it or learned to live a fulfilling life, even if not cured, are especially helpful as volunteer buddies.

Third, Jewish organizations should facilitate the creation of spiritual support groups, for example, for cancer patients. In these groups, those who are sick could discuss their pain and illness and how they cope with similar needs. Giving primacy to the wisdom of the group, attendees can share and build a Jewish spiritual structure. They will find some purpose or meaning from their experience, however painful, including a sense of having achieved things from the illness, such as improved self-esteem and personal adequacy, that would otherwise not be possible. They will also find inner strength in their own spiritual resources.

Spiritual practices engage our capacity for hope and healing. Each of us needs to find an outlet for his or her spiritual needs. What works for you may not work for others. Personalized prayer, meditation, and visualization, as well as group worship and a renewed sense of purpose in life can, individually and collectively, play a significant role in healing for sufferers.

At times we all experience negative attitudes to spiritual practices. It is not always possible to stay on track when we pray, meditate, or visualize. It is all right to feel that sometimes you are a failure at one or more of these spiritual practices. If your prayers are not answered, it may be some sort of a blessing in disguise.

The essential point is that your well-being is not in your control; ultimately, your life is in God's hands. However, you do not know God's plan for you. Your healing, your wholeness, and your inner peace of mind boils down to how you interpret what happens to you. Accept a concept of healing that allows for continued pain and suffering, even death. Some things cannot be cured. By changing your attitude to your pain and suffering you can live with them, easing the intensity of your symptoms and improving your ability to function.

Our vulnerability to illness, to pain and suffering, and ultimately to death are part of our lives. Immortality is simply impossible. Accept that death is a fact of life. No one lives forever.

Fight the good fight for life. Do everything you can in conjunction with health care professionals and alternative practitioners to get better. Live as fully as you can; however, we all will die. The realization of the inevitability of death often results in impassioned living. You have a limited amount of time on earth. How are you going to live until you die?

Then, there comes a time to surrender and let go. You should be willing to die if it comes to that. There is a time to give your life and the experience of your earthly existence over to God.

Realize the transcendent nature of your existence. You are more than your physical body. The end of earthly living is not the end of your existence. We are all part of something much bigger than this life, than this earthly world. According to the Jewish tradition, we are our eternal souls.

NOTES

1. I have drawn on Rabbi Morris Lichtenstein, *Jewish Science and Health: The Textbook of Jewish Science* (New York: Society of Jewish Science, 1986), pp. 57–86 and 104–109; Rabbi Morris Lichtenstein, *Peace of Mind: Jewish Science Essays* (New York: Society of Jewish Science, 1970), pp. 233–240 and 321-326; Rabbi Morris Lichtenstein, *How to Live: Jewish Science Essays* (New York: Society of Jewish Science, 1957), pp. 48–56 and 342–348; Rabbi Morris Lichtenstein, *Joy of Life: Jewish Science Essays* (New York: Society of Jewish Science, 1938), pp. 308–315.

2. Herbert Benson, M.D., with Marg Stark, *Timeless Healing: The Power and Biology of Belief* (New York: Scribner, 1996), pp. 228-230.

3. Ibid., p. 206.

4. Ibid., pp. 174–175.

5. Jeffrey S. Levin, "Religion and Health: Is There an Association, Is It Valid, and Is It Causal?" *Social Science and Medicine* 38:11 (1994): 1475–1482.

6. Thomas Oxman, M.D., Daniel H. Freeman Jr., Ph.D., and Eric D. Manheimer, M.D., "Lack of Social Participation or Religious Strength and Comfort As Risk Factors for Death After Cardiac Surgery in the Elderly," *Psychosomatic Medicine* 57 (1995): 5–15. Religious attendance did not, however, predict mortality.

7. Ronna Casar Harris, Mary Amanda Dew, Ann Lee, Michael Amaya, Laurie Buches, Deloura Reetz, and Greta Coleman, "The Role of Religion in Heart-Transplant Recipients' Long-Term Health and Well-Being," *Journal of Religion and Health* 34:1 (Spring 1995): 17–31.

8. Peter Pressman, M.A., John S. Lyons, Ph.D., David B. Larson, M.D., M.S.P.A., and James J. Strain, M.D., "Religious Belief, Depression, and Ambulation Status in Elderly Women with Broken Hips," *American Journal of Psychiatry* 147:6 (1990): 758–760. The study did not, however, control for age.

9. Kimberly A. Sherrill, M.D., and David B. Larson, M.D., "Adult Burn Patients: The Role of Religion in Recovery," *Southern Medical Journal* 81:7 (July 1988): 821–829.

10. Jeffrey S. Levin, "How Religion Influences Morbidity and Health: Reflections on Natural History, Salutogenesis, and Host Resistance," *Social Science and Medicine* 43:5 (1996): 849–864 (quote appears on p. 854).

11. Levin, "Religion and Health," p. 1476; Benson, *Timeless Healing*, p. 176. Experts have noted, however, that the association between attendance and health may be questionable because numerous methodological problems characterize these studies: for instance, individuals with reduced physical mobility (and poorer health) are less likely to attend religious services. See Jeffrey S. Levin and Harold Y. Vanderpool, "Is Frequent Religious Attendance *Really* Conducive to Better Health?: Toward an Epidemiology of Religion," *Social Science and Medicine* 24:7 (1989): 589–600. Yet these same scholars, in a review of nearly twenty studies, found that the greater the degree of religious commitment, regardless of how measured, the lower the blood pressure. See Jeffrey S. Levin and Harold Y. Vanderpool, "Is Religion Therapeutically Significant for Hypertension?" *Social Science and Medicine* 29:1 (1989) : 69-78.

In a study of 407 males free from hypertension and cardiovascular disease, David B. Larson, Harold G. Koenig, Berton H. Kaplan, Raymond S. Greenberg, Everett Logue, and Herman A. Thyroler, "The Impact of Religion on Men's Blood Pressure," *Journal of Religion and Health* 28:4 (Winter 1989): 265–278, confirmed the correlation between high church attendance and high religious importance with lower blood pressure, with the importance of religion having an even greater association with lower blood pressure than church attendance. These differences persisted even after adjustments for age, socioeconomic status, smoking, and weight-height ratio.

12. Benson, *Timeless Healing*, pp. 176 and 300; Dale A. Matthews, M.D., with Connie Clark, *The Faith Factor: Proof of the Healing Power of Prayer* (New York: Viking, 1998), pp. 45, 49, 186–191.

13. Larry Dossey, M.D., *Prayer Is Good Medicine: How to Reap the Healing Benefits of Prayer* (San Francisco: HarperSan Francisco, 1996), pp. 144–145; Levin, "Religion and Health," p. 1478.

14. Christopher G. Ellison and Linda K. George, "Religious Involvement, Social Ties, and Social Support in a Southeastern Community," *Journal for Scientific Study of Religion* 33:1 (1994): 46–61.

15. William J. Strawbridge, Ph.D., Richard D. Cohen, M.A., Sarah J. Shema, M.S., and George A. Kaplan, Ph.D., "Frequent Attendance at Religious Services and Mortality Over 28 Years," *American Journal of Public Health* 87:6 (June 1997): 957–961.

16. Benson, *Timeless Healing*, pp. 177 and 179.

17. Philip J. Hilts, "Health Maintenance Organizations Turn to Spiritual Healing," *New York Times*, 27 December 1995, C10.

18. Benson, *Timeless Healing*, pp. 146–147.

19. Ibid., p. 286.

20. Larry Dossey, M.D., *Healing Words: The Power of Prayer and the Practice of Medicine* (New York: HarperCollins, 1993), p. 100 (italics omitted).

21. Ibid., p. 104 (italics omitted).

22. Randolph C. Byrd, M.D., "Positive Therapeutic Effects of Intercessory Prayer in a Coronary Care Unit Population," *Southern Medical Journal* 81:7 (July 1988): 826–829.

23. Fred Sicher, M.A., Elisabeth Targ, M.D., Dan Moore II, Ph.D., and Helene S. Smith, Ph.D., "A Randomized Double-Blind Study of the Effect of Distant Healing in an Advanced AIDS Population: Report of a Small-Scale Study," *Western Journal of Medicine* 169:6 (December 1998): 356-363; Jeff Stryker, "Hallelujah! Science Looks at Prayer for Friend and Fungus," *New York Times*, 5 April 1998, Section 4, p. 2. However, in a study of forty-two alcoholics entering a treatment center, one-half were placed in an intercessory prayer group receiving prayers from anonymous intercessors during the six-month treatment program and the other half received no prayers. The study found no appreciable difference in "drinking outcomes" after treatment between the prayer group and the control. See Scott Walker, M.D., J. Scott Tonigan, Ph.D., William R. Miller, Ph.D., Stephen Comer, Ed.D., Linda Kahlich, B.A., "Intercessory Prayer in the Treatment of Alcohol Abuse and Dependence: A Pilot Investigation," *Alternative Therapies* 3:6 (November 1997): 79–86.

24. Dossey, *Prayer is Good Medicine*, p. 49.

25. Ibid., pp. 66 and 129; Dossey, *Healing Words*, pp. 169–195 and Appendix 1, Controlled Experimental Trials of Healing, pp. 211–235; Daniel J. Benor, M.D., "Survey of Spiritual Healing Research," *Complementary Medical Research* 4:3 (September 1990): 9–33.

26. Dossey, *Healing Words*, p. 2.

27. Ibid., p. 83.

28. Ibid., p. 97.

29. Adapted from *The Hasidic Anthology: Tales and Teachings of the Hasidim*, trans. Louis I. Newman (Northvale, NJ: Jason Aronson, 1987), p. 63.

30. Melvin Morse, M.D., with Paul Perry, *Transformed by the Light: The Powerful Effect of Near Death Experiences on People's Lives* (New York: Villard, 1992), pp. 138–139.

31. *Healing of Soul, Healing of Body: Spiritual Leaders Unfold the Strength and Solace in Psalms*, ed. Rabbi Simkha Y. Weintraub, CSW (Woodstock, VT: Jewish Lights Publishing, 1994).

32. Ronald H. Isaacs offers an overview of the Jewish world of angels in *Ascending Jacob's Ladder: Jewish Views of Angels, Demons, and Evil Spirits* (Northvale, NJ: Jason Aronson, 1998).

33. Jeanne Achterberg, *Imagery in Healing: Shamanism and Modern Medicine* (Boston: New Science Library, 1985), pp. 75–112; O. Carl Simonton, M.D., Stephanie Matthews-Simonton, and James Creighton, *Getting Well Again: A Step-by-Step, Self-Help Guide to Overcoming Cancer for Patients and Their Families* (Los Angeles: J. P. Tarcher, 1978), pp. 125–163; Martin L. Rossman, M.D., *Healing Yourself: A Step-by-Step Program for Better Health Through Imagery* (New York: Walker, 1987), pp. 14–78.

34. Adapted from Rossman, *Healing Yourself*, pp. 79–83.

35. Adapted from Dr. Joseph H. Hertz, *The Authorized Daily Prayer Book*, rev. ed. (New York: Block, 1985), p. 141.

36. Bernie S. Siegel, M.D., *Love, Medicine and Miracles: Lessons Learned About Self-Healing from a Surgeon's Experiences with Exceptional Patients* (New York: Harper & Row, 1986), pp. 161–204. See also Jeanne Achterberg, Stephanie Matthews-Simonton, and O. Carol Simonton, "Psychology of the Exceptional Cancer Patient: A Description of Patients Who Outlive Predicted Life Expectancies," *Psychotherapy: Theory, Research, and Practice* 14:4 (Winter 1977): 416–422.

37. Catherine Classen, Cheryl Koopman, Karyn Angell, and David Spiegel, "Coping Styles Associated with Psychological Adjustment to Advanced Breast Cancer," *Health Psychology* 15:6 (1996): 434–437. (In a study of 101 women, a fighting spirit and emotional expressiveness were found to be associated with better adjustment to metastatic breast cancer.)

38. Norman Cousins, *Anatomy of an Illness as Perceived by the Patient: Reflections on Healing and Regeneration* (New York: Norton, 1979).

39. David Mahoney and Richard Restak, M.D., *The Longevity Strategy: How to Live to 100 Using the Brain-Body Connection* (New York: John Wiley, 1998), p. 84.

40. Philip J. Hilts, "Pessimism Is Hazardous to Health, a Study Finds," *New York Times*, 29 November 1995, C10; Robert Anda, David Williamson, Diane Jones, Carol Macera, Elaine Eaker, Alexander Glassman, and James Marks, "Depressed Affect, Hopelessness, and the Risk of Ischemic Heart Disease in a Cohort of U.S. Adults," *Epidemiology* 4:4 (July 1993): 285–294 (study of 2,832 adults age 45–77, adjusted for demographic and risk factors).

41. Robert M. Sapolsky, *Why Zebras Don't Get Ulcers: A Guide to Stress, Stress-Related Diseases, and Coping* (New York: W. H. Freeman, 1994), p. 279.

42. *Rabbi Nachman's Stories*, trans. Rabbi Aryeh Kaplan (Brooklyn: The Breslov Research Institute, 1983), pp. 354–437.

43. C. S. Lewis, *The Problem of Pain* (New York: MacMillan, 1962), p. 93.

44. Gale Warner with David Kreger, M.D., *Dancing at the Edge of Life: A Memoir* (New York: Hyperion, 1998), pp. 77 and 86.

45. Allan Luks with Peggy Payne, *The Healing Power of Doing Good: The Health and Spiritual Benefits of Helping Others* (New York: Fawcett Columbine, 1991).

46. Ibid., pp. 82 and 88–91.

47. Ibid., 60–61 and 67–68.

48. Ibid., pp. 113–130.

49. Sheldon Cohen, William J. Doyle, David P. Skoner, Bruce S. Rabin, and Jack M. Gwaltney, Jr., "Social Ties and Susceptibility to the Common Cold," *Journal of the American Medical Association* 277:24 (June 25, 1997): 1940–1944.

50. David Spiegel, Joan R. Bloom, Helen C. Kraemer, and Ellen Gottheil, "Effect of Psychosocial Treatment on Survival of Patients with Metastatic Breast Cancer," *Lancet* 334:8668 (14 October 1989): 888-891. Manuel M. Kogon, M.D., Amitava Biswas, M.D., Deidre Pearl, M.D., Robert W. Carson, M.D., and David Spiegel, M.D., "Effects of Medical and Psychotherapeutic Treatment on the Survival of Women with Metastatic Breast Carcinoma," *Cancer* 80:2 (July 15, 1997): 225-230 conclude that support group participation was the determining factor in the survival of these participants. Only insignificant differences existed in the treatments and the causes of death between the patients participating in a support group and those who did not.

Researchers have also found that the addition of psychosocial intervention, mainly supportive counselling and relaxation techniques, to standard cardiac rehabilitation cut the post-heart attack death rate by forty-one percent. See Wolfgang Linden, Carmen Stossel, and Jeffrey Maurice, "Psychological Interventions for Patients with Coronary Artery Disease: A Meta-Analysis," *Archives of Internal Medicine* 156:7 (April 8, 1996): 745-752.

51. Joseph S. Ozarowski, *To Walk in God's Ways: Jewish Pastoral Perspectives on Illness and Bereavement* (Northvale, NJ: Jason Aronson, 1995), pp. 21-51.

CHAPTER TWELVE

Facing Terminal
Illness and Death:
The Process of Dying

Although difficult for nearly all of us to contemplate, we should not fear the process of dying and the death moment, according to Jewish sages. Despite all the pain and suffering we may experience in our life prior to death, the exact moment of death will mark a time of peaceful transition as we embark on the postmortem journey of the soul, affording us incredible possibilities for spiritual growth.

According to the Jewish mystical tradition, we generally experience four "death moment" visions—internal, subjective visions—immediately prior to, at, or shortly after death. This chapter discusses these four visions, namely, seeing the Clear Light, encountering previously deceased relatives and angels, undergoing a life review, and ultimately passing through a tunnel.[1] From the perspective of Jewish Spirituality, the life review, which consists of the details of one's life becoming clear to him or her, is especially important. Because our purpose in life, especially in our interactions with others, centers on loving unconditionally, extending forgiveness, and being truthful, we will be judged someday by this standard.

This chapter examines various deathbed rituals in the Jewish tradition, including the Deathbed Confessional Prayer as well as meditations and visualizations. The chapter also discusses how loved ones can help a terminally ill person deal with the dying process, death moment visions, and the death moment, thereby enhancing and deepening his or her spiritual path.[2]

THE DYING PROCESS

During the process of dying, the elements of the physical body dissolve and separate. The mystical Jewish tradition teaches:

> We have [learned] that on the [dreaded] day when man's time comes to depart from the world, four quarters of the world indict him, and punishments rise up from all four quarters, and four elements fall to quarreling and seek to depart each to its own side. (*Zohar* II, 218b)

Although this cryptic passage fails to describe the four elements, the author likely refers to the four essential elements of human existence—earth (or flesh), water (or bodily fluids), fire (or bodily heat), and air (or breath)—as they dissolve and leave the human body. The quarreling may connote the tumultuous and rather upsetting process taking place in the dying person's consciousness.[3]

On a physical level, the process of dying involves a gradual withdrawal, a shutting down of different life functions. Someone very close to death generally is drained of energy. Her body becomes heavy and she encounters difficulty in standing or even moving her limbs. A dying individual often experiences dehydration and feels extremely thirsty, needing ice chips on her face, mouth, and lips to avoid becoming parched. Losing the ability to control bodily fluids, she typically becomes incontinent. Her body loses heat and her limbs become cold. Finally, it becomes harder and harder to breathe. Inbreaths become shallower and outbreaths longer. Ultimately her breath stops, as does her brain activity; the moment of physical death has arrived.

DEATH MOMENT VISIONS

With death imminent, we enjoy the ability to see elements in worlds generally otherwise unavailable to us. According to the Jewish mystical tradition:

> . . . [W]hen a man's [judgment] hour is near, [an angel] commences to call to him, and no one knows [except] the patient himself, as we

have [learned], that when a man is ill and his time is approaching to depart from the world a new spirit enters into him from above, in virtue of which he sees things that he could not see before, and then he departs from the world. (*Zohar* II, 218b)

During the dying process, most individuals encounter four visionary experiences: (1) seeing the Clear Light, (2) encountering previously deceased relatives and friends as well as angels, (3) undergoing a life review, and (4) passing through a tunnel.[4] The order in which these internal, subjective visions occur varies from person to person, depending on the circumstances of death and extent of the person's spiritual development. The point is that even after physical death, the internal process of dissolution likely continues.

Descriptions of near death experiences (NDEs), as well as NDE studies, corroborate the portrayal of the four death moment visions we shall see in Jewish texts and tales. The extensive body of NDE literature began nearly twenty-five years ago when Raymond Moody published his celebrated book on NDEs, *Life After Life*.[5] Based on interviews with one hundred fifty people who claimed to have had an NDE, the books offered firsthand accounts of the afterlife. After describing the dying process, most subjects reported going rapidly through a dark tunnel to a point of light, many times brighter than anything they had ever seen, but warm, loving, and accepting. Some reported communications with previously deceased relatives. A few described undergoing a life review consisting of a replay of all of their thoughts, words, and deeds and the impact of their existence on others.

EXPERIENCING THE CLEAR LIGHT

During the dying process, an individual may experience a glimpse of the Clear Light, a beautiful and intense light much brighter than anything experienced on earth. This is the radiant light of the soul's higher, more spiritual aspects.

Jewish mystical sources describe how, at this time, a departed (or soon-to-depart) soul takes a dip in the River of Light and is cleansed from many of earthly life's defilements. The immersion in the River of Light assists in restoring the soul to its initial radiance. The encounter with the River of Light not only helps the dying person leave the physical world but also aids his or her soul to become more identified with the spiritual realms.

In addition, a dying person may be blessed with a brief glimpse of God's Presence, the feminine aspect of the Divine (the Shekhinah, mentioned in chapter 11 in connection with the guardian angel meditation), appearing as a formless, glowing image. According to the Jewish mystical tradition: "No man dies before he sees the Shekhinah and because of its deep yearning for the Shekhinah the soul departs in order to greet her." (*Zohar* III, 88a) Thus, the soul may fleetingly see the radiant image of God's luminescence. As we are "surrounded by total and absolute unconditional love, understanding and compassion . . . we become aware of our potential, of what we could be like, of what we could have lived like."[6]

According to Jewish sages, some "righteous" individuals may recognize the Clear Light, representing the upper levels of the soul's inner luminosity, and glory in its radiance. For others, the sight of the Clear Light may engender fear. Some may be completely unaware of the vision of the Clear Light that occurs during this phase of the soul's postdeath journey.

ENCOUNTERING DECEASED RELATIVES, FRIENDS, AND ANGELS

During the dying process, according to Jewish tradition, each of us encounters beloved, deceased relatives and close friends as well as angels. (Angels in biblical and rabbinic literature were discussed in chapter 11.) Prior to or at the death moment, the spirits of deceased relatives and friends, those who loved us the most, visit a dying person to offer a welcome and ease the transition from the world of the living to the postdeath world of the souls.

The Jewish mystical tradition describes the deathbed vision of deceased loved ones as follows:

> Rabbi Simeon then said to Rabbi Isaac: Have you seen today the image of your father? For so we have [learned] that at the hour of a man's departure from the world, his father and his relatives gather round him, and he sees them and recognizes them, and likewise all with whom he associated in this world, and they accompany his soul to the place where it is to abide. (*Zohar* II, 218a)

Numerous near death experiencers (NDErs) report seeing one or more loving relatives who are prepared to assist the individual make the transition to the world beyond. For each of the NDErs, however, the beloved tells the person that his or her time to depart earthly life has not arrived.

In describing various angels, Jewish literature, both rabbinic and medieval, refers to a vicious, destroying angel, the Angel of Death, who has the task of taking the soul from the physical body. When the Angel of Death completes his work, another angel, Dumah, arrives on the scene. Dumah serves as the caretaker for and the guardian of the soul of a deceased.

The rabbinic and mystical literature also refers to three angels, or in some interpretations, three groups of angels, who appear at the moment of death or soon thereafter. Greeting the soul and offering an initiation into the postmortem realms, the trio of angels accompany the soul as it embarks on its afterlife journey.

Drawing on ancient rabbinic teachings, the writings of the Jewish mystics also describe a catapult used to purify certain souls. Two angels appear after death and toss a soul back and forth from one end of the universe to the other end. The catapult purifies a soul of the accumulated debris that obscures the higher, more spiritual levels of the soul's pure radiance. The catapult helps shake out a soul's extraneous thoughts so that the soul gets closer to its unalloyed essence and attains a greater measure of inner peace. Immersion of the soul in this cosmic centrifuge further prepares it for its continued journey in the postdeath realms.[7]

UNDERGOING A LIFE REVIEW

Each of us also undergoes a life review of his or her immediate past life experiences and is held accountable for his or her earthly deeds, words, and thoughts. You receive an instantaneous, extraordinarily rapid, full-color, three-dimensional, panoramic review of everything in your life, good and bad.

All the details of a person's life experience are revealed, as though the person's entire life occurs at once. He or she knows every thought he or she ever had during earthly life. He or she recalls every word ever spoken and remembers each deed. The Talmud records, "At the hour of departure to his eternal home, all his deeds are enumerated before him, and the angels say to him: 'You did such and such in such and such a place and on such and such a day.'" (*Ta'anit* 11a)

The soul understands the reasons for and consequences of every one of life's thoughts, words, and actions. Events are put in perspective. You see how your conduct affected others, including strangers. You perceive how everyone's life is intertwined.

Because each of us has angels assigned to maintain records of our good and bad deeds, words, and thoughts, the balance of one's life experience in the Divine data bank becomes immediately apparent. Building on the concept of a past-life review contained in the rabbinic literature, and coupled with a just reward or retribution for each person according to his or her actions, words, and thoughts, the Jewish mystical tradition describes the life review process as follows:

> Rabbi Eleazar said: On the day when a man's time arrives to depart from the world . . . [t]hree messengers [the Angel of Love, who records a person's merits; the Angel of Judgment, who records a person's sins; and the Angel of Mercy, who notes the length of a person's life] stand over him and take an account of his life and of all that he has done in this world, and he admits all with his mouth and signs the account with his hand. . . . the whole account is signed with his hand so that he should be judged in the next world for his actions, former and later, old and new, not one of them is forgotten. . . . (*Zohar* I, 78b–79a)

The life review, which occurs before three members of the Heavenly Tribunal, culminates in the soul metaphorically signing a confession containing his or her record and acknowledging the justice of the verdict. We do not blame the Heavenly Tribunal or God for the verdict or our fate. We see what our life could have been like, what potential we had. According to death-and-dying pioneer Elizabeth Kübler-Ross:

> . . . [Y]ou will know that you yourself were your own worst enemy since you are now accusing yourself of having neglected so many opportunities to grow. Now you know that long ago when your house burned down, when your child died, when your husband hurt himself, or when you yourself suffered a heart attack, all fatal blows were merely some of the many possibilities for you to grow; to grow in understanding, to grow in love, to grow in all these things which we still have to learn.[8]

The life review typically occurs at the time of death or shortly thereafter. However, in the case of a slow, lingering death, the life review may take place more slowly. In this situation, the life review may occur over many days.

An ethical foundation underpins the Jewish teachings regarding the life review. From the perspective of Jewish Spirituality, we are responsible for our thoughts, words, and deeds during life. The central ethic of unconditional love, forgiveness, and truthfulness underpins the life review. Because our purpose in life centers on loving and forgiving other humans, as well as being truthful, we will be judged by the standards of love, forgiveness, and honesty. Near death experiencers report being asked the question they found most difficult to answer: "What service have you rendered to others?"

PASSING THROUGH A TUNNEL

At some point during the dying process, a soul passes through a tunnel or celestial pathway on its journey from the physical realm to the world beyond. Some near death experiencers recall it as a river, a gate, or a stairway. This tunnel serves as the bridge between life and death. Once the soul crosses the tunnel—a sort of boundary line—death becomes irreversible. The "silver cord" (Ecclesiastes 12:6) linking the physical body and the soul is severed. For Jewish mystics, the soul's postmortem journey begins.

THE DEATH MOMENT

In the Jewish tradition, the exact moment of physical death is painless. Death, at least for the "righteous," is effortless. Like drawing hair out of milk,[9] there is no resistance, only blissful peace, in death. Even the terminally ill, ravaged by pain and suffering, at death typically manifest a peaceful radiance, a tranquil smile of comfort and quietude. Loved ones often describe their faces as "radiant, peaceful at long last."

However, a gentle death is not universal. For the "wicked," the rabbinic literature, using a variety of metaphors, such as "pulling a tangled rope through a narrow opening,"[10] describes the moment of death as a painful experience, a time of considerable agitation.

For Jews steeped in the mystical tradition, death did not evoke anxiety. Rather, the Jewish mystics saw it as another phase in the soul's evolution. They viewed death as a peaceful process transporting an individual from the material world to other realms of disembodied consciousness. With an awesome sense of calmness and fearlessness, the pious of old made the transition from earthly life prior to their physical demise.

The death of the Baal Shem Tov continues to serve, some two hundred forty years later, as an ideal model for dying. Fully accepting death and living with the sense of a transcendent meaning to life, the Baal Shem Tov maintained inner confidence and peace of mind; his control and connectedness with self, others, and God; and his love of and devotion for others:

> When the Baal Shem Tov fell ill shortly before his death, he would not take to his bed. His body grew weak, his voice faint, and he would sit alone in his room meditating. On the eve of [the Jewish holiday of Shavuot], the last evening of his life, his [disciples] were gathered around him and he preached to them about the giving of the Torah. In the morning he requested that all of them gather together in his room and he taught them how they should care for his body after death. Afterward he asked for a [prayer book], and said: "I wish to commune yet a while with [the Name, may God be blessed]."
>
> Afterward they heard him talking to someone and they inquired with whom he was speaking. He replied, "Do you not see the Angel of Death? He always flees from me, but now he has been given permission to come and flaps his wings and is full of joy." Afterward all the men of the city gathered together to greet him on the holiday and he spoke words of Torah to them. Afterward he said, "Until now I have treated you with [lovingkindness]. Now you must treat me with [lovingkindness]." [The burial is considered the truest act of lovingkindness, because there can be no repayment.] He gave them a sign that at his death the two clocks in the house would stop.
>
> While he was washing his hands, the large clock stopped and some of the men immediately stood in front of it so that the others should not see it. He said to them, "I am not worried about myself, for I know clearly that I shall go from this door and immediately I shall enter another door." He spoke words of Torah and ordered them to recite the verse "And let Your graciousness, O [Eternal] our God, be upon us; establish You also the work of our hands for us. . . . " He lay down and sat up many times and prayed with great devotion, until the syllables of his words could no longer be distinguished. He told them to cover him with blankets and began to shake and tremble as he used to do when he prayed the Silent Prayer. Then little by little he grew quiet. At that moment they saw that the small clock too had stopped. They waited and saw that he had died.[11]

The Hasidic rebbes and their followers strove to go through death, particularly the death moment, fully conscious and in contact with God. They made the transition from earthly life with calmness and equanimity. In fearlessly accepting death, they affirmed life and our Godlike nature.

HOW SPIRITUAL SEEKERS CAN BETTER FACE DEATH

The ongoing, physically painful agony experienced by a terminally ill person, often hooked up to tubes and monitors in a sterile hospital room, offers the potential for a beautiful sharing experience. New emotional and spiritual horizons for awareness and transcendence exist beyond the outwardly bleak, immediate concerns.

People diagnosed with a terminal illness often are jolted into a new mindfulness about their lives. For however brief a period of time, what a teacher illness is, as we saw in chapter 11. They ask themselves: Who am I? What is my life about? What have I accomplished in my life? What do I need to express? What unfinished emotional business do I need to complete? How am I going to spend the rest of my limited days?

The process of dying, earthly life's final chapter, no matter how messy and painful, offers the gravely ill opportunities to grow within themselves and with others. Recognizing that death can be transforming and liberating, emotionally and spiritually,[12] loved ones should create an emotionally satisfying, spiritually oriented environment that offers a time for reflection, forgiveness, reconciliation, and ultimately closure. In addition to offering their unconditional love, compassion, and acceptance, the beloved can help the dying person through prayer and guided meditations and visualizations and in dealing with interpersonal issues, unexpressed emotions, and his or her death moment visions.

THE IMPORTANCE OF LOVED ONES OFFERING THEIR UNCONDITIONAL LOVE, COMPASSION, AND ACCEPTANCE

Do not leave a dying person—whether in a hospital, a hospice, or at home—alone and scared. He or she needs to be surrounded by family and friends so that he or she does not feel abandoned or isolated. Rather, provide the warm sun of loving attention.

Let a terminally ill individual die in dignity, surrounded by his or her loved ones. If at all possible, do not allow a dying person to make the passage unaided. Being with someone when he or she is dying represents one of the best acts of lovingkindness, so important from the perspective of Jewish Spirituality.

At the bedside, be present for and learn to listen to—really listen to—the terminally ill person: to what is said, both verbally and nonverbally, and to what is unstated but implied. Think of yourself as a heart with big ears. "Be there" and "go with the flow." Silence can be golden.

Allow a dying individual to bring up whatever he or she wants to talk about or needs to say—thoughts, fears, hopes, regrets, feelings about death and dying, good and bad memories, etc. Let the patient guide the discussion. It is important to make a dying person feel safe, no matter what he or she reveals.

By opening their hearts to the dying person and offering their total support, the beloved send their unconditional love, compassion, and acceptance, without judgment or criticism. Often sitting quietly and holding a hand (or touching the face) is sufficient. Make a dying person feel loved, accepted, and understood.

Following the model of the Baal Shem Tov's departure from life, transmit a sense of equanimity and a peaceful acceptance of death to a terminally ill person. Make certain he or she understands that, according to the Jewish tradition, death, particularly the moment of death, generally will be a peaceful, painless experience.

Studies of the near death experience confirm that death serves as a serene transition. Near death experiencers report that after being pronounced dead, they typically felt blissful. They experienced "peace, comfort, ease—just quietness."[13] It is as if they have seen something wonderful. Perhaps, just a second before the soul leaves the body, we understand so much so deeply.

Do not transmit any "negative" thoughts or feelings, such as fear, sadness, or attachment. Let your optimal attitude and verbalizations as well as your accompanying actions and emotional expressions convey an openhearted love for the dying person. The beloved can say: "We love you; your love will remain with us and your immortal soul will survive on its afterlife journey."

Give a terminally ill person who is tired and ready to go permission to die. Reassure him or her that the survivors will be all right. Tell him or her: "It's okay if you want to die. Don't worry about us; we'll be able to make it through the grieving process."

Even if the dying person is in a coma, loved ones can communicate compassionate thoughts through various means, including touch, eye contact, or music. It is still not too late for them to use their minds and hearts in positive ways. Express your regrets, saying, "I'm sorry." Tell a parent, "I love you." Or say, "It's OK. You can let go. I'll be all right." You can always express your love and compassion through your heart.

Offer the dying person the calm certainty of knowing that, according to Jewish tradition, he or she is and will continue to be safely held in God's loving arms. In time, his or her soul will experience, as discussed more fully in chapter 13, healing, rebirth, and ultimately union with God.

PRAYER AND GUIDED MEDITATION

Dying individuals often find the Deathbed Confessional Prayer (the *Viddui*) and the Guardian Angel Meditation (see chapter 11) to be of considerable help in facilitating the soul's transition. Gravely ill individuals who are lucid can use the *Viddui* prayer as a meditation (or a guided meditation) to aid in the departure of the soul from the physical body and the transference of consciousness.

The Deathbed Confessional Prayer is outwardly directed. Based on a sentence in Proverbs, "People who confess and forsake their sins will obtain mercy" (Proverbs 28:13), this prayer enables a dying individual to speak directly to and make peace with God. Through this deathbed prayer, such an individual confesses his or her sins, acknowledges his or her guilt, and expresses feelings of regret for failing to live up to his or her potential or fulfill his or her obligations. In accounting to God for a life that is about to end, he or she asks for and indicates a willingness to receive the Eternal's forgiveness.

The Deathbed Confessional Prayer, which follows, can be read by or to a dying person:

> *Deathbed Confessional (Viddui).* I acknowledge unto You, O Eternal my God and God of my ancestors, that both my cure and my death are in Your hands. May it be Your Will to send me a perfect healing. Yet if my death be fully determined by You, I will in love accept it at Your hand. O may my death be an atonement for all the sins, iniquities, and transgressions of which I have been guilty against

You. Grant me the abounding happiness that is treasured up for the righteous. Make known to me the path of life: in Your presence is the fullness of joy; at Your right hand bliss for evermore.

You Who are the protector of the bereaved and the helpless watch over my loved ones with whose soul my own is linked. Into Your hand I commit my spirit; redeem it, O Eternal God of truth.[14]

By affirming that life and death are in God's hands, the Deathbed Confessional Prayer serves several purposes. First, it represents an individual's turning from evil. As a petitionary prayer, the confessional asks for something for the dying person. A gravely ill person offers repentance and seeks forgiveness from the Supreme Sovereign.

Second, the deathbed confessional serves as a prayer of surrender to God: Your will be done, O Eternal.

Third, the confessional may lead a dying person to try to settle all unfinished emotional issues before his or her demise. By focusing on major interpersonal relationships and how he or she feels about each, the recitation of the confessional may trigger one final attempt by a gravely ill person to make amends and achieve a lasting reconciliation with family members and friends.

Fourth, the deathbed confessional may enable a dying individual to explore his or her inner life, feelings about God and the fate of his or her soul, and the meaning of his or her earthly life and death. In asking for Divine forgiveness, he or she also realizes the presence of the Eternal's unconditional love and compassion for each of us. It facilitates the healing of wholeness.

Fifth, according to Jewish sages, the *Viddui* helps clear a path for the soul, our deeper essence, to exit the physical body. Whether as a prayer or a meditation, the confession of sins facilitates the transition of a dying person from the world of the living to the world of souls. It helps usher the soul to the next realm.

GUIDED VISUALIZATION

If asked by a dying person, loved ones can center into a dialogue as a means of exploring beliefs about the afterlife. By altering our ordinary perspective of reality, a guided visualization enables a dying person to travel on an inner journey to the postdeath realms and freely form his or her own internal images of the afterlife. This assists in investigating these other realms, thereby lessening fears of the unknown.

The Guided Spiritual Journey Visualization can be used to provide spiritual support for a dying person to explore his or her beliefs about the afterlife. If you are the guide, try to take a terminally ill person through this visualization for ten to fifteen minutes.

Guided Spiritual Journey Visualization: Introduction: As the guide, try to create a warm, welcoming atmosphere, an environment of serenity and spaciousness for the journey within. Lower the lights, if possible. Although difficult in a hospital room, candles can set a mood that enhances the visualization.

Ask the dying individual to close his or her eyes; sit quietly; calm and relax his or her body by sitting, reclining, or lying down; and breathe in and out normally, feeling where the breath flows into and out of the body. Adjust the breaths so that the in and out breaths are the same length, thereby bringing about both a relaxation of the body and an alertness of the mind. (Obviously, you need to vary these instructions depending on the individual's physical condition.)

Ask the terminally ill individual to visualize his or her own death and what he or she thinks will happen at the death moment. Specifically, ask him or her to explore the transcendent realms; visualize the image of God and identify with the universal, transpersonal Higher Soul; and experience the ultimate destination—union with the Eternal. Invite him or her to visualize the transference of his or her consciousness and the ongoing journey of his or her soul.

Invite the dying person to see how God immerses him or her in radiant, unconditional love and compassion.

Concluding Instructions: As the guide, now invite the dying individual to come back to the here and now. Take time to ease him or her back. Slowly bring awareness back into his or her body, feeling himself or herself back in the room and opening his or her eyes.

Afterward, the guide can encourage the terminally ill person to verbalize, if possible, this guided visualization. The Guided Spiritual Journey Visualization and the ensuing verbalization enable loved ones to better provide spiritual support for departure of the dying person's soul as it begins its afterlife journey.

DEALING WITH INTERPERSONAL ISSUES:
FORGIVENESS AND COMMUNICATING
PREVIOUSLY UNEXPRESSED EMOTIONS

During the process of dying, as part of the acceptance of death, individuals often need to clean up and heal old, previously unfinished emotional and relationship "baggage."[15] Be particularly sensitive to a dying person's efforts to communicate previously unexpressed feelings and emotions—such as guilt, jealousy, greed, anger, desire, or anxiety—and to come to terms with others.[16]

The dying process can be a time for profound reconciliation, transformation, and closure. Encourage a terminally ill person, if he or she is receptive, to make up with family members and friends by addressing failed relationships, old grievances, and hurts inflicted on or by others. By being more openhearted, he or she may be ready to ask for forgiveness from others, to send forgiveness and make amends to others, and to forgive himself or herself.

Although forgiveness represents an important part of Jewish Spirituality, as discussed in chapter 6, it is often quite difficult. Each of us continues to fear being hurt or rejected again. We may be unable to let go of our past perceptions. What has been done to us in the past may approach being unforgivable.

Encouraging an admission of past mistakes, asking for forgiveness, and making amends is often quite powerful. It opens the possibility for healing old wounds and tapping the power of love, thereby allowing a dying person to be at peace. Without conflict in his or her life, he or she no longer suffers emotional or spiritual pain. By facilitating reconciliation between estranged children, parents, siblings, and others, the quest for forgiveness often enables a terminally ill person to reach closure with and open unconditionally into love for his or her closest relatives as well as friends.

In contrast to a sudden, unexpected death such as a heart attack, car accident, or plane crash, a slowly developing illness with a fatal outcome, like cancer or AIDS, gives the survivors time to ask for forgiveness and a chance to resolve old, unfinished emotional business or communicate previously unfinished, unexpressed feelings. With the AIDS epidemic, parents can do the same thing with their dying adult children. For instance, a father who previously rejected a homosexual son can ask for forgiveness, avoiding a lifetime burden of guilt.

Although another may view unsolicited expressions of forgiveness as an attack, encourage a terminally ill person, either face to face or over the telephone, to try to heal old resentments and fears and make amends for anything he or she did or did not do that might have hurt or harmed another person in any way. If there is not sufficient time or energy for the dying person to do this, various prayers or meditations can be used to open the heart and enable a gravely ill person to let go of the resentments that block his or her openheartedness toward others.

A dying person can use the Deathbed Confessional (*Viddui*) as a prayer or meditation not only to ask for forgiveness from God but also to seek forgiveness from and of other humans. Listening to a deathbed confession, particularly as an expression of interpersonal forgiveness, takes considerable sensitivity. Remember that a terminally ill individual may not want to reveal well kept secrets, the scars of failed interpersonal relationships, or hurts inflicted on others that generate feelings of guilt and emotional distress. Try to provide a safe space for the expression of the regrets, fears, or sadness resulting from past actions, words, and thoughts.

Acting as a guide, loved ones can use the Guided Forgiveness and Lovingkindness Meditation-Visualization to facilitate the process of reconciliation before death, thereby bringing about a lasting healing to previously troubled relationships. If you are a guide, try to take a terminally ill person through this meditation-visualization for ten to fifteen minutes daily, for several days, if possible.

Guided Forgiveness and Lovingkindness Meditation-Visualization. Introduction: As the guide, try to create a warm, welcoming atmos-phere, an environment of serenity and spaciousness for the journey within. Lower the lights, if possible. Although difficult in a hospital room, candles can set a mood that enhances meditation or visualization.

Ask the dying individual to close his or her eyes; sit quietly; calm and relax his or her body by sitting, reclining, or lying down; and breathe in and out normally, feeling where the breath flows into and out of the body. Adjust the breaths so that the in and out breaths are the same length, thereby bringing about both a relaxation of the body and an alertness of the mind. (Obviously, you need to vary these instructions depending on the individual's physical condition.)

Ask the dying individual to feel himself or herself surrounded by warmth and love—allow any anger to dissolve into the warmth and love. With each breath, breathe in warmth. Feel the nourishing warmth.

Breathe in love and feel the openness that love creates. Allow the warmth and love to give rise to forgiveness. The power of forgiveness is so great. Ask the dying individual to contemplate forgiveness—its meaning and what it might mean to bring forgiveness into his or her life.

Ask the dying individual to visualize another person whom he or she resents and, with a new state of openness, invite that person into his or her heart. The dying person should notice whatever blocks the approach to his or her heart—the problem, the hurt, the fear, the anger, or whatever it is. The dying person should enter into and continue a dialogue with that person, until there is nothing more to say.

Now, the dying person should try to let that person through to his or her heart. Let go of the pride that holds onto resentment. Allow the pain of old hurts to dissolve. In his or her heart, the dying person should say, "I forgive you for whatever you did in the past, whether intentionally or unintentionally, through your deeds, words, or thoughts, that caused me pain or hurt." Repeat the words: "I forgive you." Allowing the forgiveness to grow, the dying person should let go of resentments and open unconditionally into love and compassion.

Then, the dying person should repeat this for others whom he or she resents.

Next, the dying person should visualize someone who resents him or her—someone whom he or she has caused pain or hurt, someone who has put the dying one out of his or her heart, and, with a new state of openness, invite that person into his or her heart. Notice what blocks that individual's approach to his or her heart—fear, guilt, or whatever it is. Try to let that person through to his or her heart. From the bottom of his or her heart, the dying person should ask for forgiveness: "I ask for your forgiveness for what I did in the past, whether intentionally or unintentionally, through my deeds, words, or thoughts, that caused you pain or hurt." Repeat the words: "Please forgive me." Again, the dying person should be touched by the possibility of forgiveness. Ask him or her to let that individual back into his or her heart.

Then, the dying person should repeat this for others whom he or she may have hurt.

Let the dying person's heart fill with forgiveness and lovingkindness for himself or herself. Repeat: "May I be happy and at peace. May I be free from anger, envy, pride, greed, desire, fear, sorrow, and doubt. May I be filled with love."

Concluding Instructions: As the guide, now invite the dying individual to come back to the here and now. Take time to ease back. Slowly bring awareness back into his or her body, feeling himself or herself back in the room and opening his or her eyes.

Apart from asking for or expressing forgiveness, a dying person may wish to communicate previously unsaid sentiments that otherwise contribute to a sense of emotional incompleteness. For example, a parent could tell his or her children how much he or she loves and admires them. Other previously unexpressed items could include things the terminally ill person wished he or she had said or done for someone (or did not say or do) or things he or she wished another had or had not said or done. Encourage the expression of both positive and negative emotional statements.[17]

By engaging in an emotional cleansing and finishing relationship "business" prior to death, both the survivors and a terminally ill individual help alleviate the departed soul's suffering in the postdeath realms, according to the Jewish tradition, as discussed in chapter 13. The successful resolution and completion of difficult relationships between the dying individual and his or her family members and friends as well as the expression of previously unexpressed emotions also make the subsequent grief and bereavement process, as we shall see, significantly easier for the survivors.[18]

DEALING WITH DEATH MOMENT VISIONS

When family members and friends visit a dying person who knows (or who wishes to learn) about the Jewish teachings on the afterlife, strive to validate his or her death visions and experiences and try to honor his or her inner, subjective realities. Calmly explain that one or more visions are part of the dying process, thereby alleviating deathbed fears and making it easier for a gravely ill individual to die peacefully. However, continually respect a dying person's wishes and needs.

Specifically, beloved ones can assist an individual facing death deal with the life review, the encounter with previously departed relatives and friends as well as angels, and the Clear Light.

FACILITATING A LIFE REVIEW

If possible, try to facilitate a life review as a way of helping a dying individual sort through what has gone before, particularly his or her unresolved life experiences and previously unexpressed emotions; engage in the emotional and spiritual preparation for death; and clear the path for the hereafter. A life review also enables a terminally ill person to share his or her personal history and legacy with family members and close friends and to come to terms with his or her unfulfilled dreams and regrets.

Encourage a life review, either in the form of a monologue or a dialogue between loved ones and a gravely ill person, if the latter is receptive. Facing the inevitability of death may encourage a new openness of communication and an illumination of the past with a newfound love, compassion, forgiveness, and honesty. However, if there has been past trauma or abuse, it is probably best not to force such memories.

> The life review should be quite comprehensive and encompassing:
> Happy moments and sad occasions;
> Expressions of gratitude and appreciation for goodness and beauty in life, including the experience of love;
> Accomplishments and virtues, experiences of growth, and instances of overcoming a limitation or a challenge;
> Regrets, grievances, old hurts, unrealized hopes and dreams, undeveloped talents, missed opportunities, failed relationships, and harm inflicted on or by others;
> Important people, from both a positive and a negative standpoint, in his or her life;
> Final expressions of emotions and feelings as well as previously unrevealed family secrets.

Gently, and as sensitively as possible, ask open-ended questions, such as: Is there anything you hold against others (or you think they hold against you)? Do you want to bring these matters to a resolution? Do you have any unexpressed emotions and feelings you wish to communicate to others? Although some risk exists that the life review may aggravate a dying individual, causing additional and unnecessary pain and suffering, a pattern of a life of worthwhileness and meaningfulness often emerges from these open-ended questions and the accompanying answers.

Loved ones find the following guided meditation and journal exercise useful in facilitating a life review. As a guide, take a dying person through this meditation for ten to fifteen minutes.

Guided Life Review Meditation.   Introduction: As the guide, create a warm, welcoming atmosphere, an environment of serenity and spaciousness for the journey within. Lower the lights, if possible. Although difficult in a hospital room, candles can set a mood that enhances meditation.

Ask the dying individual to close his or her eyes; sit quietly; calm and relax his or her body by sitting, reclining, or lying down; and breathe in and out normally, feeling where the breath flows into and out of the body. Adjust the breaths so that the in and out breaths are the same length, thereby bringing about both a relaxation of the body and an alertness of the mind. (Obviously, you need to vary these instructions depending on the individual's physical condition.)

Invite the dying person to contemplate what he or she is grateful for, including happy times, good friends, special moments, and love and compassion extended to him or her.

Then, invite each special person separately to enter the dying person's openheartedness and engage in a dialogue with him or her. Invite the saying of separate goodbyes and thanks to each special person.

Next, invite the terminally ill person to contemplate moments and memories associated with frustration, anger, envy, guilt, desire, remorse, sorrow, fear, pride, or anxiety. These form the unfinished relational business needing closure.

Also invite the dying person to reflect on his or her unfinished or unexpressed emotions. These comprise another aspect of relational business needing closure.

Concluding Instructions: As the guide, now invite the dying individual to back to the here and now. Take time to ease back. Slowly bring his or hear awareness back into the body, feeling himself or herself back in the room and opening his or her eyes.

Dying individuals often find it helpful to make notes on their earthly journey—distinct memories and the accompanying states of mind—in a journal, on separate pieces of paper in a notebook, in some sort of visual form, or on an audio or videotape. This can be a particularly liberating exercise. Leaving a message or tape of love and encouragement, among other unexpressed emotions, often helps survivors surmount their grief.

In connection with the life review, loved ones may also want to guide a terminally ill person through the Guided Forgiveness and Lovingkindness Meditation-Visualization as a technique for asking for and extending forgiveness.

Do not pressure a dying person to engage in an oral or written life review. Loved ones can only provide a safe space, which may be difficult in a busy and often intrusive hospital environment, in which a terminally ill individual can discuss—orally, in writing, or on audio or videotape—the events and relationships of a lifetime, express what is in his or her heart, ask for forgiveness for past hurts and harms to and from others, make his or her apologies, and achieve reconciliation.

The earthly life review also assists a dying person to question and broadly reflect on the meaning and purpose not only of his or her life but also his or her present pain and suffering. This process hopefully helps him or her achieve an inner peace of mind regarding all that he or she has been through during earthly life.

VISUALIZING DECEASED FAMILY MEMBERS, FRIENDS, AND ANGELS

Visualizing contact, now and in the future, with deceased family members and friends, as well as angels, opens new vistas for exploring the meaning of eternal life and the soul's afterlife journey. If a gravely ill person is receptive, loved ones can use this guided visualization for ten to fifteen minutes.

Guided Visualization of Deceased Family Members and Friends. Introduction: As the guide, create a warm, welcoming atmosphere, an environment of serenity and spaciousness for the journey within. Lower the lights, if possible. Although difficult in a hospital room, candles can set a mood that enhances meditation.

Ask the dying individual to close his or her eyes; sit quietly; calm and relax his or her body by sitting, reclining, or lying down; and breathe in and out normally, feeling where the breath flows into and out of the body. Adjust the breaths so that the in and out breaths are the same length, thereby bringing about both a relaxation of the body and a calmness of the mind. (Obviously, you need to vary these instructions depending on the individual's physical condition.)

Ask the terminally ill person to imagine his or her guardian angel, perhaps one of the four from the Guardian Angel Meditation in chapter 11, or another angel.

Inviting communication with his or her guardian angel (or another angel), ask: When did the angel come into his or her life? What is it doing for him or her now? What will it do for him or her in the future?

Focusing on complete relaxation, invite the guardian angel (or other angel) to describe various stages of the soul's afterlife journey: the death moment and the immediate postdeath transition, particularly deceased family members and friends who will serve as guides in the postmortem realms.

If appropriate, invite the guardian angel (or another angel) to also describe the soul's ongoing afterlife journey.

Concluding Instructions: As the guide, now invite the dying individual to come back to the here and now. Take time to ease back. Slowly bring his or her awareness back into the body, feeling himself or herself back in the room and opening his or her eyes.

SURRENDERING TO AND ENTERING THE CLEAR LIGHT

Gently urge the dying person to surrender to and enter the Clear Light appearing at the death moment or immediately thereafter. Following the example of the Baal Shem Tov, encourage a terminally ill person to let go of earthly attachments and desires, slowly and consciously exit the material world, and remain open to the Clear Light and the afterlife realms. Facilitate this process when the dying individual is declining physically but prior to the time when death is imminent as characterized by the gradual shutting down of various life functions discussed earlier in this chapter. Obviously, the timing of this discussion represents a difficult judgment call, as a gravely ill person may still have weeks or days left prior to his or her demise.

DISIDENTIFYING WITH THE PHYSICAL BODY

In addition to encouraging a life review, the visualization of previously deceased relatives and friends as well as angels, and the surrender to and entering into the Clear Light, it is good to facilitate a dying person's disidentification with his or her physical body and attachments to the earthly plane. In striving to break the linkage with his or her body, a person ceases to identify with the material dimension of his or her being as well as the earthly realm and begins to focus awareness on his or her timeless, immortal soul and its afterlife journey. Recognizing that our bodes are not all that we are, reduced attachment to the physical, materialistic aspects of life assists the soul to leave the body and opens us to the next stage of our existence.

The following guided meditation (or visualization) encourages the process of letting go and facilitates identification with the spiritual dimensions of one's inner life. But remember that letting go takes time. Each of us needs time to overcome our attachment to the material world and our physical body. Guide a dying person through this meditation (or visualization) for ten to fifteen minutes daily, for one week, if possible.

Guided Bodily Disidentification Meditation (or Visualization). Introduction: As the guide, create a warm, welcoming atmosphere, an environment of serenity and spaciousness for the journey within. Lower the lights, if possible. Although difficult in a hospital room, candles can set a mood that enhances meditation.

Ask the dying individual to close his or her eyes; sit quietly; calm and relax his or her body by sitting, reclining, or lying down; and breathe in and out normally, feeling where the breath flows into and out of the body. Adjust the breaths so that the in and out breaths are the same length, thereby bringing about both a relaxation of the body and a calmness of the mind. (Obviously, you need to vary these instructions depending on the individual's physical condition.)

Invite the dying person to feel his or her body. Feel the weight of his or her head. Feel the weight of his or her arms and hands. Feel the weight of his or her torso. Feel the weight of his or her legs and feet. Feel the pull of gravity on his or her body.

Ask him or her to open his or her heart to subtler and lighter sensations, to his or her immortal soul. With each inbreath, invite him or her to see how it is received by the soul. Feel the contact with his or her soul. See how each breath sustains the soul.

Then imagine that each breath is his or her last breath. The connection between his or her soul and body is severed. Let his or her last breath go, forever. Let go gently and die. Let go of attachments, desires, fears, and thoughts. Let him or her die and go gently into the Clear Light.

See his or her soul float free from his or her body. With an open heart, let go of his or her identification with his or her body, this earthly world, material possessions, and anything else that holds him or her back. Let his or her soul float free. Let him or her die. Let him or her be free from this earthly incarnation. Open to his or her soul floating free of his or her body.

Concluding Instructions: As the guide, now invite the dying individual to come back to the here and now. Take time to ease back. Slowly bring his or her awareness back into the body, feeling himself or herself back in the room and opening his or her eyes.

PRACTICAL SUGGESTIONS FOR CAREGIVERS

Make a gravely ill person as comfortable as possible, thereby lessening any unnecessary pain and suffering. Whether an individual dies at home or in a hospice or hospital, make certain that the dying person's physical care needs are met. This may require the continuous presence of family members and friends throughout the day.

As life ebbs for the terminally ill, particular attention should focus on the use of pain control medication. Be certain that the dying person does not experience, if at all possible, severe, uncontrolled pain. Concerns about drug usage, including unreasonable fears about addiction to pain control medication, may cause physicians to underutilize pain medicine. For the terminally ill, these fears are simply ridiculous. Because he or she is going to die anyway, prevail on physicians to allow a loved one to take as much pain medication as needed to be comfortable.

It is paramount that a dying person's pain be adequately controlled. In nearly all situations, this is now medically feasible.[19] Allow the patient, if lucid, to control how much painkiller to take and when.

The use of pain control medication must, however, take into account the reality of the death moment visions, which help a person exit the earthly world and enter the postmortem realms as a disembodied soul. Although minimizing physical pain, the medication should permit, if possible, the patient to remain conscious. Because the moment of death represents the point in time when the soul begins to leave the physical body, see to it that a dying individual goes through the dying process, as the Baal Shem Tov did, fully lucid.

In addition to focusing on controlling and managing a dying person's pain, make certain that he or she is comfortable. A limitless number of physical concerns may arise, including breathing and bowel movement difficulties, nausea and vomiting, and sleep disorders. Deal with all of these physical needs. The requisite medical technology and knowledge currently exist to control just about every form of physical distress among the dying.

Remember that various relaxation strategies, such as the Relaxation Response discussed in chapter 10, can help a patient cope with arduous treatments and as supplements to procedures and medication. Also suggest that a terminally ill individual learn a cognitive approach, found in chapter 10, in which he or she reframes pain by looking at it from a different perspective.

Saying our final goodbyes to a family member or a close friend is, of course, difficult for all of us. Be aware of the expected emotional reactions as the last goodbyes are said. We experience great grief at the impending physical separation. Tears come with remembrance and memories. We seem unable to let go. However, as developed in this chapter, the souls of peaceful living beings can help the soon-to-depart soul overcome its attachment to earthly life on its transition to the afterlife realms.

NOTES

1. Chapter 5 of my book *The Jewish Book of Living and Dying* (Northvale, NJ: Jason Aronson, 1999) discusses in more detail the death moment visions.

2. Chapter 4 of *The Jewish Book of Living and Dying* considers both deathbed rituals in the Jewish tradition and techniques for assisting the terminally ill prior to death.

3. Simcha Paull Raphael, *Jewish Views of the Afterlife* (Northvale, NJ: Jason Aronson, 1994), pp. 295–296 and 378–379.

4. Ibid., pp. 132–136, 288–291, 294, 342, 379–380.

5. Raymond A. Moody Jr., *Life After Life: The Investigation of a Phenomenon—Survival of Bodily Death* (New York: Bantam Books, 1976). Near death experiences (NDEs) are also discussed in Michael B. Sabom, *Recollections of Death: A Medical Investigation* (New York: Harper and Row, 1982) (interviews with 116 persons having a close brush with death, 71 reporting a near death experience); and Kenneth Ring, *Life at Death: A Scientific Investigation of the Near-Death Experience* (New York: Coward, McCann & Geoghegan, 1980) (study of 102 persons who had a close brush with death). Patrick Glynn, *God: The Evidence: The Reconciliation of Faith and Reason in a Postsecular World* (Rocklin, CA: Forum, 1997), pp. 99–137, summarizes the evidence.

6. Elizabeth Kübler-Ross, *On Life After Death* (Berkeley, CA: Celestial Arts, 1991), p. 61.

7. Raphael, *Afterlife*, p. 294; and Anne Brener, *Mourning & Mitzvah: A Guided Journal for Walking the Mourner's Path Through Grief to Healing* (Woodstock, VT: Jewish Lights Publishing, 1993), p. 197.

8. Kübler-Ross, *On Life After Death*, p. 18.

9. *Midrash on Psalms* 11:6, trans. William G. Braude (New Haven, CT: Yale University Press, 1959).

10. Ibid.

11. Adapted from *Jewish Reflections on Death*, ed. Jack Riemer (New York: Schocken, 1974), pp. 26–27.

12. Simcha Steven Paull, *Judaism's Contribution to the Psychology of Death and Dying* (Ph.D. dissertation, California Institute of Integral Studies, 1986), pp. 336–338.

13. Moody, *Life After Life*, p. 37.

14. Adapted from Dr. Joseph H. Hertz, *The Authorized Daily Prayer Book*, rev. ed. (New York: Bloch, 1985), p. 1065.

15. Stephen Levine, *Who Dies? An Investigation of Conscious Living and Conscious Dying* (Garden City, NY: Anchor, 1982), pp. 73–83.

16. John W. James and Russell Friedman, *The Grief Recovery Handbook: The Action Program for Moving Beyond Death, Divorce, and Other Losses*, rev. ed. (New York: Harper Perennial, 1998), pp. 109–114.

17. Ibid., pp. 140–141.

18. Paull, *Judaism's Contribution*, p. 338.

19. A technical analysis of pain control, useful to a layperson, is provided by Cicely M. Saunders and Mary Baines, *Living with Dying: The Management of Terminal Disease*, 2nd ed. (New York: Oxford University Press, 1989).

CHAPTER THIRTEEN

Death, Grieving, and the Soul's Afterlife Journey

This chapter presents a spiritually based, universally applicable model of life after death, based on Jewish sources. It delineates an approach to the soul's afterlife journey and offers spiritual suggestions for understanding the human encounter with death and the afterlife.[1]

Death represents a source of great anxiety for nearly all of us. We are gripped with fear when we think about our ultimate destiny. However, the Jewish tradition urges us to see life and death as a continuum. God did not create us to destroy us. The Eternal created us for growth and development, not annihilation. The Divine goodness is as active in the hereafter as in our material world.

We are eternal beings. Our soul, our spiritual essence, is immortal, infinite in time and space. After we leave our physical body behind and are liberated from its weaknesses and hindrances, our soul enjoys eternal life. Death should hold no terror for us. Because our earthly death marks a new destination for us, our fear of annihilation should vanish.

In exploring the soul's afterlife journey, the first part of this chapter offers a four-part model of the afterlife journey: first, the separation of the soul from the physical body—the pangs of the grave; second, the purification of the soul in Purgatory for a finite time period; third, the heavenly visions of the soul in Paradise, a realm of emotional, intellectual, and spiritual bliss; and fourth, spiritual unification consisting of return of the soul to the Source of Life, reincarnation on the earth, and, ultimately, union with God.

The second part of this chapter sets forth various soul-guiding techniques[2] designed so that the living can assist a soul on its afterlife journey. These soul-guiding techniques not only help the soul of a departed loved one lessen the pangs of the grave in the immediate postdeath transition but also promote the interconnectedness between the survivors and the soul. These techniques assist individuals seeking to establish a new (or to continue to strengthen their) relationship with the immortal soul of a decedent, based upon a belief that a window of communication, albeit separated by some sort of thin veil, exists between the living and the dead. An active bond endures between the living and the soul of a departed loved one, not a wall of silence, despite the seeming finality of bodily death. The thoughts, words, and actions of the living impact on the departed soul. Using these soul-guiding techniques, the survivors can assist a soul to make its afterlife voyage. In addition, the soul, as explained in this chapter, may also help the living.

A QUICK TOUR THROUGH THE WORLD OF SOULS

Let us begin by taking a quick tour through the world of the souls, beginning with the pangs of the grave a soul experiences immediately after death, followed by Purgatory, Paradise, return to the Source of Life, reincarnation, and, finally, union with God.

THE PANGS OF THE GRAVE

In the anguish of the grave, the soul undergoes a painful ordeal Jewish sources refer to as the "pangs of the grave." The soul remains close to its physical body, struggling to hold onto life and only slowly releasing its attachment to the body and the material world.[3]

Unwilling to surrender its attachment to the earthly realm, the soul—particularly its physical level, closely identified with the body and material existence—experiences considerable torment during the three-to-seven-day period immediately after death. As the mystical teachings note: "Throughout the seven days the soul goes from his house to his grave, and from his grave to his house, and mourns for the body. . . . It goes and dwells in his house. It sees them all grief-stricken, and it mourns." (*Zohar II*, 218a–219a)

A soul with physical realm attachments often remains earthbound during this time frame, traveling between the grave holding the physical body and his or her former residence, where grieving family members and material possessions are located. The mystical sources suggest that the soul, aware of the family's thoughts and emotions, may try to talk to the survivors and make use of familiar objects. Seeing their weeping, the soul begins to realize there has been a death—his or hers.

During the three-to-seven-day postdeath period, the soul remains close to its physical body and may even try to reenter it. With the body's decomposition and the soul's realization that it no longer has a body to make a shadow or cast a reflection in a mirror, the soul leaves its body and sets out on its afterlife journey.

The mystical teachings indicate that many souls do not experience a painless transition out of their physical body, only gradually yielding the entrapments of the earthly plane. For most of us, the soul's withdrawal or separation from the body results in an emotional, often tormenting upheaval, as explained in this excerpt:

> "For love is strong as death" [Song of Songs 8:6]: It is as strong like the parting of the spirit from the body, as we have [learned] that when a man is about to depart from the world and he sees strange things, his spirit courses through all his limbs and goes up and down like a boatman without oars who is tossed up and down on the sea and makes no progress. It then asks leave of each limb; and its separation is only effected with great violence. (*Zohar I*, 245a)

What we are most attached to in life may result in considerable suffering after death. The soul of an individual who lived a life too fully focused on the body's physical aspects or its sensual delights, who was attached to the material world or addicted to nicotine, alcohol, or drugs, experiences, in his or her clinging, a severely difficult time in overcoming the pangs of the grave. This individual encounters the world of confusion, a realm of painful torment, in seeing his or her body decompose and in severing concerns with earthly matters. However, this tenacious craving, like any addiction, cannot really be satisfied.

For those individuals who refuse, during their lives, to relinquish, or at least lessen, their attachments to the physical body and more generally to the material plane (or those who have died violently or suddenly), their souls' separation from the body not only creates much discomfort but also may require a considerably longer time period. The souls of these decedents may remain in the world of confusion for far more than three or seven days.

Conversely, the period of separation from the physical body is easier and more rapid for certain individuals who have lived a "purer" life. According to the Jewish sages, those falling into this category include those who have avoided various addictions as well as those who have cultivated the spiritual, nonmaterial dimensions of life, a more balanced earthly existence, not overly identifying with the physical body and the material world. Because in life they have discerned that their sense of self transcends the body and the earthly plane, the pangs of the grave can be lessened or even avoided.

Building on Jewish Spirituality's emphasis on lovingkindness, forgiveness, and truthfulness in our dealings with others, a life of "good" conduct, words, and thoughts makes it easier for the soul to leave the physical body. For the "righteous," the separation of the soul from the body need not be an overly painful or lengthy task.

THE SOUL'S PURIFICATION IN PURGATORY

After surrendering any attachment to its physical body, the soul undergoes a process of purification in Purgatory (*Gehenna* in Hebrew). Variously described by Jewish sources, the process of purgation consists of a healing transformation in which the soul's defilements and impurities are further cleansed. For some souls, the journey through Purgatory will be very difficult; for others, this journey represents a far less painful encounter. Each experience in Purgatory not only reflects the soul's immediate past life behavior, words, and thoughts but also the depth and nature of the soul's unresolved relationship issues and unexpressed emotions.

During the process of purification in Purgatory, each soul atones for its earthly wrongdoings. Various impurities of the soul are cleansed, including harmful actions and unkind words as well as destructive thoughts, harmful attitudes, and negative emotions: hate, aggression, anger, fear, hostility, shame, guilt, anxiety, grasping, greed, pride, envy, jealousy, lust, manipulation, revenge, blame, desire, sadness, resentment, fault finding, and an inability to forgive.

This period of inner dissolution in Purgatory marks the beginning of the end of the soul's desires, attachments, and fears, as well as the termination of its selfishness and greed. During its journey through Purgatory, each soul discovers a deeper sense of inner peace of mind, characterized by humility, joy, and equanimity, as well as an enhanced ability to be loving, compassionate, forgiving, and truthful.

TIME SPENT IN PURGATORY

Jewish resources generally view the period of time a soul spends in Purgatory as finite.[4] In other words, damnation in the Jewish tradition is not eternal. The soul's journey through Purgatory and the accompanying purification of earthly life's defilements eventually ends.

Jewish sages throughout the ages have reiterated that the soul typically completes its period of purgation and purification in Purgatory after a maximum of twelve months. According to tradition, one year represents the length of time needed to extract the soul's impurities and prepare it for the ongoing afterlife journey. Because time does not exist in the hereafter, however, who knows what one year in Purgatory feels like?

The teaching of an eternal punishment for souls in Purgatory remained a minority view among Jewish sages. According to the mainstream of the Jewish tradition, nearly all souls, after a transitory experience in Purgatory, are sufficiently purified to enter the realm of Paradise. It is important to note that only very few souls skip Purgatory and go directly to Paradise. The more "righteous" experience a far shorter and easier purification process in Purgatory than do the less.

THE REALM OF PARADISE

In the realm of Paradise, the soul continues its evolutionary journey of emotional, intellectual, and spiritual growth. Paradise represents neither a static experience nor a soul's final destination. It is "rest and recreation" for the soul. On its postdeath journey, the soul ultimately advances from Lower Paradise to the even higher, more transcendent spiritual levels of Upper Paradise. Paradise, whether Lower or Upper, represents a heavenly realm where souls, as disembodied states of consciousness, reside for an unspecified but not eternal time frame.

Lower Paradise

Lower Paradise serves as a transit stage between Purgatory and Upper Paradise. In the Lower Paradise, each soul continues the purification process begun in Purgatory and prepares for entry into Upper Paradise.

Souls who do not immediately merit admission from Purgatory into Upper Paradise are assigned to a subordinate realm, Lower Paradise. There, each soul experiences the emotional, intellectual, and spiritual bliss appropriate to its most recent past attainments.

The last vestiges of the decedent's earthly personality and his or her personal life just ended play out in Lower Paradise.[5] Incomplete desires, attachments, and emotions are experienced there. What is personal and impermanent gradually dissipates.

The Soul's Restful Journey in Upper Paradise

The soul eventually leaves Lower Paradise and enters Upper Paradise, the realm of heavenly bliss, a region designed for the soul's higher dimensions. In Upper Paradise, the soul attains an even higher level of emotional, intellectual, and spiritual fulfillment and ecstasy, as well as the joy of being close to God.

On entering Upper Paradise, the soul once again takes a dip in the River of Light and experiences a second Life Review. (These two steps were discussed in chapter 12 in connection with the Death Moment Visions.) This second immersion in the River of Light further heals the soul and purges it of any remaining impurities and impressions from its immediate past earthly existence, enabling it to perceive the glory manifest in Upper Paradise.

In addition to a second immersion in the River of Light, the second Life Review is equally significant. The events of the deceased's life just completed are again viewed, this time from the perspective of the immortal soul's many lifetimes. The meaning of what the deceased experienced in his or her most recent life becomes clearer and more enduring from the viewpoint of the soul's eternal self.

The Jewish mystics regard Upper Paradise as a world of transcendental bliss. Each soul dwells in a level of Paradise (there are said to be seven realms) according to the merits of and as a reward for its beneficent deeds, words, and thoughts accumulated during its immediate past life. Each soul finds other kindred spirits: loving, compassionate, forgiving, truthful, joyful, courageous, and humble.

Putting behind its immediate past life's desires, attachments, and emotions and without any jealousy, guilt, anger, hatred, bitterness, or pride, each soul experiences, in Upper Paradise, the delight of studying and meditating on the Divine harmony and mysteries of the cosmos. Like-minded souls gather together in what the mystics metaphorically describe as the Celestial Academy. There, each soul attains a majestic, blissful understanding of God. The Eternal appears daily in the Celestial Academy and shares the Divine Wisdom with the souls dwelling there, who are said by Jewish sages to derive great, almost unimaginable, joy from being close to God.

A glimpse of Upper Paradise may be gained from the near death experiencers studied by Raymond Moody who express a newfound respect for knowledge and learning, for life's intellectual aspects. Some realize that learning does not end when you die. You continue to learn and to grow. Others describe an entire afterlife realm set aside for passionately pursuing knowledge, what one woman described as a "big university."[6]

As the soul's intellectual aspects come to the fore, the souls as disembodied states of consciousness, according to the mystical tradition, passionately engage in the pursuit of knowledge. The Jewish mystics view the souls in Upper Paradise as engrossed in deep, ongoing conversations about the cosmos, human existence, and universal wholeness. They ponder timeless questions, including the meaning and purpose of our earthly life and why many humans endure much pain, suffering, and tragedy during their mortal lifetimes.

According to the mystics, in Upper Paradise the soul uses its newly acquired knowledge to further its personal wholeness and to perceive the interrelatedness of all humans.[7] This knowledge allows the soul to feel complete again in all of its aspects: physical, emotional, mental, and spiritual. The soul reflects within itself the Wholeness that is God.

Each soul is said to gain a transcendent, transpersonal awareness. It achieves a richer, deeper understanding of earthly life. The intellectual and spiritual maturity attained in Upper Paradise, particularly the expanded view of the world and the cosmos, permits each soul to become even more inclusive in its worldview.

Perceptions of awe and wonder abound in the midst of a grand, majestic order. The distinctions between any one soul and the infinite God gradually become blurred. Each soul lives before the Eternal, bathed in unconditional love, compassion, and forgiveness, experiencing the glories of inner peace of mind and spiritual fulfillment.

Reflecting the interconnectedness between the world of the living and what a soul experiences in Paradise, the mystics indicate that our lifetime of deeds, words, and thoughts have consequences large and small, and impact on the destiny of each of us in the afterlife realms. By living a more balanced, more spiritually oriented existence in the here and now, each of us creates beneficial experiences for his or her soul in the world beyond. The mystical tradition suggests these spiritually attuned and questing souls will reap the rewards of their earthly spiritual pursuits and are better and more easily able to enjoy the transcendent bliss of the lofty reaches of Upper Paradise.

THE SOUL'S RETURN TO THE SOURCE OF LIFE

After a soul completes its evolution in Paradise but before being reborn, it gathers together with other souls in what the Jewish tradition describes as the transcendent realm of the souls. Each soul returns to the Divine Source of all life, to the realm of being with God.

Jewish sources refer to the soul as returning to the Divine Storehouse of Souls, the place of the origin and the termination of all souls. The Divine Treasury of Souls is often equated with the biblical bond of life, the bundle of the living (1 Samuel 25:29).

The rabbis repeatedly spoke of the Divine Treasure House, a realm where righteous souls gather. They perceived this transcendent realm of souls as a postdeath gathering place, a storehouse for the righteous souls in the highest Divine spheres, where each disembodied soul prepares for rebirth in a new physical body.

REINCARNATION: THE SOUL'S REBIRTH
IN A NEW PHYSICAL BODY

Reincarnation in the earthly world marks the full circle of the soul's journey. Rebirth gives each soul the opportunity to atone for any past misdeeds and actualize its potential by improving its physical, emotional, intellectual, and spiritual evolution through its earthly thoughts, speech, and conduct.

Although the concept of reincarnation fires the modern mind, it remains a challenge for empirical proof. However, some intriguing evidence exists. Dr. Ian Stevenson, a professor of psychiatry, has spent his professional career investigating cases of young children, especially in India, who spontaneously recall past lives.[8] Stevenson has documented more than 2,600 cases suggestive of reincarnation. These children, when brought into contact with their families from prior lives, recognize spouses, siblings, or parents without any prompting. Stevenson also found examples in which birthmarks in this life correspond to wounds inflicted on the body in a previous earthly existence.

Evidence of reincarnation also comes as a result of past life regression under hypnosis. In his best-selling book, *Many Lives, Many Masters*,[9] psychiatrist Brian L. Weiss, M.D., tells the story of Catherine, a young laboratory technician who came into his office complaining of her chronic fears of water, choking, darkness, and dying. Following one year of unsuccessful conventional psychotherapy, Weiss encouraged her to try hypnosis. After several sessions, he instructed her to go back to the time from when her symptoms first arose. Catherine described herself as a young woman living in 1863 B.C.E. She recalled a tidal wave destroying her village. As Catherine revealed more of her past lives, more of her emotional and physical symptoms subsided.

Stepping back from these modern case studies, the belief in the Jewish tradition that a soul enters a new body is not found in the Bible or the rabbinic literature. Rather, the Jewish mystics speak of reincarnation (*gilgul* in Hebrew) as marking the rebirth of the soul and its reentry on earth in a new physical body.

Building on kabbalistic thought, particularly the *Zohar*, a major mystical text, reincarnation plays a central role among Hasidic Jews. For instance, the Baal Shem Tov proclaimed himself to be a reincarnation of Rabbi Saadia Gaon, the first eminent philosopher of medieval Judaism, who lived from 882 to 942 C.E.[10]

Reincarnation serves a significant purpose in the Jewish tradition. Through rebirth, a soul can improve its good deeds, words, and thoughts—perhaps remedying any wrongdoing it committed in its immediate past life. The soul can also attain further physical, emotional, intellectual, and spiritual purification, completing its tasks—particularly fulfilling its spiritual potential, which varies from person to person—before reaching its ultimate destination, union with God. In addition to striving to attain perfection for its own benefit, rebirth also affords a righteous soul the opportunity to provide others with love, compassion, and forgiveness and generally to be of selfless service to humanity.

Reincarnation: Some Further Details

Through the ages, Jewish sages have wondered: Who is reincarnated?[11] Jewish mystics first viewed reincarnation as open just to evildoers, and subsequently to evildoers, ordinary or middling people, and the righteous. Through reincarnation, a righteous person could help other humans attain a higher degree of spiritual perfection.

Beyond the general notion of reincarnation, the details remain quite fuzzy. The Jewish mystics were (and are) unable to agree on a number of tantalizing details, including who comes back and the length of time between incarnations. The number of times a soul comes back, according to Jewish sages, has varied from four incarnations for righteous souls all the way up to one hundred or even one thousand rebirths for a wicked soul.[12] Seemingly, no limit exists on the number of reincarnations for the righteous whose souls are reborn for the good of the entire world.

Disputes also focused on when the soul is implanted in a new physical body. The range of possibilities include: at conception, forty days after conception, just before or at the moment of birth, or up to five days after birth. It is also unclear whether an individual is reborn as the same or the opposite sex.

Some Jewish mystics espoused the concept of transmigration, a notion basic to Eastern religious traditions. Transmigration connotes the incarnation of an individual guilty of grave transgressions as an animal, particularly a chicken or a dog; a plant or flower; or even an inanimate object, such as a stone. Most Jewish mystics, however, reached the conclusion that souls are reborn again only as human beings. Their reasoning is quite simple: Only rebirth as a human enables a soul to continue its process of evolution and purification.

Despite these quibbles, one thing is clear. The Jewish tradition indicates that only very few souls do not require reincarnation.

Reincarnation: A Reality Check

If we undergo reincarnation, why do most of us not remember our past lives? One explanation is found in a medieval text describing how a soul prepares for its rebirth into the earthly world. According to this writer, two angels are said to accompany the soul before it is placed in the womb or when it is in the womb. A light, set above the soul, enables the soul to see from one end of the world to the other. One angel accompanies the soul to Paradise to see the fate of righteous souls. Then, the soul is shown the fate of the wicked in Purgatory. The soul is briefed, receiving a coming life preview, including where it will reside, die, and be buried. This author continues:

> When the time arrives for [the soul] to emerge from the womb into the open world, [an] angel addresses the soul, "The time has come for you to go [forth] into the open world." The soul demurs, "Why [do you] want to make me go forth into the open world?" The angel replies: "Know that as [you were] formed against [your] will, so now [you will] be born against [your] will, and against [your] will [you shall] die, and against [your] will give account of [yourself] before the [Blessed Holy One]." But the soul is reluctant to leave her place. The angel [touches] the babe on the nose, extinguishes the light at his head, and brings him forth into the world against his will. Immediately the child forgets all his soul has seen and [learned], and he comes into the world crying, for he loses a place of shelter and security and rest.[13]

So why don't most of us remember our past lives? There is a ring of logic to our present amnesia. Each of us has a role to play in earthly life, here and now. Knowledge about our past roles might, therefore, interfere with our current role as well as our free will. According to one researcher of past life regression through hypnosis, "This amnesia is invaluable in that it prevents endless pining and homesickness for the grandeur that has been left behind and allows the individual to embark on the new life unhindered by confusing echoes of past deeds and misdeeds."[14]

What the soul retains, perhaps, are those enduring lessons and truths of significance for its physical, emotional, intellectual, and spiritual evolution in its present incarnation. However, most of us cannot recall specific information, including past identity or the names of people, dates, or places we knew in former lifetimes. The positive lessons and truths and the wisdom, but not the details, the soul previously learned hopefully will be used for the benefit of not only one individual but also, more generally, for humanity.

In the Jewish tradition, the soul's next earthly incarnation involves a mixture of God's control, Divine providence, and mercy, as well as human free will. Charting the soul's future course, the mystics suggest, the Eternal tells each soul, particularly less developed souls, what its mission will be and how to fulfill it. The soul obtains its instructions and the specific lessons it needs to learn to achieve a higher degree of perfection. A soul may be assigned a spirit guide. More advanced souls may receive only a general outline. Each soul is reborn with the task of not only mending itself but also helping perfect the world.

Incarnations may be more difficult as the soul evolves. An impaired physical body, a difficult interpersonal relationship, or grinding poverty, to take but three examples, all serve a purpose in the Divine plan.

At the same time, the Jewish tradition insists on free will. You are free to respond to the circumstances in which you find yourself, how you perceive and experience them, how you interpret what happens to you, and the choices you make in life. Using your creative imagination and your constructive will, you are responsible for who you are and what you make of your life.

Through your mind and your way of thinking, you create your world. How you interpret what happens to you determines your inner peace of mind (or lack of it). Do your best to work with what God has given you. Thus, for each of us, the future is not made in the womb or at birth; rather it is within our wills to create it—subject, of course, to certain parameters.

In the midst of this rather uneasy balance between Divine control over our lives and free will, it is important to realize that profound reasons exist for our being and what happens to us in our earthly sojourn, although we may be unable to discern them. Each experience contains a lesson; every relationship has its lesson; each task presents a lesson. There are no accidents in God's plan for you. Each situation provides a means for you to become more aware of the Divine Presence and Love. A time of challenge and difficulty offers an opportunity to discover (or rediscover) your own deeper spiritual essence.

The Holy One sends us a vast array of experiences—the people we meet, the relationships we form, the physical and emotional pain and suffering we experience, and other adversities we face—as learning opportunities, often quite difficult and demanding but designed to help us grow spiritually and purify and perfect ourselves. In particular, free will is given us, from the viewpoint of Jewish Spirituality, to love, forgive, and be truthful with others and make positive choices that benefit humanity.

The experiences we encounter as reborn souls in the earthly realm serve a vital purpose in the larger scheme of things. As an educational process, these interactions give meaning and purpose to our lives and hopefully reinforce our perception of an enduring spiritual—not the all-too-visible materialistic—reality.

THE SOUL'S ULTIMATE DESTINATION: UNION WITH GOD

With new opportunities for performing good deeds, expressing kind words, and thinking beneficent thoughts on earth, reincarnation enables a soul to fully actualize its potential and attain a higher degree of physical, emotional, intellectual, and spiritual perfection. Successive rebirths enable each soul to evolve and obtain a sense of the more profound dimensions of God. As a soul continually reincarnates, it ultimately achieves complete purification and perfection.

For the mystics, the soul gradually progresses to its final goal: union with God, thereby ending its cycles of birth and death in the earthly world.[15] If we view God as an independent Being, then perhaps the concept of union with the Supreme Sovereign may best be seen as a soul touching the Eternal or as the merging of an individual's will with that of the Divine so that the two are essentially the same.

In the soul's long and arduous spiritual journey, time is a relative criterion. Some righteous souls achieve the desired realization of a spiritual life, union with God, much quicker than others.

HOW SPIRITUAL SEEKERS CAN ASSIST THE SOULS OF DEPARTED LOVED ONES AND HEAL THEMSELVES

Bereaved spiritual seekers wrestling with grief or intense emotional suffering can engage in a number of practices designed to overcome the initial shock, heal their grief, and accept the searing reality of death; help the soul detach from its physical body; and interconnect the soul of the departed with the world of the living, using various soul-guiding techniques.

Let us consider three phases: first, immediately after death; second, the first year or so of mourning; and third, beyond the first year after a loved one's death. There is a gradual movement toward building a new normalcy, characterized by moving on, and letting go and liberation from an attachment to the deceased. The living gradually achieve both an intellectual and emotional acceptance of death.

THE IMMEDIATE POSTDEATH PERIOD

Immediately after the death of a loved one is a time of great shock, as the bereaved struggle with their grief. They experience a profound numbness, confusion, and disbelief that temporarily insulate them from the reality of death. As a sort of anesthetic, the numbness and disbelief provide a means of survival, giving loved ones a breather to enable them to catch up emotionally with what their mind is telling them. Some experience a delayed grief after their exhaustion ends.

Throughout the immediate postmortem period, it is important for the living to remember that the deceased is much more than his or her physical body. He or she has a soul, and it has departed earthly life. Let us consider, in turn, three time frames: first, the period from death to the funeral (or memorial) service; second, at the funeral (or memorial) and burial services; and third, the immediate mourning period.

FROM DEATH TO THE FUNERAL SERVICE

From the time of death until either the funeral service (a service held in the presence of the body) or memorial service (a service without the body present), despite your numbness and disbelief you should provide the soul of a departed loved one the maximum amount of support you possibly can. Your support helps the soul lessen its attachment to the material world—the pangs of the grave—and assists in its entrance into the afterlife realms. Give the soul your thoughtful attention and assistance as the last remnants of consciousness leave the earthly plane.

If possible, stay with the body for a few hours after death. Some hospitals and hospices will cooperate, especially if it is prearranged. As you say your goodbyes one more time, the deceased's inner peace becomes apparent, silently radiating "Things are O.K." As the reality of death sets in, this time with the decedent's physical body will help you begin to adjust to your loss.

Recognize that your thoughts, words, and practices help a soul in a number of positive ways. Through your prayers, urge the soul to let go and to move onward, now that his or her earthly work is complete. By attuning your thoughts to the departed, you aid the soul to become free from the pangs of the grave and find its way in the afterlife.

Coming from the heart, telling the soul, "Go onward," also offers you the possibility to start to adjust to your loss and heal your grief, even at this early stage.

At the Funeral and Gravesite Services

At the funeral or memorial service, either of which help make apparent and confirm the reality of death, open your heart to your grief in the midst of outwardly expressing your thoughts and feelings—your sadness, anxiety, fear, guilt, regret, anger, and loneliness—and shedding your tears. In addition to talking about the deceased, continue to send your loving thoughts to the departed. Let go of your attachment to him or her but treasure his or her memory and let go with love.

At many Jewish funeral services, a traditional prayer for the soul (*El Malai Rachamim*) is recited. This prayer calls on God to embrace the soul of the deceased under the nurturing wings of the Divine's feminine aspect (the Shekhinah). Family and friends pray as follows that the soul will encounter the Eternal's love and compassion on its afterlife journey:

> Compassionate God, Eternal Spirit of the universe, God of forgiveness, mercy, and abounding lovingkindness, pardon his/her transgressions and grant perfect rest in the shadow of Your wings to ———— who has entered eternity. O God of compassion, remember him/her for all the meritorious deeds that he/she did on earth. Open to him/her the gates of righteousness and light, the gates of mercy and grace. Let the departed find refuge in Your eternal presence. Let his/her soul be bound up in the bond of eternal life. God is his/her inheritance. May he/she rest in peace.[16]

For many bereaved, it is still much too soon to focus on forgiveness or a letting go of the past. They are still in the midst of the initial shock and the accompanying numbness and disbelief. They are disconnected from the world around them. In addition to a reduced ability to concentrate, disorganization, confusion, and forgetfulness, they begin to experience a gamut of emotions accompanying their grief: rage, anger, hostility, guilt, regret, despair, sadness, emptiness, anxiety, irritability, fear, panic, loneliness, and hopelessness. Grief is usually sporadic; there are good days and bad days. It is important to express your grief and not ignore it. A number of physical symptoms also typically occur, including sleeplessness, appetite disturbances, dizziness, headaches, heart palpitations, breathlessness, loss of energy, and stomach pains.[17]

At this early stage of the mourning process, only a few survivors are able to begin to ask the deceased to forgive any hurt they caused him or her. Only these few are able to contemplate any unresolved and previously unexpressed feelings and emotions, including anger, resentment, bitterness, powerlessness, disappointment, fear, and the sense of being wronged, regarding the deceased.

In asking for or communicating forgiveness, as appropriate, use the Forgiveness and Lovingkindness Meditation (or Visualization) daily, for ten to fifteen minutes, to facilitate the process of forgiveness and reconciliation with the deceased as well as to forgive yourself. Visualizing the deceased and talking to him or her can be very powerful. Gradually, as the days and months pass, more and more mourners, realizing the magnitude of their loss, and as their feelings slowly return and they overcome their numbness, can beneficially use this exercise.

Forgiveness and Lovingkindness Meditation and Visualization. Introduction: Create a warm, welcoming atmosphere, an environment of serenity and spaciousness for the journey within. Lower the lights in your room. Close your eyes, sit quietly, calm and relax your body, breathe in and out normally, feeling where your breath flows into and out of your body. Adjust your breaths so that the in and out breaths are of the same length.

Feel yourself surrounded by warmth and love. Allow any anger, envy, or other emotion you feel to dissolve into the warmth. Feel the warmth nourishing you. Breathe in love and feel the openness that love creates in you. Allow the warmth and love to give rise to forgiveness. The power of forgiveness is so very great.

Visualize the deceased. Within a new state of openness, invite the deceased into your heart. Try to let the deceased through to your heart. Notice what blocks his or her approach to your heart—the problem, the hurt, the fear, the anger, the envy, the guilt, or whatever it is. Enter into and continue a dialogue with the deceased until there is nothing more to say. Then try again to let the deceased through to your heart. Let go of the pride that holds onto resentment. Allow the pain of old hurts to dissolve.

In your heart say, "I forgive you for whatever you did in the past, whether intentionally or unintentionally, through your deeds, words, or thoughts, that caused me pain or hurt." Repeat the words "I forgive you." Allowing the forgiveness to grow, let go of your resentments, your anger, and your hurt and open unconditionally into love and compassion.

Continue to visualize the deceased. Does he or she resent you? Did you cause him or her pain? Did the deceased put you out of his or her heart? With a new state of openness invite the deceased into your heart. Notice whatever blocks his or her approach to your heart. Try to let the deceased through to your heart.

From the bottom of your heart ask for forgiveness. Say: "I ask for your forgiveness for what I did in the past, whether intentionally or unintentionally, through my deeds, words, or thoughts, that caused you pain or hurt." Repeat the words "Please forgive me." Again, let yourself be touched by the possibility of forgiveness. Ask him or her to let go of his or her anger and hurt and let you back into his/her heart. Feel his or her forgiveness.

Let your heart fill with forgiveness and lovingkindness for yourself. Say to yourself: "May I be happy and at peace, free from anger, pain, fear, and doubt. May I be filled with love."

Concluding Instructions: Come back to the here and now. Take time to ease yourself back. Slowly bring your awareness back to your body. Feel yourself back in the room and open your eyes.

You can choose to forgive at any time, whenever you are ready to forgive or ask for forgiveness.

At the funeral or memorial service, the beloved also have an opportunity to attune their consciousness to the departed soul's consciousness. Realizing that we are not just physical bodies, remind yourself that there is so much more to life and to living.

Try to connect with and direct your thoughts to the soul of the departed. Through your expressions of love, compassion, and forgiveness, invite the soul to float freely on its postdeath journey and not cling to the physical body left behind. Conveying feelings of lovingkindness and compassion assists the soul in separating from its physical body and recognizing that it is no longer part of the material world.

Look into your own heart, mind, and soul. Ask yourself: What is your Divine mission and are you fulfilling it? Death may force you to rethink your own goals and priorities.

At the gravesite service, a stark reminder of the finality of death, again attune your thoughts to the soul, urging it to leave behind its attachment to the earthly plane. Relying on the mystical tradition, describe the realms the soul will encounter as a disembodied state of consciousness.

THE JEWISH TRADITION'S FORMAL MOURNING PERIOD

From the perspective of Jewish Spirituality, the length and style of mourning, the process occurring after death, represents a personal decision. This section offers an introduction to traditional Jewish rituals of mourning as well as a spiritual perspective on grieving and helpful soul-guiding techniques.

Immediately following the funeral begins the formal mourning period (*shivah* in Hebrew), which extends for three to seven days, with the longer period (suspended by the Sabbath and major Jewish holidays) following traditional Jewish practice.[18] The pangs of the grave, described earlier in this chapter, corresponds to the *shivah* period in which friends and relatives provide emotional and spiritual support for the mourners, thus comforting the bereaved.

The *shivah* process affirms community and family ties; offers a social support network for the bereaved, providing a source of comfort to the mourners and relieving the burden of intense loneliness; and begins the lengthy period of emotional healing. Family and friends come and extend their love and support. Through his or her presence, a visitor indicates: "I'm here because I care about you. I don't want you to be alone."

During the *shivah* period, the mourners have the opportunity to begin to grieve the deceased's loss and express the gamut of feelings that follow a loved one's death. Within a community context, they receive helpful emotional and spiritual support from visits by family members and friends, who often engage in animated conversation, telling stories about the departed and sharing cherished memories, some tears, and even some good laughs. They reminisce about the past. Surrounded by a supportive community, the mourners are encouraged to talk about their loss and to face and gradually accept the reality of death, thereby beginning to overcome their tendency to deny the permanence of the void in their lives.

Although often viewed as a frivolous social occasion, an opportunity for an ongoing cocktail party marked by food, drink, and insipid talk, the formal mourning period affords an excellent opportunity for a soul-guiding dimension. In the mourning period include time for spontaneous, unstructured prayers from the heart; silent meditations; and visualizations. Using these techniques daily, if possible, will help you connect personally with the soul of a departed loved one by sending it love, support, and forgiveness and communicating previously unexpressed feelings and emotions.

Align your thoughts and consciousness with the soul, helping it finish its business with this world and speeding it on its after-life journey. Encourage the soul to complete its business in this realm, leave behind the material world, let go of its attachments to the earthly plane and its physical body, and begin its postmortem journey.

Strive to connect in a deep, personal manner with the soul and to communicate previously unexpressed or unresolved emotions. Pouring out the feelings that each of the survivors holds in his or her own heart is of value for both the soul and the living, who are aided in giving up their attachment to the deceased.

As discussed in chapter 4, loved ones may want to begin to open their hearts to God using the practice of the Breslov Hasidim, the followers of Rabbi Nachman of Breslov. The Breslovers go outside daily and scream to God, often for an hour at a time. You can do this at home, while driving in your car, or anyplace where you are alone and can shout above your normal voice. You likely need a catharsis; recognize and release your feelings.

Open your heart to God. Ask God from the bottom of your heart: "Please help me." Use everyday language, not the liturgy of prayer. Express what is in your heart. Tell it to God; pour out your feelings to the Holy One. Say: "Please open and heal my heart." Express your grief, pain, sorrow, loneliness, helplessness, disbelief, guilt, fear, isolation, anxiety, panic, frustration, confusion, dependence, anger, despair, and resentment. Acknowledge and accept your feelings and your loss. Ask for God's help from the bottom of your heart. Let your sad feelings surface and your tears flow. Get your outrage with the Supreme Sovereign off your chest.

Visualize God responding, sending rays of light filling you with love and compassion, transforming your pain and suffering, and bringing you unconditional acceptance and love. Remember, God loves you with an everlasting love. Feeling the Divine Presence even in the midst of your grief and loneliness leads to an enormous relief and an increased sense of control over your life.

You may want to recite a prayer, based on the traditional prayer for the soul set out earlier in this chapter, to help you, in a more structured manner, visualize the outpouring of God's unconditional love and compassion for the departed soul.

Opening your heart to God or reciting a prayer for the soul helps you give up your attachment to the departed and assists the disembodied soul in its time of transition. Gradually, your longing for the deceased will lessen.

Many have found that selecting and reciting (or listening to) favorite spiritual teachings, poems, or songs—theirs or the deceased's—helps in saying goodbye and letting go. This technique not only aids loved ones accept the reality of death, it may also ease the passage of the soul.

To facilitate the letting go and the sending on of a soul, put a photo (or a special keepsake) of the departed on a table near you. Carve out a special time each day, for ten or fifteen minutes, to sit with your loved one. Tell him or her to let go of attachments to the earthly realm and continue on his or her journey.

This is also a time for the living to begin to open a window of communication with the soul of the departed and build a relationship that does not rely on a physical, earthly presence. Express your previously unstated emotional messages.

For some, this time of intense grief represents an opportunity for personal growth and development. They find that they are able to get in touch with otherwise inaccessible places within them. They reach something essential in their beings. They realize there is no place to hide. Their immense grief sometimes turns their lives around. For the rest of their lives, they come to open their hearts to others and are more loving, compassionate, forgiving, and truthful.

THE FIRST YEAR OF GRIEVING AND MOURNING

Beginning with the day of the funeral and each day thereafter for eleven months, a special memorial prayer, the Mourner's *Kaddish*, is traditionally recited at Jewish communal worship services by those who have lost a parent. Those who have lost a child (who lived for at least thirty days), a spouse, or a sibling say *Kaddish* only for thirty days. According to the Jewish tradition, those who are obligated say *Kaddish* and to be mourned for are a parent, a child, a spouse, or a sibling. Although originally recited only by sons (though now by both sons and daughters, at least in non-Orthodox congregations) for a parent, survivors now recite the Mourner's *Kaddish* for a child, spouse, sibling, or other close relatives such as a grandparent.

The period for saying the Mourner's *Kaddish*, eleven months for parents, corresponds roughly with the twelve months that Jewish sages proclaim a soul spends in Purgatory. Mourners recite the *Kaddish* for only eleven months to avoid any implication that the soul of a parent or other relative who is being remembered requires the full term in Purgatory.

Public recitation of the *Kaddish* offers the possibility of becoming part of an ongoing social support system as well as creating a sense of community and helping overcome the isolation and loneliness often encountered in bereavement. The saying of *Kaddish* also unites a group of mourners in the embrace of others, who regularly attend worship services, in a time of seeming helplessness and despair.

The Mourner's *Kaddish* represents a prayer of praise for and glorification of God, a supplication for the Divine rule, and for peace for all humanity. It does not refer to the dead, mourning, or the afterlife. Rather it is concerned with life in this world and the day when the earth will reflect Godliness. It is a message of comfort, hope, and peace.

In the *Kaddish* prayer, the mourner publicly declares his or her great faith in the Holy One's exalted greatness and goodness as well as his or her submission to the Eternal's will and justness as follows:

> Let the glory of God be extolled, let the Eternal's great Name be magnified and sanctified in the world created according to the Divine Will. May God's spiritual foundation soon prevail in our own day, in our own lives, and in the life of all of Israel, and let us say: Amen.
>
> Let God's great Name be blessed now and for ever and ever.
>
> Let the Name and the Presence of the Blessed Holy One be praised, glorified, exalted, extolled, and honored, though the Almighty is beyond all praises, songs, and expressions that we can utter, and let us say: Amen.
>
> For us and for everyone, may the abundance of peace and the promise of life's goodness come true, and let us say: Amen.
>
> May God, who causes peace to reign in the high heavens, bring peace to us, to all Israel, and to everyone, and let us say: Amen.[19]

Perceiving that the living and the departed are interconnected, the *Kaddish* process performs an important soul-guiding function[20] in enabling the bereaved and the soul of a deceased loved one to engage in an interactive dialogue. The living communicate with the departed on two levels. First, saying *Kaddish* helps mediate the continuing relationship between the survivors and the soul. Second, recital of the Mourner's Prayer by the living may help redeem a soul during its purification in Purgatory. In other words, saying *Kaddish* impacts on the afterlife destiny of the soul in Purgatory.

The recitation of the *Kaddish* facilitates the completion of the relationship in Purgatory between the living and the soul, particularly a highly ambivalent relationship marked by a good deal of unexpressed hostility or other strong emotions. In some family situations, the bereaved use the eleven-month (or thirty-day) postdeath period to continue to work out their previous stormy relationships with the soul of a loved one. The mourning process, specifically the recital of the *Kaddish* prayer, enables them to finish their old emotional business and deal with a variety of the predeath negative and often unstated emotions and resentments.

For these families, Purgatory may be viewed as the process of purging the emotional "stuff" swept under the rug between (and among) family members during the life just lived. The *Kaddish* process represents a time for healing relationships not mended during the deceased's lifetime, issues not worked out, difficulties never really confronted, or emotions never expressed.

Going through the rather lengthy *Kaddish* process helps the mourner resolve his or her churning, often incomplete emotions regarding a departed family member, particularly a parent or a child. The mourner may pour out his or her previously unexpressed feelings, ask for answers to serious questions, and tell the stories that have been kept secret or perhaps reflect negatively on the departed. Asking for forgiveness, a survivor may be more open to listening to the decedent's response, which may take the form of an apology and a request for reconciliation. By getting things off their chests, reciting the Mourner's Prayer gradually aids the survivors to reclaim their lives and frees them to go on living unburdened by whatever was previously unresolved with the deceased.

Pleasant thoughts often replace painful memories. A parent and a child, for instance, achieve a new opening as the gulf previously separating them over the years dissolves into love and forgiveness. Through an exploration of issues, even after death, a relationship can evolve in a positive direction, sometimes imperceptibly. *Kaddish* keeps the dialogue going until the living say all that they need to say to the soul.

The *Kaddish* process may also impact the destiny of the soul in the postmortem realms. The mystical tradition suggests that saying *Kaddish* assists a parent's (or close relative's) soul during its purification in Purgatory. By attaining a sense of inner peace of mind and resolving emotional issues pertaining to a loved one and his or her demise, the mourner affects the soul during its period of cleansing. As the living recite the Mourner's Prayer and enter into a dialogue with the departed, the soul may gradually perceive and feel the consequences of its negative conduct, words, and thoughts during its immediate past life. Forgiving a parent (or other close relative) for any hurt or harm, the mystics maintain, helps the parent's (or close relative's) soul resolve its feelings of guilt, regret, and shame. Forgiveness assists the soul in cleaning the slate and gradually purifying its incomplete emotions. By saying *Kaddish*, the living provide a source of inspiration and guidance for the soul, thereby diminishing its suffering in Purgatory.

From the viewpoint of Jewish Spirituality, observance of the *Kaddish* ritual and recital of the Mourner's Prayer is far less important than the soul-guiding concepts underpinning the process. In other words, it is the process more than any formalistic prayer or ritual.

Bereaved spiritual seekers who want to escape tradition and devise something personal often find it helpful to set aside time on a regular basis each day for a number of weeks or months (and in some cases, even a year or more) to grieve freely, express and sort out their feelings as well as shed some tears, and continue to forge a link between the world of the survivors and the realm of the dead. Let us separate and consider two quite different family situations: first healthy and then troubled relationships.

HEALTHY RELATIONSHIPS

Through spontaneous, unstructured, personal prayers from the heart; silent meditations; and visualizations, stay in contact with the soul of a departed loved one and experience the continued sense of your ongoing relationship. Continue to say your goodbyes; express your respect and gratitude; and send loving, freeing thoughts to the deceased, not thoughts that would continue the soul's attachment to the material world. Consider making notes in a journal, taking long walks even in an urban environment, or looking at old photo albums or a piece of jewelry. Although tears come with remembrance, whatever works as a focal point for an individualized means of healing your grief is good.

As difficult as it is with a beloved family member or friend, try not to brood unnecessarily over the departed. According to the Talmud, Jewish sages taught: Don't weep for the dead in excess or moan beyond measure (*Moed Kattan* 27b). Let your tears flow, but do not cry excessively. Express your respect, honor, and love for the departed. Do not let go of your fond memories.

As the Jewish tradition teaches, trust in God. The Divine, as the essence of goodness, did not create us to destroy us. Each soul is destined for higher development and a better existence.

Expressing positive sentiments, particularly praying for cleansing and healing as well as sending compassion to the soul, facilitates, Jewish sages teach, the completion of its purification process in Purgatory more quickly and more thoroughly. By opening your heart to the Eternal, invoke the Holy One's love for the soul. Thus, the living can assist and elevate a soul on its journey in the afterlife realms.

TROUBLED RELATIONSHIPS

In troubled, ambivalent family relationships, the postdeath spiritual process helps in sorting out, healing, and completing the interactions between the living and the soul of the departed. In these situations, focus on the unresolved emotional issues involving the deceased, painful memories and regrets, and any lingering feelings. Try to communicate what was unfinished or unstated in the relationship.

As we have seen in chapter 6, forgiveness plays a large role in Jewish Spirituality. The living help the soul of a departed loved one by reviewing their relationships; asking for the soul's forgiveness for any past transgressions on their parts; expressing their willingness to forgive the deceased for his or her prior deeds, words, or thoughts; and encouraging self-forgiveness.

Strive to openly and honestly express your continuing gratitude to and lingering resentments of and tensions with the departed. Try to see from the decedent's perspective—not your viewpoint—any emotions, particularly previously unexpressed feelings, you now perceive as a "negative" in your relationship, including regrets, fears, anger, envy, guilt, sorrow, loneliness, or anxiety.

In pouring out and releasing your feelings; striving to make amends; and unburdening your guilt, your anger, and your regrets, diligently listen for the departed's response, which may consist of an expression of forgiveness and a hope for reconciliation. As is true of many situations, both sides probably need to acknowledge their joint responsibility to overcome the anger, the fears, and the guilt emanating from the mistakes in their botched relationship.

Many find the Forgiveness and Lovingkindness Meditation (or Visualization) useful in opening (or continuing to facilitate) the channel of communication between themselves and the soul of a departed loved one, achieving a sense of completeness with respect to previously unresolved issues and uncommunicated emotions, and quieting their minds and nourishing their inner essences. Speaking from your inner heart, try to enter into a dialogue with the deceased and honestly express what lies at the root of your continued separation. An ongoing, truthful, interactive dialogue focusing on forgiveness and letting go of the past, even now, opens lines of communication permitting the previous estrangement and alienation to fall away.

To sort out your previously troubled relationship with the departed, you may find it useful, as many others have, to put in a journal, notebook, pieces of paper, or perhaps in a letter to the deceased, the specific unresolved issues never worked out, the exact difficulties never adequately confronted, and previously unspoken words and uncommunicated thoughts and feelings—your anger, your sadness, anything you yearn for—saying whatever you need to say. This detailed, focused, written expression, particularly where there was a troubled relationship, enables you to enter into a dialogue with the deceased and offers the possibility of your seeing things from his or her viewpoint. You should also write down several of the departed's redeeming, positive qualities, his or her nonmaterial gifts left to you and others. End your letter with a truthful closing statement. If "I love you" is not appropriate, then perhaps "I have let go of my pain and confusion." To achieve emotional closure, close with "Goodbye."

In addition to caring friends and relatives who will listen without judging, many mourners find that they need some sort of a social support system, whether or not they observe the *Kaddish* process through communal worship services. A support group composed of bereaved persons, in which people come together regularly and share death, grieving, and mourning as a common bond, often helps. You will benefit from a connectedness with people who have recently experienced death in their lives. To be most useful, individuals in your social support system must appreciate the impact of your loss on you. They should enable you to express your grief, long after the death. Allow yourself permission to talk about your grief with those who understand and can support you in a compassionate, nonjudgmental manner.

Over the course of the year (or even more), your feelings toward the decedent gradually shift, enabling you to work out any unfinished relationship business as well as incomplete emotions and get on with the concerns of living your life. You will be able to finally say your genuine and lasting goodbyes.

We each grieve in our own way and in our own time frame. The process takes time; it is slow and time-consuming. Grieve, but do not allow your grief to overwhelm you.

Gradually the living, although maintaining their love and respect for the deceased, accept the reality of death: The person is dead and will not return. They let go of their identity with and attachment to the departed. Their pain and sadness lessen. They are able to think of the deceased without pain or sadness. They realize that the relationship—good or bad (for most of us, a mix of good and bad)—is over. A sense of loss remains, but somehow it is much softer and more gentle. Regaining an interest in life and feeling more hopeful, they are free to go on with life, to live their own agenda filled with new activities and interests, not the deceased's. They move forward in life and reach out to others, renew old friendships, cultivate new relationships—recognizing that the deceased can never be replaced. Developing a new self-identity, a new sense of who they are, their faith in God and humanity is gradually restored.

AFTER THE FIRST YEAR OF
GRIEVING AND MOURNING

During a survivor's lifetime, two ongoing Jewish postdeath rituals exist: the recitation of the Mourner's Prayer (*Kaddish*) annually on the anniversary in the Hebrew calendar of the death of a parent or other close relative (the *Yahrzeit*) and the recitation of a memorial prayer (*Yizkor*) at four Jewish holiday religious services each year.[21] These rituals are designed so that the living will never forget the dead.

In addition to or apart from these traditional rituals, spiritual seekers, while letting go of the deceased, can continue to honor his or her memory in other meaningful ways and engage in various soul-guiding practices.

YAHRZEIT: A TRADITIONAL RITUAL

On the anniversary of the death of a parent or a close relative (the *Yahrzeit*), the bereaved engage in a number of rituals, including reciting the Mourner's Prayer, the *Kaddish*, in the deceased's memory at the daily, communal worship services held at a synagogue. If there is a synagogue memorial plaque, it is illuminated on the day of the *Yahrzeit*.

On the evening before the death anniversary, a loved one also lights, at home, a *Yahrzeit* candle that burns for twenty-four hours. The memorial candle symbolizes the immortal soul of a departed. In lighting the *Yahrzeit* candle, a survivor symbolically aligns himself or herself with the deceased's eternal spirit.

The *Yahrzeit* is observed by visiting the gravesite. Loved ones also perform good deeds and acts of kindness, such as making charitable contributions, in the decedent's memory, to promote and fulfill his or her aspirations.

The *Yahrzeit* serves one simple but important function. It provides a time for the living to remember the dead. This is especially important as the years pass and the memory of the departed fades. Observing a *Yahrzeit* allows an individual to remain in touch with the decedent's memory.

Through the annual recitation of the Mourner's Prayer, the *Kaddish*, on the anniversary of a parent's (or other close relative's) death, the mystical tradition suggests that the living provide a spiritual benefit for the soul of a departed loved one. The merit of remembering the dead helps the soul rise to higher and higher realms of Paradise on its ongoing journey in the afterlife world.

YIZKOR: A TRADITIONAL JEWISH RITUAL

The bereaved also attend special memorial services (*Yizkor*) at a synagogue or temple. *Yizkor* services are held four times a year: the Day of Atonement (Yom Kippur), discussed in chapter 6; Shemini Atsaret, the day between the last day of Sukkoth (a fall harvest festival) and Simcha Torah (when the annual Torah reading cycle ends and begins anew); the last day of Passover (a festival discussed in chapter 9 that, according to tradition, commemorates the biblical Exodus of the Jews from Egypt); and on the second day of Shavuot (a spring festival, that according to tradition marks the giving of the Torah to Moses).

The seasonal cycle of four *Yizkor* services provides a context for remembering loved ones. By limiting the seasons of ongoing mourning, Jewish rituals provide a circumscribed vehicle for remembrance and the accompanying emotional responses.

At these communal memorial services, the beloved recite various prayers, including the *Yizkor* prayer (May God Remember), in which each individual inserts the names of his or her departed relatives—parents, grandparents, spouse, children, and others. It has become a common practice to also recite the remembrance prayer on behalf of the six million Jews who perished in the Holocaust.

The special *Yizkor* prayer, included as part of the memorial service or recited by the beloved by himself or herself at home, is as follows:

> May God remember the soul of my dear ———, who has gone to his/her eternal rest. May his/her soul be bound up in the bond of life. May his/her rest be glorious, with the fullness of the joy in Your presence and the eternal bliss at Your right hand.[22]

The prayers recited during the memorial services call on God to remember and provide merciful treatment for the soul. Thus according to the Jewish mystics, reciting the *Yizkor* prayer (May God Remember) at a memorial service, like the *Yahrzeit* observance, helps elevate the soul to an even higher level of Paradise. Saying the *Yizkor* prayer also assists in strengthening the spiritual bonds between the living and the departed soul. This spiritual bond, linking the past to the present, allows us to prepare for the future with hope and with a sense of connectedness to those we have known and loved.

In addition to the living attending a memorial service and offering the *Yizkor* prayer for the benefit of a soul on its postmortem journey, the memorial prayer performs another function. The survivors hope, based on mystical teachings, that reciting the *Yizkor* prayer will facilitate an intercession before God by the soul of the deceased, producing various benefits—physical, spiritual, emotional, or material—for the living.

Strengthening their interconnectedness with the soul of a departed loved one may also help the survivors find greater meaning and purpose in their lives. Perhaps the lessons the soul learns in its postmortem journey may in some form, Jewish sources suggest, be transmitted back to earth, assisting loved ones live with greater fervor and enabling them, from the viewpoint of Jewish Spirituality, to be more loving, more forgiving, and more truthful.

OTHER MEANINGFUL SPIRITUAL PRACTICES

Apart from the observance of the traditional rituals, strive to set aside time for reflection, at least annually on the anniversary of the death (or the birth) of a parent (or other close relative) and periodically on one or more other special occasions as appropriate, such as holidays that were shared, during the year. Also, communicate with the soul periodically throughout the year. Building on the interrelationship between the earthly world and the realm of the dead, strengthen this linkage and find a continued sense of partnership in your relationship with the soul of a deceased loved one. It is important for you to reconnect not only with your feelings and memories regarding the earthly departed but also with his or her soul.

Create a sacred time and space where you can open your heart and mind to a genuine interconnection with beloved family members and friends who have left the world of the living. There are many techniques you can use to strengthen an avenue of connection between the living and the dead.

You may find a symbol of remembrance—a picture, a letter, a song, a memorial plaque or fund (i.e., donating to a special charity)—helpful in remembering your loved one and renewing your linkage with his or her soul.

Striving to remain in contact with a soul, spend time in personalized prayer, silent meditation, visualization, or some special way in which you can communicate with the departed. Recall your gratitude to the deceased. Give thanks for what you received and what you learned from him or her.

As you open your heart to God in spontaneous, unstructured prayer, hopefully you will be able to reach beyond yourself. By crying out to and seeking to touch the Divine, you can seek continued compassion and mercy for the soul on its afterlife journey.

The following visualization may assist you in continuing to remember a deceased and aid the soul in the postdeath realms. This visualization also helps strengthen your interconnectedness with his or her soul. You should engage in this visualization, for ten to fifteen minutes, on one or more special days throughout the year.

Remembrance Visualization. Introduction: Create a warm, welcoming atmosphere, an environment of serenity and spaciousness for going beyond your ordinary perspective of reality. Lower the lights in your room. Close your eyes, sit quietly, calm and relax your body, breathe in and out normally, feeling where you breath flows into and out of your body. Adjust your breaths so that the in and out breaths are of the same length.

Feel yourself surrounded by warmth and love. With each breath, breathe in warmth, feel the warmth nourishing you.

Take your time. There is no reason to hurry.

Visualize your departed dear one. Imagine his or her face before you. See his or her smile. Hear his or her words. Feel his or her presence. In your heart and in your mind, allow a conversation to unfold.

Ask him or her what it is like where he or she presently is.

Ask the departed to enter into a dialogue with you, telling you what he or she feels most proud of having done during his or her lifetime. Ask what he or she feels most ashamed of? What does he or she most regret doing (or saying) or not doing (or saying)?

Ask the beloved what would be the single most important thing he or she would do differently if he or she could live his or her life again.

Focus on a specific situation that occurred between you and the deceased. Try to visualize how the departed would have wished the event to have occurred so that he or she (or you) would have no regrets.

Ask: What still remains unspoken, unresolved? Listen. Let the radiance of his or her love and compassion be with you.

Ask the departed how he or she would like to be remembered.

Concluding Instructions: Promise to remain in contact. Say your goodbyes, giving your beloved a big hug. Come back to the here and now. Take time to ease yourself back. Slowly bring your awareness back into your body. Feel yourself back in the room and open your eyes.

Using the Remembrance Visualization, along with the Forgiveness and Lovingkindness Meditation (or Visualization) set out in this chapter, helps you keep your memories of the departed alive and enables you to send forgiving and loving messages to his or her soul.

The Forgiveness and Lovingkindness Meditation (or Visualization) continues to be useful in mending a stormy past relationship with the departed and in dealing with unresolved issues and unstated emotions. Strive to work out lingering resentments and unexpressed feelings, whatever is holding you back from changing and growing. Sending lovingkindness and forgiveness to the soul of a loved one often encompasses both the living and the dead in the embrace of radiant love.

Over the years, feelings change and soften. Most of us achieve a new clearing with our departed loved ones. We free ourselves from the past and are able to move forward.

Forging a new relationship also helps heal the departed soul, enabling it to achieve a greater degree of emotional, intellectual, and spiritual bliss. In reframing our memories of the past, we practice forgiveness—not only for ourselves, but also for the soul of a deceased loved one.

Even after reincarnation, a linkage still remains. Whatever you dedicate on the deceased's behalf will benefit him or her by removing obstacles in his or her new life and furthering his or her emotional, intellectual, and spiritual progress. You can attain additional merit for a reincarnated soul through your good and beautiful thoughts, words, and deeds.

Feeling the pain and hurt of death, the survivors can grow from their experience with grief and the process of mourning. The living should ponder: How am I responding to events and environments? Am I able to go beyond and surmount them? Or will I be defeated?

Our mortality is unavoidable, as are the tragedies we encounter in life. However, constructive responses to life's vicissitudes and hardships heighten the soul's consciousness and awareness, particularly its spiritual development, thereby enabling you, through successive incarnations, to come closer to God. Through your mind and your way of thinking, you can find meaning and purpose in life and create your own future, based on how you face life's events. You decide how to react to and what to do with your life's pain, suffering, and tragedies.

In facing adversities, recognize that every situation and experience contains the seeds for our good and for our spiritual benefit. Life's difficulties are given to us for a reason: for our spirit, our essence. Handled "correctly," through the process of trial and error, these experiences make us stronger, more knowledgeable, and more perceptive. No matter how hidden, strive to find a response to each hardship you encounter that is creative, growth-oriented, and life-affirming. Times of challenge represent an exceptional opportunity to rediscover the lasting truth of your deeper, spiritual nature. Remember that it is difficult to tell which situations, however painful and tragic, bring the greatest blessing.

Live fully in the face of the personal tragedies you will encounter. Do not surrender to despair. Do not fear death, because you will be transported into another state of consciousness closer to God. Your fear of death interferes with your joys, limits your aspirations, and provides fertile ground for pessimism. Thus, you can discover the message of life within the meaning of pain, suffering, and, ultimately, death.

NOTES

1. Chapters 6 through 9 of my book *The Jewish Book of Living and Dying* (Northvale, NJ: Jason Aronson, 1999) contain a much fuller exposition of the ideas presented in this chapter.

2. Dr. Simcha Paull Raphael's original concept of soul guiding as a linkage between the world of the living and the world of the dead originated in his doctoral dissertation, Simcha Steven Paull, *Judaism's Contribution to the Psychology of Death and Dying* (Ph.D. dissertation, California Institute of Integral Studies, 1986), pp. 349–350, 358–359, 362–364, 368–371. The theme of soul guiding is developed in his monumental scholarly work, Simcha Paull Raphael, *Jewish Views of the Afterlife* (Northvale, NJ: Jason Aronson, 1994), pp. 383, 387–388, 391–392.

3. Ibid., pp. 139–140, 166–167, 291–294, 344–345, 381–384.

4. Ibid., pp. 144–145 and 303–305.

5. Ibid., p. 389.

6. Raymond A. Moody Jr., M.D., with Paul Perry, *The Light Beyond* (New York: Bantam, 1988), p. 43.

7. Raphael, *Afterlife*, pp. 390–391.

8. Ian Stevenson, M.D., *Twenty Cases Suggestive of Reincarnation*, rev. ed. (Charlottesville, VA: University Press of Virginia, 1981). The evidence in support of the concept of reincarnation is summarized in Liz Hodgkinson, *Reincarnation: The Evidence* (London: Piatkus, 1989).

9. Brian L. Weiss, M.D., *Many Lives, Many Masters* (New York: Simon & Schuster, 1988).

10. *In Praise of the Baal Shem Tov: The Earliest Collection of Legends About the Founder of Hasidism*, ed. and trans. Dan Ben-Amos and Jerome R. Mintz (Northvale, NJ: Jason Aronson, 1993), pp. 106–107.

11. Raphael, *Afterlife*, pp. 314–320 and 392–394; Gershom Scholem, *On the Mystical Shape of the Godhead: Basic Concepts in the Kabbalah*, ed. Jonathan Chipman, trans. Joachim Neugroschel (New York: Schocken, 1991), pp. 197–250; David A. Cooper, *God Is a Verb: Kabbalah and the Practice of Mystical Judaism* (New York: Riverhead, 1997), pp. 117–120 and 265–269; Rifat Sonsino and Daniel B. Syme, *What Happens After I Die? Jewish Views of Life After Death* (New York: UAHC Press, 1990), pp. 46–53; Yonassan Gershom, *Beyond the Ashes: Cases of Reincarnation from the Holocaust* (Virginia Beach, VA: A.R.E. Press, 1992), pp. 70–80 and 196–205; and Gershon Winkler, *The Soul of the Matter: A Psychological and Philosophical Study of the Jewish Perspective on the Odyssey of the Human Soul Before, During, and After "Life"* (New York: The Judaica Press, 1982), pp. 17–19.

12. Scholem, *Godhead*, p. 201; Gedalyah Nigal, *Magic, Mysticism, and Hasidism: The Supernatural in Jewish Thought*, trans. Edward Levin (Northvale, NJ: Jason Aronson, 1994), pp. 53 and n.12, pp. 238–239; Gershom, *Beyond the Ashes*, pp. 76 and 196–197.

13. *Legends of the Jews*, vol. 1, ed. Louis Ginzburg, trans. Henrietta Szold (Philadelphia: Jewish Publication Society, 1968), pp. 57–58; "The Formation of the Child," in *The Chronicles of Jerahmeel* IX: 8, ed. and trans. Moses Gaster (New York: Ktav, 1971), p. 21.

14. Joel L. Whitton, M.D., Ph.D., and Joe Fisher, *Life Between Life: Scientific Explorations into the Void Separating One Incarnation from the Next* (Garden City, NY: Doubleday, 1986), p. 49.

15. Raphael, *Afterlife*, p. 326; Gershom, *Beyond the Ashes*, p. 187.

16. Adapted from Dr. Joseph H. Hertz, *The Authorized Daily Prayer Book*, rev. ed. (New York: Bloch, 1985), p. 1073.

17. Helen Fitzgerald, *The Mourning Handbook: A Complete Guide for the Bereaved* (New York: Simon & Schuster, 1994), pp. 72–105. One expert conceptualizes the four tasks (or dimensions) of mourning, the process occurring after death, as follows: first, acceptance of the reality of loss, that death is irreversible and the person is gone and will not return; second, working through, experiencing, and expressing the pain of grief, a broad range of feelings and behavior; third, adjusting to an environment where the deceased is missing, including analyzing the different roles the deceased played in a survivor's life, developing coping skills, and moving forward with a reassessed view of the world; and fourth, emotionally relocating the deceased and moving on with life, including establishing a new identity and finding a new life direction. See J. William Worden, Ph.D., *Grief Counseling and Grief Therapy: A Handbook for the Mental Health Practitioner*, 2nd ed. (New York: Springer, 1991), pp. 10–18.

18. Tzvi Rabinowicz, *A Guide to Life: Jewish Laws and Customs of Mourning* (Northvale, NJ: Jason Aronson, 1989), pp. 45–54 and 81–89; Maurice Lamm, *The Jewish Way in Death and Mourning* (New York: Jonathan David, 1969), pp. 77–146 and 175–187; Central Conference of American Rabbis, *Rabbi's Manual* (New York: Central Conference of American Rabbis, 1988), pp. 252–

254; *Jewish Insights on Death and Mourning*, ed. Jack Riemer (New York: Schocken, 1995), pp. 141–167 and 186–198.

19. Adapted from Hertz, *The Authorized Daily Prayer Book*, p. 213; and Central Conference of American Rabbis, *Gates of Prayer: The New Union Prayerbook* (New York: Central Conference of American Rabbis, 1975), pp. 629–630.

20. Paull, *Judaism's Contribution*, p. 368–370.

21. For further background on the Jewish laws and customs pertaining to *Yahrzeit* and *Yizkor* see Rabinowicz, *A Guide to Life*, pp. 90–100; Lamm, *The Jewish Way*, pp. 196–207; *Rabbi's Manual*, pp. 256–257; *Jewish Insights*, pp. 194–220; and Gershom, *Beyond the Ashes*, pp. 69–70.

22. Adapted from Hertz, *The Authorized Daily Prayer Book*, p. 1107.

PART SIX

CONCLUSION

CHAPTER FOURTEEN

Placing Jewish Spirituality in an Institutional Context

Throughout this book, I have discussed how Jewish Spirituality helps meet human needs, in life and death. I have focused on having faith in God, remembering that the Eternal's ways are beyond human comprehension, and trusting that God will do what is best for you. God, Who is concerned with each human being, watches over you. Everything happens for a reason, even if it does not make sense to you, viewed from your limited perspective.

This chapter places Jewish Spirituality in an institutional context. After examining communal worship services and do-it-yourself, home-based discussion and worship groups, I will also briefly consider the revamping of Jewish supplemental school education.

REVITALIZING COMMUNAL WORSHIP SERVICES

The synagogue, an institution that arose after the destruction of the Second Temple in Jerusalem in 70 C.E., enabled Judaism to be transported around the world. As an enduring hallmark of Judaism, worship services allowed Jews to come together as a community and engage in sacred ceremonies. Traditionally, Jews have been expected to pray with one another, not apart from human fellowship. Through prayer in a group context, worshippers find strength and support throughout life, particularly in difficult moments such as the death of a loved one.

The performance of a traditional prayer service requires a quorum, a critical mass (*minyan* in Hebrew), of ten adult males (ten men and women in an egalitarian era). Prayer for everyone's welfare and betterment serves as the focus of a *minyan*. The language of Jewish prayer is first person plural: "Forgive us," and, more broadly, connects our personal needs to the praying of the Jewish community at large. Serving as a cohesive social force, prayer makes each one who prays in a worship service more empathetic with others, those with whom at first glance he or she seems to have little if anything in common. Commonality and compassion for others are seen as arising from the collective worship and the prayer experience.

So much for the ideal!

Sterility often characterizes conventional synagogue or temple worship. The services are routinized, tedious, and staid. They are often boring and irrelevant. They take too long. The liturgy and the music is generally sterile, uninspiring, and outmoded. There is a need for much more than the rote recital of preset prayers at great speed. God does not need so much praise—I am sure that the Divine's self-esteem is fairly high. Spiritual seekers often do not find or experience God in a typical Jewish worship service.

Looking to restructure communal worship services, to make the synagogue a more spiritual place, and to go beyond the present, rather bloodless and devitalized Judaism, I offer the following "Ten Suggestions for Worship Revitalization":

(1) Limit worship services to a maximum of ninety minutes—even better sixty minutes—including a short, fifteen-minute, high-quality sermon. Period, end of discussion—and consider a discussion in place of a sermon.

(2) Departing from a twenty-five-hundred-year-old tradition, introduced by Ezra in the fifth century B.C.E., stop reading from the Torah as the focal point of Saturday morning and holiday worship services. The weekly Torah portions or even those read on holidays, similar to the services in general, are typically quite boring and irrelevant. As developed in chapter 2, the Torah evolved as a work of humans, not as a product of Divine revelation. Therefore, we can de-emphasize the Torah and its study. Simply put, most of the time the weekly and holiday Torah portions constitute a meaningless waste of

time. If a reading from the Hebrew Bible is needed as part of a worship service, use a brief—make that a very brief, perhaps one minute—excerpt from the prophets, one of the psalms, or the Book of Proverbs as part of the liturgy or as a lead into (or as part of) a sermon.

(3) Through prayer we reestablish our connection, or at least our awareness of a connection, with God. The worship service experience should focus on God-talk. Those who gather yearn to express their belief in the existence of the Divine and to speak about and to the Eternal. Restructure prayers so they help us establish an intimate relationship with God, Who is near to us.

Spiritual seekers want to find a personal connection with God. Rather than a fixed liturgy that often makes this connection with the Eternal quite difficult, they want to offer petitionary and affirmative prayers expressing their personal needs as well as prayers of thanksgiving to express their gratitude for life and its bounty.

(4) Focus the liturgy and sermons on "real life" from a spiritual perspective, not Zionism, political issues, "social justice," or making people feel ignorant or guilty. Worshippers want help in grappling with an increasingly complex, chaotic, stressful world, marked by loneliness and isolation and the emptiness of contemporary, consumption-oriented American culture. Hopefully, Jewish Spirituality as outlined in this book and as further developed by others in communal worship services will focus on the tough issues of everyday life: How do you live and love? How do you deal with stress and the use of your time and money? How do you face and deal with illness and tragedy, pain and suffering, death and grief? What values do you (and should you) transmit to your children?

As we contemplate restructuring worship services, remember that a variety of spiritual practices including prayer, meditation, and visualization help heal our mind, body, and spirit. An array of spiritual practices can assist in changing the physical world including our bodies and our minds. Thus, Jewish Spirituality should encourage and facilitate the development of stand-alone services designed to promote healing on a number of levels—physical, mental, emotional, and spiritual—together with a continued exploration of the relationship between faith and healing—a wholeness of mind, body, and spirit.

(5) Offer more participation and interaction beyond the congregation watching the rabbi and cantor perform. This, of course, is difficult with a large group, for instance, on the High Holidays.

However, many worshippers desire to go beyond perfunctory and dutiful observances and find constructive outlets to release their feelings and emotions of failure, meaninglessness, guilt, and self-reproach; to find passion and re-enchantment; and experience a spiritual connection with others and the Eternal rather than a dry, lifeless Judaism.

Complement the world of the mind, Judaism's traditional emphasis on the intellectual side of life, with the world of the heart and the soul. Worshippers want to be fully engaged on four levels: mental, physical, spiritual, and emotional. They want to talk about and to share their experiences, to meditate, to cry, and to dance. Music and dance heighten and enhance the nonverbal aspects of services. Encourage laughter and the joining of hands.

(6) Make more imaginative use of different, eclectic, even contemporary, music and literature. Song and movement engage the body in what the heart and mind feel and believe.

(7) Provide more moments of silence for contemplation, personal prayer, meditation, or visualization. This takes some getting accustomed to. Jews are generally a very verbal group; if they do not communicate verbally they feel as if they do not know who they are. Less verbiage in worship services provides more time for quiet reflection and relief from the chaos and complexity of modern life—a place to go within our messy, confused lives to be safe and to be ourselves. During these periods of silence, some worshippers, their eyes closed, their palms loosely opened on their laps, may attain (or at least strive to attain) a connection with God. Also, provide worshipers with sufficient time to ask and reflect on such questions as: Who am I? What am I here to do? What is the purpose of my existence, the meaning of my life, and my place in the cosmos?

(8) De-emphasize the child-centered aspects of Judaism, particularly routinized Saturday morning bar/bat mitzvahs. Rather, focus on reaching out and meeting the spiritual needs of adults, not children.

(9) Creatively use the latest-high tech advances: big-screen television, CD sound, electronic keyboards, video projectors and screens, and audio mixing boards. Use clips from movies or videos to demonstrate the lessons of Jewish Spirituality. Utilize skits and other live, dramatic techniques to bring the spiritual essence of Judaism to life.

(10) While recognizing that holidays have become regular events for large numbers of Jews, dramatizing their commitment to the Jewish people and values, serving as vehicles to promote Jewish identity, and expressing solidarity with Jews past and present, some traditional Jewish holidays are not worth saving. Although retaining

Rosh Hashanah (chapter 3), Yom Kippur (chapter 6), and Passover and Hanukkah (chapter 9), we can jettison Shavuot, Purim, and Sukkoth.

Shavuot, a spring festival commemorating the legendary giving of the Torah by God to Moses, lacks historical validity, as discussed in chapter 2. There is also no need for Simcha Torah, which revolves around completing and beginning the annual cycle of weekly Torah readings, something, as noted above, we can dispense with.

Likewise, Purim, also observed within the synagogue, is devoid of a basis in historical reality.[1] There never was a Queen Esther or a Mordecai. Emphasis on a history of persecution, with the evil Haman as a prototype for Hitler in shaping a sense of Jewish identity, only reinforces a feeling of separation and negative thinking on the part of Jews. Jewish Spirituality, as demonstrated throughout this book, strives to move far beyond uniting Jews in victimhood. While we are on the topic of victimology, let us stop celebrating the destruction of the First and Second Temples in Jerusalem (*Tisha be-Av* in Hebrew) and Holocaust Remembrance Day (*Yom ha-shoah* in Hebrew).

Finally, Sukkoth, the holiday of booths, marked by the building of a small outdoor tent-like structure, a *sukkah*, has no historical foundation. As noted in chapter 9, there was no Exodus of the Jews from Egypt and they did not wander for forty years in the wilderness using tent-like booths. Furthermore, there is no need for another autumn holiday on top of the High Holidays, Rosh Hashanah and Yom Kippur.

As restructured, communal services would provide an inspiring, uplifting worship experience in an entertaining manner, coupled with a meaningful message and quality music, all designed to make the synagogue or temple more of a spiritual place. Based on the spiritual essence of Judaism, to make worship services interesting and attractive we should focus on God, our behavior toward others, personal virtues and character traits, and dealing with life and all its complexities. We should emphasize responsibility for our choices and our actions, not victimhood or trauma.

All this experimentation with a far looser structure, a more contemporary or even no liturgy, will "turn off" those comfortable with traditional Reform or Conservative services—never mind Jewish fundamentalists. Those basking in "tradition" will, however, still find plenty of Jewish places of worship where they can mindlessly drone on through their regimented prayers.

THE GROWTH OF HOME-BASED WORSHIP
AND DISCUSSION GROUPS

Realizing that many synagogues and temples are too large, too impersonal, and too passionless, the past twenty-five years have witnessed the growth of *havurot*—small, home-based, lay-led study, worship, ritual celebration, discussion, and friendship groups. These grass roots gatherings, often formed by synagogues and temples, strive to create a more personal, participatory, and intimate spiritual experience. In these informal, do-it-yourself, living room settings, the participants teach and learn from each other rather than one person serving as the leader in a rigid, formal worship service. In other words, these groups depend more on the skills of their members and less on professional clergy.

In the future, the growing individualized and personalized culture of Judaism, a keynote of Jewish Spirituality, will fuel the development of home-based worship services. Striving to move beyond the joyless, rigid, spiritually vapid institutional worship and religious ritualism now the focal point of Jewish existence, I expect more and more Jews to claim and establish spiritual space for themselves. They will realize you do not need an organized, institutionalized physical place for worship. Home-based worship in someone's living room for ten to fifteen people, small fellowships of independent Jewish worshippers, will likely flourish in the twenty-first century and make synagogues and temples less and less necessary.

Because God is everywhere, it is possible to carve out a sacred space in the midst of routine life, as Jews do for the traditional home-based Passover seder or the lighting of the Hanukkah menorah. The sacred and the profane intersect and interact all the time. The home serves as an appropriate setting for lay-led, small-scale worship, study, discussion, and other forms of spiritual gatherings.

These small groups provide a sense of community and safety, enabling attendees to meet their spiritual needs and receive warmth and support from others. In offering the spiritual connectedness many long for, these groups can help members deal with everyday existence and "real life" problems—finding a spouse, parenthood, divorce, illness, death of a loved one, and work-related issues—through faith and trust in the Eternal, not through the guilt engendered by what you eat (or do not eat) or how strictly you observe the Sabbath. In these small gatherings, following the insights of Martin Buber developed in chapter

4, individuals can enter into a dialogue and experience genuine encounters with others.

RETHINKING THE TRADITION OF GROUP WORSHIP

Beyond small, informal worship and discussion groups—say, once a month on a Friday night—many Jews will recapture the spiritual depth of the Jewish tradition through personalized approaches to prayer, meditation, visualization, and even crying out to God. Although difficult for institutional Judaism to admit, worship involves more than going to a synagogue or temple and reading words on a printed page, often by rote. It is perfectly acceptable to pray or meditate from your own heart, to engage in quiet reflection, at home, in your office, while on your way to work, or wherever you are. More Jews, now and in the future, want to exercise their faith on their own terms and in their own ways.

Meaningful prayer, meditation, and visualization can take place when you are entirely alone. They take place in your heart and mind when you enter into an intimate conversation with the Eternal. Open yourself to the possibility of an encounter with the Divine outside a synagogue or a temple. You can establish this personal intimacy, a direct relationship with God, through spontaneous prayers and meditations. You can meet your spiritual needs without any sort of institutional, group worship.

The emphasis of Jewish Spirituality on communing with God through individualized, improvised prayers and meditations will, of course, negatively impact on traditional Jewish institutions, in particular, synagogues and temples. For two thousand years, the synagogue has served as the focal point of Judaism. It functions as a house of prayer, study, and community. It is a sanctuary where Jews conduct public worship. It offers Jewish instruction mainly to children but also to adults. As a house of assembly, Jews seek out other Jews and strengthen their Jewish identity.

Yet, at the beginning of the twenty-first century, Jewish commitment to institutional affiliation has significantly weakened, as part of the diminishing loyalty of many Americans to institutions in general. This is seen in decreasing membership in religious groups, parent-teacher associations, and even bowling leagues.[2] Jews are abandoning traditional synagogues and temples in droves. Less than forty percent of Jewish households report having someone who is a synagogue or temple member.[3] In other words, in a majority of Jewish households not one person belongs to a synagogue or temple.

Expressing a desire to be free of institutional Judaism, more and more Jews are voting with their feet (and their dollars). These spiritual seekers want the Jewish tradition to offer them more of a focus on personal fulfillment; well-being in all its dimensions—physical, mental, emotional, and spiritual; peace of mind; and the transcendent meaning of life. Developing a one-on-one relationship with God, a Friend to Whom they can talk anytime, about anything, they are discovering, need not exist only in an institutional religious context with all of its trappings, including a formal house of worship and prayers devised by others.

Many of these spiritual seekers do not find God in a traditional synagogue or temple. They are realizing that they can commune with the Supreme Sovereign at home or in any place of solitude. You can cry out to God as words, thoughts, or emotions spontaneously burst forth. For some, these spiritual moments may occur in a natural, outdoor setting. Thus, more and more of us may find that bringing the spiritual back into our daily lives does not require a physical place to go for dutiful observance and congregational worship.

IMPROVING JEWISH SUPPLEMENTAL SCHOOL EDUCATION

In the twenty-first century, it is almost axiomatic that improvements must take place in Jewish education for children and adults. Beyond funneling resources and improving the quality of teachers, Jewish education requires a significant refocusing, particularly with respect to the limited time available for after school and Sunday morning classes for children.

Jewish supplemental school education faces any number of distressing difficulties: sporadic attendance, discipline problems, a low level of achievement, and a high dropout rate (more than fifty percent) after bar/bat mitzvah.[4] These schools do a poor job of imparting Jewish knowledge. They do not guide children toward increased Jewish involvement. If anything, they contribute toward negative Jewish attitudes. Thus, a need exists for far more than instruction in biblical narratives stressing miraculous and supernatural events and stories and a bare bones grounding in Jewish rites, holidays, and worship skills.

We should attune Jewish education of children and adults toward the highest ideals of Jewish Spirituality: a deep God-realization, our conduct toward others, and personal virtues.[5] In addition to providing a spiritual and moral foundation, Jewish supplemental schooling should include an introduction to Jewish history; the teachings of the Jewish prophets and sages; and Jewish Wisdom Literature, notably the Psalms and Proverbs.

Education comprises a lifelong process. As part of this ongoing process, we should seek to teach children (and adults) about God. They need to have faith in the Holy One and to be aware of the Divine presence, the Eternal's oneness, goodness, and bountiful love. As developed in chapter 3, God, our Creator and our Sustainer, an historical and ongoing Reality, loves, guards, and guides us. With a caring, loving Eternal, a true Protector and Helper Who is always there for us, there is no need to fear, worry, or to be sorrowful. God's presence and goodness dwells in each human being, comprising our noblest aspect. Each of us is a sacred being. Through this type of education, children as well as adults will come to love not only God but also all of humanity.

In addition to offering an introduction to Jewish holidays and restructured group worship services reflecting Jewish Spirituality's turn to a more personal religion focusing on inner experiences rather than on outward observances, we should initiate children and adults into the importance of private prayer, meditation, and visualization. So instructed, they will be better able to seek out and appeal to God in moments of need, difficulty, and distress. Initiation into the efficacy of personal prayer, meditation, and visualization helps spiritually fortify individuals against life's complexities, onslaughts, and vicissitudes. Being able to appeal for God's assistance and guidance in times of difficulty, perplexity, or sorrow will prevent children and adults from being thrown into panic or despair. To face life with courage, hope, and peace of mind, children and adults can turn to the Eternal for help, realizing the Divine ever-protecting Presence.

We need to impart the enduring ethics and virtues that lie at the heart of Jewish Spirituality. God wants just, sincere, and loving relationships between and among individuals. We should focus on the development of a humble, joyous, and serene nature within each person and emphasize the quest for meaning and transcendence in life. In short, Jewish education should teach children and adults how to live in their bodies, in their families, and in the marketplace based on a spiritual, moral foundation resting on faith and trust in God.

Most importantly, the loftiest reaches of education enable us to open our eyes and think for ourselves. Do not ever be pressured to conform or to accept unquestioningly or blindly the Jewish tradition and its accompanying beliefs, rules, and rituals. Living and dying involves change and growth. Each day of your life, resolve to change and grow. Accept your time on earth—your present incarnation—as a special gift. Do not waste your life!

NOTES

1. Norman F. Cantor, *The Sacred Chain: The History of the Jews* (New York: HarperCollins, 1994), p. 111.

2. Robert D. Putnam, "Bowling Alone: America's Declining Social Capital," *Journal of Democracy* 6:1 (1995): 65–78. A different viewpoint is offered by Everett Carl Ladd, "The American Way—Civic Engagement—Thrives," *Christian Science Monitor*, 1 March 1999, p. 9.

3. Elliott Abrams, *Faith or Fear: How Jews Can Survive in a Christian America* (New York: Free Press, 1997), p. 128.

4. Isa Aron, "The Malaise of Jewish Education," *Tikkun* 4:3 (1989): 32–34.

5. I have drawn on Rabbi Morris Lichtenstein, *Judaism: A Presentation of Its Essence and a Suggestion for Its Preservation* (New York: Society of Jewish Science, 1934), pp. 193–206.

SELECTED
BIBLIOGRAPHY

Benson, Herbert, M.D., with Marg Stark. *Timeless Healing: The Power and Biology of Belief.* New York: Scribner, 1996.

Cantor, Norman F. *The Sacred Chain: The History of the Jews.* New York: HarperCollins, 1994.

Cooper, Rabbi David A. *God Is A Verb: Kabbalah and the Practice of Mystical Judaism.* New York: Riverhead, 1997.

Dossey, Larry, M.D. *Healing Words: The Power of Prayer and the Practice of Medicine.* New York: HarperCollins, 1993.

———. *Prayer Is Good Medicine: How To Reap the Healing Benefits of Prayer.* San Francisco: HarperSan Francisco, 1996.

Friedman, Richard Elliott. *Who Wrote the Bible?* Englewood Cliffs, NJ: Prentice Hall, 1987.

Glynn, Patrick. *God: The Evidence: The Reconciliation of Faith and Reason in a Postsecular World.* Rocklin, CA: Forum, 1997.

Goldstein, Niles E. and Steven S. Mason. *Judaism and Spiritual Ethics.* New York: UAHC Press, 1996.

Lichtenstein, Rabbi Morris. *How to Live: Jewish Science Essays.* New York: Society of Jewish Science, 1957.

———. *Jewish Science and Health: The Textbook of Jewish Science.* New York: Society of Jewish Science, 1986.

———. *Joys of Life: Jewish Science Essays.* New York: Society of Jewish Science Publishing, 1938.

———. *Judaism: A Presentation of Its Essence and a Suggestion for Its Preservation.* New York: Society of Jewish Science, 1934.

————. *Peace of Mind: Jewish Science Essays.* New York: Society of Jewish Science, 1970.

Raphael, Simcha Paull. *Jewish Views of the Afterlife.* Northvale, NJ: Jason Aronson, 1994.

Ribner, Melinda. *Everyday Kabbalah: A Practical Guide to Jewish Meditation, Healing, and Personal Growth.* Secaucus, NJ: Citadel Press, 1998.

Seligman, Martin E.P. *Learned Optimism.* New York: Knopf, 1991.

Sherwin, Byron L. and Seymour J. Cohen. *How To Be A Jew: Ethical Teachings of Judaism.* Northvale, NJ: Jason Aronson, 1992.

Solomon, Lewis D. *The Jewish Book of Living and Dying.* Northvale, NJ: Jason Aronson, 1999.

Wine, Sherwin T. *Judaism Beyond God.* Hoboken, NJ: Ktav, 1995.

Index

ABOUT THE AUTHOR

Lewis D. Solomon, an ordained rabbi, is the Theodore Rinehart Professor of Business at The George Washington University Law School, where he has taught corporate and tax law for over twenty years. He holds a B.A. from Cornell University, a J.D. from Yale Law School, and is a member of the Bar of the State of New York. He received his ordination from the Rabbinical Studies Department of The New Seminary, has served as a guest rabbi at Jewish houses of worship, and has officiated at numerous life cycle events. Rabbi Solomon is a member of the International Fellowship of Rabbis, and is the author of *The Jewish Book of Living and Dying* (Jason Aronson Inc.). He received Clinical Training in Mind/Body Medicine from the Harvard Medical School. He resides in Washington, D.C. with his wife Jane Stern Solomon. They have a son, Michael.